# CHEMISTRY & ART

*Further Adventures of a Chemist Collector*

# CHEMISTRY & ART

*Further Adventures of a
Chemist Collector*

ALFRED BADER

Weidenfeld & Nicolson
LONDON

First published in Great Britain in 2008
by Weidenfeld & Nicolson
An Hachette Livre UK Company

10 9 8 7 6 5 4 3 2 1

A CIP catalogue record for this book is
available from the British Library.

ISBN 978 0 297 85512 5

Typeset by Input Data Services Ltd, Frome

Printed and bound in the UK by CPI Mackays, Chatham ME5 8TD

The Orion Publishing Group's policy is to use papers that
are natural, renewable and recyclable products and made
from wood grown in sustainable forests. The logging and
manufacturing processes are expected to conform to the
environmental regulations of the country of origin.

Weidenfeld & Nicolson
The Orion Publishing Group Ltd
Orion House
5 Upper St Martin's Lane
London WC2H 9EA

www.orionbooks.co.uk
www.hachettelivre.co.uk

For Isabel

# Contents

# Author's Note

## Summary of *Adventures of a Chemist Collector*

W hat follows here is a summary of my first book, *Adventures of a Chemist Collector* (Weidenfeld & Nicolson, 1995), to give readers some background of the people, places, and events in my life leading up to *Chemistry and Art*.

My life has been described as a "case of hard study and work." Born in Vienna in 1924, I was sent to England at age fourteen before the outbreak of World War II, in the first Kindertransport leaving Vienna. This humanitarian effort ultimately enabled nearly ten thousand children to escape the Nazis. Although a Jewish refugee, I was interned in 1940 along with other "enemy aliens" and sent to a Canadian prisoner-of-war camp.

After obtaining my release in 1941, I was accepted at Queen's University in Kingston, Ontario, where I studied engineering chemistry, then gained a fellowship in organic chemistry at Harvard University, where I obtained my doctorate. In 1949, traveling from Quebec to Liverpool, I met Isabel Overton, the daughter of a deeply religious Protestant family in northern Ontario. We fell in love, but I am a believing Jew, and Isabel eventually decided that she could not be the Jewish wife I needed and stopped writing to me.

Work as a research chemist for the Pittsburgh Plate Glass Company took me to Milwaukee, Wisconsin, where in 1951 I co-founded the Aldrich Chemical Company, a manufacturer of fine chemicals.

In 1952 I married Helen (Danny) Daniels and our sons, David and Daniel, were born in 1958 and 1961. However, we divorced in 1981, and Isabel and I were married in 1982.

After spending more than forty years building the distinctive reputation of Aldrich, which as Sigma-Aldrich became the world's largest supplier of research chemicals, I was thrown off the Board of Directors in 1992.

Parallel to my work as a chemist, I began collecting art, in particular old master paintings. After leaving Sigma-Aldrich, I have continued a fruitful career as an art collector and dealer. My special interest has always been the works of Rembrandt and his students.

Isabel and I have also become involved in philanthropy, primarily in the fields of chemistry, education, and Jewish interests. The last chapter of my first book gives the story of our gift to Queen's University to purchase and renovate Herstmonceux Castle in Sussex, England, for an International Study Centre.

I would like to thank the many people who have helped me with my account of our adventures since that time: Carolyn Kott Washburne, my editor in Milwaukee; Jeffrey Simmons, my literary agent in London; Ann Zuehlke, my secretary, who by now is close to knowing some chapters by heart; as well as scores of chemists, art historians, and art dealers who have been so helpful. And, of course, Isabel, my guardian angel for twenty-five years, who has read and re-read my drafts and improved these immensely.

I hope you will enjoy this second story of my passions: art, the Bible, and chemistry.

# Introduction

## Alfred and Isabel Bader

One of my greatest joys since coming to Queen's in 2004 has been my relationship with Alfred and Isabel Bader. Philanthropists are generally a happy breed, but the Baders are uniquely so. Whether as gracious hosts at their home in Milwaukee, or as guides around the grounds and the castle of the International Study Centre in England, they are an extraordinary couple who relish each moment. Their giving is reflective of their generosity of spirit, their deep caring for others, and their enduring sense of the wonder, magic, and joyful "accidents" of existence.

Over the years, they have sought out and supported deserving causes, chemists, and art historians at universities throughout North America, Europe, and Israel. At Queen's University, Alfred's *alma mater*, their gifts have contributed to academic excellence through chairs, curatorships, and countless awards in many fields, all aimed at enriching the educational environment for students and ensuring that all have access to it, regardless of means.

Alfred was a newly graduated PhD from Harvard when he co-founded a chemical company in a Milwaukee garage. His astute perception of market needs, and his extraordinary ability to find new and inexpensive ways to produce chemicals and supply chemists, helped him build one of the most important and successful chemical companies in North America.

From a small operation in cramped space, Aldrich Chemical (named for his partner's fiancée) grew rapidly, moving to larger

1

premises as the company soon became widely recognized for the quality and variety of its products. When the American Chemical Society honored Dr. Bader with its top award for outstanding public service, he had earned a reputation as a "fascinating mixture of ego, modesty, and almost boundless energy."

Aldrich resisted buyout offers but in 1975 merged with Sigma of St. Louis, thereby becoming a leading supplier of organic and biochemicals. Alfred was president of the merged company, Sigma-Aldrich, and spent long years building the company's reputation. In 1992, Alfred left Sigma-Aldrich a proud legacy that included the ABCs of his life—art, the Bible, and chemistry. He was revered as the chemist who visited laboratories with Isabel, noted for asking, "What can we do better?" He continues to respond on a personal basis to calls for help and advice from chemists worldwide.

Leaving the company meant more time for art-dealing activities. He moved Alfred Bader Fine Arts (a company he had established in 1961) into Milwaukee's historic Astor Hotel. Although he is well known to international art auction houses, he takes particular pleasure in buying dirty old paintings in antique stores or at auctions and flea markets, hoping that cleaning will reveal great works. His special skill is his capacity to distinguish works by Rembrandt's students from those by the master himself. Slide-illustrated tales of such detective work have held audiences spellbound for years.

With Isabel his closest advisor and collaborator, he now spends his time dealing in paintings, writing, lecturing, and—most challenging of all in his judgment—undertaking the difficult tasks associated with philanthropy.

His relationship with the Agnes Etherington Art Centre at Queen's began in 1967, when then-curator Frances Smith asked Alfred whether he would consider donating a painting to the fledgling gallery. Pleased to be asked, he felt Queen's would be a good home for the *Salvator Mundi* that had

2

belonged to his mother's family. And so began a relationship of giving that has flourished over the decades. Alfred's gifts of paintings to the Agnes Etherington Art Centre currently number more than one hundred, and the remainder of his collection, including more than one hundred other paintings, is a promised bequest. Consisting primarily of seventeenth-century Dutch art, the Bader Collection is among the finest of its type worldwide. The collection is known among galleries and art historians around the world.

In August 2003, the Agnes Etherington Art Centre announced the gift of *Head of an Old Man in a Cap*, a painting by the celebrated seventeenth-century Dutch artist Rembrandt Harmensz van Rijn (1606–1669). *Head of an Old Man in a Cap* was only the fourth Rembrandt ever to enter a Canadian museum collection and the first in almost half a century. In September 2007, a second Rembrandt joined our first: *Head of a Man in a Turban, in Profile* is an oil on panel painted around 1661. Queen's is honored to be able to share these great works of art that enrich not only our own collection, but also the national patrimony.

The Baders' generosity ranges well beyond their interests in chemistry and art; for instance, they have supported a Queen's humanitarian aid project for disabled war victims in Bosnia-Herzegovina, as well as many other efforts to help the needy, particularly in Europe.

Alfred Bader is a survivor, an astute businessman, a connoisseur, and a scholar. It is fitting that it was the Baders—unconventional benefactors with a love of the past and with bold and extraordinary initiative—who were responsible for Queen's acquisition of the 140-room, fifteenth-century Herstmonceux Castle in England. Anyone who visits the castle will know that the Baders' belief in the promise of the remarkable structure and its grounds to provide unique opportunities for international and interdisciplinary learning was right! The castle has been renovated with their generous support and is now the unique and much-admired Queen's International Study Centre they envisioned. In the fall of 2007, the Baders attended a ribbon cutting for their latest gift—David Smith Hall, a building renovated to offer enhanced faculty accommodation and named at Alfred's request in memory of his dear friend and former Queen's principal, David C. Smith.

The Baders often say that their gift of the castle posed a serious problem for them—the challenge of what to do for an encore. They have recently responded to this challenge by purchasing a magnificent piece of waterfront land—the future site of Queen's performing arts campus, whose centerpiece will be a performing arts centre named for his beloved Isabel. The campus will benefit Queen's and the entire Kingston community—a wonderfully symbolic and practical gesture.

Alfred and Isabel Bader are a wise and remarkably devoted enabling presence for higher education and the arts. They believe passionately in education and its probable influence on men and women with uncommon potential for making contributions to the solutions for the problems of humankind. And they cherish their roles as partners in the precious activities that invent, develop, and renew the learning tapestry for these students.

Karen R. Hitchcock
Principal and Vice-Chancellor
Queen's University
Kingston, Ontario, Canada

---

Dr. Alfred Bader is quoted from his 1995 book, *Adventures of a Chemist Collector* (Weidenfeld & Nicolson).

# 1

## *Life After Expulsion*

My expulsion from Sigma-Aldrich in 1992 caused me a great deal of grief. But now, looking back, I can truly say that I am much happier. Life is better because I no longer have to work with the top people at Sigma Chemical Company, who were so convinced they were right about everything. Of the many days spent at board meetings in St. Louis, there was not a single one I could call happy. Sigma's culture and business philosophy were very different from those of Aldrich, and the pressures from Aaron Fischer and Tom Cori, two of the key executives of Sigma, were enormous. Now I can choose people with whom I enjoy working—art dealers with whom I can discuss paintings and who can sell some of the many paintings I buy, men and women like Yechiel Bar-Chaim and Adina Shapiro who help us choose and then administer many of our charitable donations intelligently, friends like Joe Bernstein to talk about investments, local charities, and problems with art. My days are just as busy as they were when I was at Sigma-Aldrich. Of course, there are personal frustrations and disappointments, but I still have the joy of learning about new chemical discoveries, of meeting great chemists from time to time, and of a much more intense involvement in art. I am a workaholic, and the pressures are mostly self-imposed.

I am wealthier because I have followed my son Daniel's advice in 1991 to sell covered call options. Tom Cori's "good" reason for expelling me was that I had bet against the company by selling call options of Sigma-Aldrich stock for my *alma mater*; his "real" reason was probably his desire to run the company without any input from me. Until that first sale and my realization that Queen's University in Kingston, Ontario, did indeed benefit from it, I had not known much about call options. Now, as I am no longer a director of Sigma-Aldrich, I am free to sell these for myself. What fun that is, and so profitable.

Of course, I am still interested in the company's progress. Since 1992, Sigma-Aldrich's performance has been very mixed, never reaching the steady 10–20 percent growth in annual sales and earnings that we had reached before. The stock hit a low in July 1994 after an unprecedented announcement of flat quarterly earnings. I realize that it is a great deal more difficult to have an annual 10–20 percent growth in sales and earnings in a large company than in a small one, and the company has indeed grown, partly as a result of acquisitions. I believe, however, that at least part of the slower growth has been caused by the absence of close contact with the academic community and hence the slower flow of new products. Another reason, I am sure, is that all decisions have been made at the very top with little communication or discussion within the company. The old Aldrich policy of encouraging the talents and suggestions of employees is long gone. In 1999, the last year under Cori's leadership, sales increased by all of 3.3 percent and net income from continuing operations declined by 6.4 percent.

An important turning point in the history of Sigma-Aldrich came in 1999 when the decision was made to find a new plan to improve performance. Eight company executives, helped by two summer interns from Washington University, worked for six months on the problem. Mike Hogan, the company's very able CFO, had previously worked on such plans at McKinsey, the management consulting company. The committee interviewed more than 650 customers and 150 Sigma-Aldrich employees.

In December 1999, in an interview with Joan Suda,

Marketing Communications Coordinator at Sigma in St. Louis, David Harvey, who had taken over as CEO from Tom Cori, explained the Strategic Plan: "...the performance of our company has not been satisfactory during recent years. 1998 was not good and this year has been only slightly better ... Over the last five years our Return on Equity has declined from 20 to 14 ... We achieved ROE of 20 in the past—so I believe we can do it again." The basic intention of the Strategic Plan was to make the company "One Company Worldwide," the goal I had made when we merged in 1975, but had found so hard to achieve, because I was so often frustrated by Sigma's unwillingness to share information or make any changes.

In the interview, David was asked, "Sigma-Aldrich has lost a lot of good people over the last year. In times of stress and uncertainty, more people might consider leaving. How can we convince them to stay?" He replied, "Regarding commitment to our company, my belief is that the answer above all is to provide job satisfaction. And we need this at all levels. Employees want to be asked for their ideas, work where excellence is rewarded, be informed how the organization is performing, and achieve personal growth. Quite candidly, we have room for lots of improvement and this was recognized in the Strategic Plan." This, of course, is just what we had aimed for from the early days at Aldrich, but we had been unable to convince Sigma management of its importance after the merger.

The company also decided to require its officers and other senior managers (about fifty worldwide) to hold shares of the company's stock valued at [one]-half to two times their annual salaries. As David explained, "They should have their own money at risk, which should be an added incentive to improve the performance of our company." Also, the company began repurchasing shares of stock, over 30 percent in the following five years.

Tom Cori moved from CEO to Chairman of the Board for one year, and David Harvey became CEO. One important result of the shakeup was the resignation of Tom Cori the following year and the replacement by David of the directors beholden to Cori with really able financial experts: W. Lee McCollum, Senior VP and CFO of S.C. Johnson; J. Pedro Reinhard, formerly the Executive VP and CFO of Dow Chemical Company; and Barrett A. Toan, CEO of Express Scripts. Cori was given an obituary-like farewell (Plate 2) in the 2000 company annual report. This reminded me of a similar farewell (Plate 1) that he had prepared for me for the 1991 annual report but that was scrapped when I vigorously protested my expulsion (Plate 3). Since his departure, Cori has had almost no contact with anyone in the company.

This is so different from my relationship with the company. I have continued to find many research samples for the library of rare chemicals and have received suggestions for new products and, occasionally, complaints, which I have relayed to chemists in Milwaukee and St. Louis. What I really enjoy are the two evenings each year, one in the spring and one in the fall, when Isabel and I invite some fifty Aldrich old-timers to join us for a simple Chinese dinner, a really fun evening.

The relationship between David Harvey and me has been mixed. Shortly after my first book, *Adventures of a Chemist Collector* (Weidenfeld & Nicolson, 1995), came out, David asked employees in Milwaukee for their anonymous comments, and I am sure that I was much happier seeing what they wrote than was David. Here are a few examples of the many given to me by Delores Menehan, who acted as David's secretary when he came to Milwaukee:

Alfred Bader's book is educational as well as incredibly interesting. It tells about a self-made man who stepped on a few toes during his lifetime, but when you start a business and try to make it go, sometimes you have to do what is necessary to keep that business. He made the only judgments he thought were correct at the time, and I believe he was a very wise, concerned individual. He tells about the hiring of a black lady with great compassion. I don't think he has a discriminatory bone in his body as far as that is concerned. He mentioned that when he first started his business, he didn't even cash his paycheck in order to pay his employees. That to me rather proves his allegiance to the employees working for him. I believe he did the best he could with what he had to work with at the time. He must have spent some sleepless nights back then worrying whether his small business could make it. I also believe he was a man of vision, determined, is religious, and is a man of great character.

I don't have much education; I'm a janitor; quit school. My friend says read the book. Learn about your company. It takes me a long time to read and understand but my friend is right, he knows a lot. My wife is reading it too. I've never read very much. My family just never had many books at home, just the ones we read in school and that wasn't much. Now we talk about it. We've never met the man, but I heard like because he is a Jew, Jews stick together and get anything they want. But man, he didn't have nothing to start with, he was real poor like a lot of us. I'm glad he done real good. He helped a lot of people like me, I have a good job that I come to every day and I try to work hard. I like working at Aldrich and I can keep this job for as long as I want to and maybe someday I can have a better job if I read and study, and learn things. If I ever meet the man I'd like to shake his hand and say "thanks, man." I tell you more when I'm done [with] the book.

Alfred Bader is a survivor. His story of his adventures told of some heavy blows dealt to him personally at a very young age and again later in life. Especially, his expulsion from the Sigma-Aldrich Board of Directors. He did a good job explaining in detail his position and the Board's decision, and I'm glad he put it in writing. I cannot for the life of me understand the fairness in the final decision and I can well imagine the effect it had on him. I think they were very narrow-minded, and also believe that Tom Cori, the leader, was determined to do it *his* mean-spirited way regardless of the consequences and the hurt it caused. It is my opinion that Tom Cori wanted Alfred Bader out of his way completely and that was the only method he had to do so. Jealousy, perhaps? This is a case of not only surviving from being struck down, but not counted out. He was dealt a raw deal in the end which was not planned, but he did not collapse. He showed resilience and coped under the circumstances, attaining a healthy self-image to the world. People admire him for his spirit and tenacity. Definitely a remarkable life adventure.

When Aldrich celebrated its fiftieth birthday in 2001, David permitted the publication of a very fair history of the company, with a reproduction of a beautiful painting I had bought years earlier. It was particularly suitable for an *Aldrichimica Acta* (Aldrich's scientific magazine) cover, since it depicts Professor Brande teaching the young Michael Faraday how to make Prussian blue (see Chapter 9).

An evening I spent with the Harveys in August 2003 was interesting and disturbing. Isabel and I had invited David and Margarete to dinner at the University Club. I had a number of questions I hoped David would answer. One was why he allowed Ralph Emanuel to be fired as a director of Sigma-Aldrich in 1980. David answered, "He was no longer useful to the company. Look how I fired some of the other directors recently." He was referring to the departure of several of Tom Cori's friends who had really made little contribution to the company, but had effectively kept Cori in power for years. In contrast, it was Ralph who had hired David in 1974. He had constantly pushed him ahead, putting him in charge of our German operations, and then urging that he come to Milwaukee to become my successor. Ralph was an astute businessman and the only one of us familiar with British law and practice, and he had a major role to play in the growth of our English company. However, in 1980, Ralph had offended Aaron Fischer and Tom Cori by voting to retain Dan Broida (who really had built Sigma) in management when they wanted to get rid of him during his fight with cancer. Talk of *good* reasons—Ralph was no longer useful—and *real* reasons!

Another question I hoped David would clear up for me was why he refused to use Bader paintings on *Aldrichimica Acta* and catalog covers. These had a long-recognized impact among world chemists and would have had a twofold advantage. It would not cost the company anything to use the paintings, and the covers could be reproduced in good color. This is difficult when the printer works only from color transparencies submitted by museums. The color of a recent Aldrich catalog cover, a painting by Fragonard in the National Gallery in Washington, was particularly poor. I had asked Joe Porwoll, the current president of Aldrich, whether he did not think it would be better to use some of my paintings again. Joe told me that he had "sent it up the flagpole and the answer was no." Up the flagpole meant to Dr. Jai Nagarkatti, former President of Aldrich, who had become the COO in St. Louis. I sent a detailed query to Jai, who advised me to speak directly to David Harvey.

David's reply that evening in August astounded me. "Certainly not," he said. "You hurt the company tremendously when you left in 1992. You spoke to many chemists about how badly we had treated you, and many of these chemists in turn talked to us. Many of us in the company were very angry. Then you asked the Milwaukee Art Museum and the St. Louis Art Museum not to help Aldrich with catalog covers." I admitted that I might well have made a mistake asking the two museums not to help, but that I had been so deeply hurt. David said that I should have left the company quietly and all would have been much calmer. To me this seemed like the world

11

upside down. I had been treated horribly, accused of betting against the company, and now once again I was the accused. I wonder if David ever asks himself whether he has made personal mistakes, like firing so many good people: Ralph, Marvin, me, and many others. When I asked why he allowed the Prussian blue painting on the *Acta* cover, he said that this was a one-time event celebrating fifty years of Aldrich, and I said again how pleased I was that he had done this.

Later on during dinner, we talked about Marvin Klitsner, and David admitted that he was the ablest attorney he had known and that he had greatly enjoyed working with him. When I reminded David that the accusation against us about "betting against the company" had happened while Marvin was in the hospital undergoing bypass surgery, David said that he had not known that. David has a selective memory. If Marvin had not been in the hospital, our defense before the Board would have been much stronger but still of little avail, since the accusation was simply an excuse.

Of course, we talked about a great many other matters. For instance, David just the month before had sold over 33,000 shares of Sigma-Aldrich stock. He told me that he planned to sell more, because with most of his assets in company stock, he should diversify. That, of course, I understand. We discussed the acquisition of other companies and our competitors. He mentioned that Roma Broida, wife of Dan Broida, would be celebrating her eightieth birthday in February 2004 and that her family was preparing a book to present to her. David actually wrote a play, "Beauty and the Beast" (Plate 5), as his contribution, which he also had printed in the Sigma-Aldrich internal newsletter (May 2004). I found this astounding, because Dan Broida was certainly not a beast; he was very demanding, but he was the remarkable builder of Sigma.

David is stridently atheist, saying time and again that he does not want to have anything to do with all that "religious mumbo-jumbo." In an interview published in the *St. Louis*

*Post-Dispatch* in September 2004, he said, "I became an atheist about the age of thirteen. My mother was Catholic. I think I once read there were 3,000 religions. What are the chances of Christianity being the right one? Nonsense!" I have known many intelligent atheists, but none who is as publicly offensive to people of faith. David has also been offensive to British chemists. Though himself a PhD from Oxford, he wrote in an editorial in *C&E News* in 2003, "... American institutions for chemical research are the best in the world." They certainly are very good, but are they better than Oxford and Cambridge and the Eidgenössische Technische Hochschule (the ETH) in Zürich? I guess I need to remind myself that it is possible to be convinced but mistaken.

There is no question in my mind that David is able and hard working, but he is also arrogant, and that must put off many people inside and outside the company. I have faulted him, but I admire his hard work and analytical ability. Since Cori's departure, the company has really prospered and morale has improved greatly. By 2003, ROE exceeded the 20 percent goal and reached 21.1 percent by 2004. Excellent acquisitions have been made, a $50 million Life Science R&D building was completed in St. Louis in 2000, and a $70 million production and distribution facility was finished in Milwaukee in 2005. The latter was helped by Milwaukee County's paying $32.5 million for Aldrich's old eight-story facility on St. Paul Ave. (Plate 4), which Marvin Klitsner and I purchased from General Electric for only $300,000 in 1966. This was because at the time the County was unwilling to pay GE fair compensation and had to construct the new freeway around the building, which GE was then very glad to sell to us.

In January 2006, Jai Nagarkatti (Plate 6) became the company's CEO with David remaining as chairman, and the company has continued to do well, still the world's most profitable chemical company. Dr. Nagarkatti, now sixty, came from India for his graduate studies at Texas A&M University where he received his PhD in 1976. He then joined Aldrich as a production chemist: very bright, well organized, somewhat of a perfectionist, frank, and really well liked. He became Manager of Aldrich Production in Milwaukee in 1978, Vice President of Manufacturing in 1985, and the president of Aldrich in 1987. During his twelve-year tenure as president of Aldrich, the company continued its unbroken record in sales and profits.

Jai then moved to St. Louis and became president of Sigma-Aldrich's Scientific Research and Fine Chemicals business units, and, in 2004, the company's president and Chief Operating Officer. In 2005, he joined Sigma-Aldrich's Board of Directors. Jai communicates well and can bring out the best in people. Soon after becoming the company's CEO, he made me very happy by asking me again to be the company's "chemist collector" of paintings for the *Aldrichimica Acta* covers (Plate 7).

As for my own life since 1992, the major decision I had to make when I was forced out of Aldrich was what I wanted to do when we returned from our summer trip to Europe at the end of July. As the realization that I had indeed been forced out became painfully clear, I knew that something absorbing must take the place of the intense effort I had put into what had been my life's work. The answer was to become much more deeply involved in art.

Alfred Bader Fine Arts (ABFA) had been founded in 1961, and for thirty years I had bought and sold paintings, a very part-time interest. Marvin Klitsner and I had eventually turned the company over, half to my sons David and Daniel, half to Marvin and Jane's grandchildren. I became the president, owning no shares myself. David, Daniel, and, by 1992, the nineteen grandchildren of Marvin and Jane were the shareholders, and I looked forward to building a successful dealership in paintings. I am sure some people have wondered why I work so hard for ABFA. The simple answer is that I love buying and selling paintings; I love my work and do not want to stop and retire.

The choice of location for the gallery, an apartment in the Astor Hotel in downtown Milwaukee, was decided quite quickly. Fifteen years of occupancy have proved me right in that. The apartment soon became a comfortable gallery, but my urgent need was for a good secretary. To my great relief, the problem was soon solved. My long-time associate from Aldrich, Marilyn Hassmann, decided to take early retirement from Aldrich and come to work for ABFA. What good fortune! We knew each other's ways, and she quickly tackled the challenge of our new venture. Sadly, I lost Marilyn's excellent help at the beginning of 1995. Experiencing great pain, she was taken to St. Joseph's Hospital in Milwaukee on a weekend. Her treatment, or lack of, was completely mishandled. Malpractice led to a stroke that left her partially paralyzed and unable to speak. Marvin recommended Gerald J. Block, an able lawyer, who sued and recovered a million dollars net for Marilyn—materially helpful, but nothing could give her back the active, useful life she had.

Good fortune again eventually brought me another able and experienced secretary, Ann Zuehlke, who has become my gallery manager. She is very good with people, both in person and on the telephone, and is a great help with our many projects, including my often complicated philanthropic efforts. Particularly useful is the fact that she is good with figures and is able to do much of ABFA's accounting. Whereas computers are a complete mystery to me, Ann is quite capable of recovering material when a computer crashes or is attacked by a virus. She has saved us from many a possible disaster, managing to remain calm in the face of seemingly insurmountable difficulties. She upgrades hardware and software regularly as the technology changes. It's a pleasure to work with her. I have been glad to see that Ann has become increasingly interested in paintings and enjoys the buying and selling, the wheeling and dealing, almost as much as I do. She checks the websites of a number of auctions around the world for paintings of interest. She and my son David have brought ABFA into the twenty-first century.

David has done a fine job of constructing our website, www.alfredbader.com, which has brought in a lot of interest from all over, though so far it has attracted more sellers than buyers. We have learned to monitor the site carefully because of an exchange we had with an Italian dealer. He bought a delightful Italian genre painting that he found on our website and sent us an e-mail expressing his delight when he received it. This turned to anger when he discovered a week later that we had not removed it from our list. "You don't think that I would be selling it for less than $5,000!" he e-mailed us. *Gott lebt im Detail.*

My son David has now taught Ann how to photograph our paintings in the gallery so that we can e-mail them and add them to the website more easily. All in all, each year we buy several hundred paintings, minor works from local auctions in Milwaukee, Chicago, and England and major works at auctions in New York, London, and Vienna. Occasionally an owner who is anxious to sell will bring a painting into the gallery. We sell largely to dealers, and I have a few collectors who have become friends. Paintings priced over $100,000 would generally not sell in Milwaukee and so are handled by my dealer friends in New York, London, and Munich.

Of course, I have never lost my love of chemistry, and so my second "job" is to invest in fledgling chemical and pharmaceutical companies. You would think that with my background, I would do uniformly well, but this has not been so. My first investment in 1992 was as successful as it was fun. I had long known Jim Jappy, a really able Scot specializing in fluoroaromatics in the south of England in a company, Yarsley, owned by the British Institute of Physics. Jim was often frustrated because he felt that he was underused. Even after the company was taken over by Shell, and he hoped for better things, promises were not kept. In 1991, Shell sold the business to British Nuclear Fuels, which did not stipulate that Jim and his two able co-workers stay on. They took the opportunity, often discussed in the past, to leave and start their own company.

They found a good location near by in Leatherhead, Surrey, and, in 1992, formed JRD Fluorochemicals Ltd. using the initials of the three partners. I had often asked Jim why he didn't strike out on his own. Once they had taken the plunge, they needed capital, so Jim asked if I would help with £48,000 for a 38 percent share of the company. I was sure he could make a success of it and readily agreed, with the understanding that I would visit twice a year and consult for them whenever they felt I could help. They were soon operational, growth was steady, and within ten years they came close to a million pounds in sales. When they began paying substantial dividends, I felt they were making a mistake. They should reinvest. But Jim did not want to expand the company. Leslie Jappy, his wife, handled the secretarial and financial work capably. One and later two very able lab technicians were hired, and with the three partners managing production, money started to accumulate. They were happy as they were, and obviously I was no longer needed. I offered my shares at a price that was accepted immediately.

My second investment, in Coelacanth Chemicals, began even more promisingly but turned into a failure. It was started by my old friends Barry and Jan Sharpless whom I have known for many years, first at MIT and Stanford, then at the Scripps Research Institute in San Diego. Barry's first review article on one of the great discoveries of the century—metal-catalyzed asymmetric epoxidation—was published in the *Aldrichimica Acta* in 1979, and since then Barry has won the Nobel Prize for this work. His grandfather had started the Sharpless Chemical Company, and Barry and Jan longed for involvement in a

chemical company of their own. Would I help kick-start Coelacanth with half a million dollars? Knowing of Barry's brilliant
chemistry, I agreed. One of his able co-workers, Hartmuth
Kolb, soon joined Coelacanth, and I thought that their joint
effort would lead to many new compounds of great interest to
pharmaceutical companies. But the man heading the company,
Seth Harrison, was not the right man. In 2001, Coelacanth
had to be rescued by Lexicon Genetics in Texas, and I sold my
stock at a substantial loss.

In my more recent investments in Cedarburg Pharma-
ceuticals and Fluorous Technologies, Inc., my son Daniel has
joined me. This has made the venture all the more pleasant. I
really value his input. He has a fine business sense, honed by
his business training at the Rochester Institute of Technology.
Daniel is now on the Board of Directors of Cedarburg Pharma-
ceuticals, a company some ten miles north of Milwaukee.
Started in 1998, it manufactures active ingredients for pharmaceutical companies. It has had a very bumpy ride so far, but
recent changes in administration point, we hope, to a much
more stable future.

The chemist founder of Fluorous Technologies in Pittsburgh
is my good friend, Professor Dennis Curran, at the University of
Pittsburgh. In 2000, Dennis won the ACS Award for Creative
Work in Synthetic Organic Chemistry sponsored by Aldrich.
The company develops fluorous products and applications
for life science market needs in drug discovery, biopolymer
synthesis, and protein science. It owns or exclusively licenses
broad seminal patents on fluorous compositions and applications, and is the world's only company dedicated to com-
mercializing this important new chemistry. Across a wide
spectrum of applications, fluorous chemistry has proven adept
at solving separation-based problems within the chemical and
biological industries. Fluorous Technologies is led by Philip
Yeske, a Pittsburgh native with experience in both small and
large organizations, having spent ten years working at Bayer

sites in the US and Germany. Philip brings a charismatic and entrepreneurial management style to Fluorous Technologies that is well suited for an early-stage company.

Ever since my experience of debating when I was an undergraduate at Queen's, I have realized how much I enjoy speaking in public, so it is not surprising that my third "job" is to give many talks, fifty or sixty a year, from a menu of twelve. I really enjoy talking to diverse audiences about the history of Aldrich, Josef Loschmidt, the Rembrandt Research Project, and my own collection, and I always look forward to the questions afterwards, which sometimes shed new light on the subject and range from serious to funny. The funniest came from a girl at Herstmonceux: "Is one of your sons still available?" It resulted in whoops of laughter.

My fourth, and perhaps the most difficult, "job" is giving money away sensibly. This can be very complicated and requires a great deal of time and input from friends as well as family. It has brought us a great deal of joy, sometimes considerable frustration, and will be a chapter of its own in this book: "Help the Neediest and Ablest."

# 2

## *Marvin Klitsner*

The greatest influence on my business life, and often on my personal life, was Marvin Klitsner (Plate 8). Our truly treasured friendship developed over a period of almost half a century. Marvin and I met in 1954 through his daughters, first Francie and then Betsy, who were in my Sunday School class at Temple Emanu-El B'ne Jeshurun on the east side in Milwaukee. The following year, he and I were together at the Bnai Brith retreat in August where we met Rabbi Abraham Joshua Heschel, a charismatic teacher. Heschel spoke about other people building "palaces in space" while Jews built a "palace in time" and called it the Sabbath.

That meeting changed the Klitsners' lives. Marvin was eager to study more. Rabbi Heschel advised him that Rabbi David Shapiro was the best possible scholar in Milwaukee. Although both of our families already attended his synagogue, Congregation Anshe Sfard, we lived on the east side and had to drive to the west side of Milwaukee. Marvin and Jane decided they would sell their home and move nearer to Rabbi Shapiro, the synagogue, and his classes. Marvin so honored the Sabbath because he felt it was such an important holiday that it was distinguished above all others. He celebrated it inspirationally with his entire family every Sabbath—even on the day of his death.

Marvin was a partner in one of Milwaukee's largest and most prestigious law firms, respected nationally: Foley, Sammond and Lardner (now Foley & Lardner), and when he finally ended his practice in 1988, was senior partner there. When I became the sole owner of Aldrich in May 1955, he really began helping the company. He became a director of Aldrich in 1961 and a member of the executive committee and, until our joint painful dismissal, was my trusted advisor and mentor at Aldrich and Sigma-Aldrich.

Thinking of what Foley & Lardner charges now for its legal services, I have to smile on reading in the first prospectus of Aldrich's common stock in December 1965, "The law firm of Foley, Sammond and Lardner, of which Marvin E. Klitsner is a partner, was paid $750 during the last fiscal year." I am glad that, as a small thank you, I persuaded him to buy 30,000 shares of Aldrich, about 5 percent of the company, at $1 a share. His advice was vital to the continued growth of the company.

We worked together on so many other projects as well. He joined me on the Board of Directors of Rabbi Shapiro's synagogue and in the founding of the Hillel Academy, Milwaukee's only Jewish day school at the time. We started the Bader-Klitsner Foundation, which helped Jewish causes in Milwaukee and Israel, and B&K Enterprises, doing business as Alfred Bader Fine Arts, which is now owned 50 percent by my two sons and 50 percent by Marvin's nineteen grandchildren. He had the great wisdom to have me give each of my sons' trusts 6.5 percent of Aldrich stock when that was worth very little. Our daily contact over more than thirty years continued after he retired from Foley & Lardner, and even after he and Jane moved to Israel in 1988.

Marvin gave me the gift of his inspiring friendship, his omniscient expertise, and his support in decision-making. Marvin was my MENTOR, my most dear friend. He was so respected, so trustworthy, so sincere, and so honest that during my divorce from my first wife, Danny, he served as attorney for her as well as for me. He helped Danny write her will, leading to the Helen Bader Foundation, and similarly helped

# Alfred Bader

Dr. Alfred Bader has had a long and very distinguished career.

Since founding Aldrich Chemical Company 41 years ago, Dr. Bader has been instrumental in building Aldrich into one of the world's foremost suppliers of high quality, fine organic and inorganic chemicals.

A native of Austria, Dr. Bader went to England and eventually to Canada, where he received several degrees from Queen's University in Ontario. Later he also earned a PhD. degree from Harvard University in Cambridge, Massachusetts.

While working in Milwaukee, he received permission from his employer to start a small business on his own, which he did in 1951 in a rented garage. When, in 1954, his employer decided to move its Milwaukee operations to Pennsylvania, Dr. Bader opted to remain in the city he had grown to love and formed Aldrich Chemical Company. It grew and prospered under his able leadership and guidance.

The early success and growth of Aldrich was due to his enthusiasm and creativity which attracted other able chemists and to his stamina and drive which were widely admired by his co-workers.

In 1975, he and Dan Broida, then the President of Sigma Chemical Company in St. Louis, led the effort which resulted in a merger of Sigma and Aldrich that year to become today's Sigma-Aldrich Corporation. Dr. Bader served as President of the new Sigma-Aldrich Corporation, with Dan Broida as Chairman. In 1980, Broida stepped aside and Dr. Bader became Chairman, a position in which he served with honor and distinction until his recent retirement.

Throughout his career, Dr. Bader has traveled extensively meeting customers and suppliers, giving lectures and becoming well known among leading chemists throughout the world. He has been the driving force in accumulating a collection of 39,000 rare chemicals which Aldrich makes available to the research community. Over the years, he has also personally helped many deserving chemists at universities with grants to underwrite their research.

Dr. Bader also has won renown as an art historian and a student of the Bible. His collection of the works of seventeenth century Dutch Masters is considered one of the finest private art collections in the world. He was named a fellow of the Royal Society of Arts in London for his achievements as an art collector and historian and for his research in art restoration.

Sigma-Aldrich has benefited significantly through the years from the influence and guidance provided by Dr. Bader. The entire Sigma-Aldrich organization is deeply grateful for his valuable contributions.

**Please Bother Us.**

## LEADERSHIP

**TOM CORI**
**30 Years Service at Sigma-Aldrich**

As the twentieth century came to a close, so ended a remarkable chapter in Sigma-Aldrich's leadership history. Tom Cori retired as Chairman after devoting 30 years of his life to building Sigma-Aldrich into a leading $1 billion Life Science and High Technology company.

Tom joined Sigma in 1970 as a production chemist and quickly rose through the ranks. He became Vice President of Sigma-Aldrich in 1975 before moving on to hold the positions of President, Chief Executive Officer (16 years!) and Chairman. He was also a director of the Company for over 25 years.

When he started, it was a very different company from the one we know today — sales were less than $10 million. Under his leadership, Sigma-Aldrich saw many years of consistent growth and increased profitability. From a base of $76 million in chemical sales, 1,400 employees in four countries and 24,000 products in 1980, the Company's sales now exceed $1 billion with 6,200 employees in 33 countries and 85,000 products.

During his tenure, total return to shareholders averaged more than 17% per year. This success is largely due to Tom's skill in focusing the Company to respond to our customers' needs to have high quality products, delivered on time anywhere in the world, all backed by superior technical support.

In building Sigma-Aldrich, Tom Cori has made a major contribution to the development of science. As he always said, "At Sigma-Aldrich we can be proud of our daily work for we are improving the quality of life for humankind."

We are proud of Tom Cori's leadership and the dedication, energy and vision he brought to Sigma-Aldrich.

PLATE 1 (above): The farewell prepared for me by Tom Cori in 1991, which was scrapped when I protested my expulsion.

PLATE 2 (above right): The similar, obituary-like farewell given to Cori in the 2000 annual report.

# Beauty and the Beast

Broida Scholarship Gives
Employees' Children an
Opportunity to Shine

In 1982, friends of Dan
Broida and Sigma-Aldrich
established a scholarship fund
to honor a man highly respected
by the international biomedical
research community. Broida
was one of the initial leaders of
Sigma Chemical Company along
with Aaron Fischer and Bernard
Fischlowitz. Broida's leadership,
honesty and dedication helped
Sigma-Aldrich become a pillar
in the scientific community.

The Broida scholarship is
the Company's way to not only
pay homage to Broida, but to
the children of Sigma-Aldrich
employees who excel in the class-
room – and are in essence, pillars
of our community. Winners of
the Broida scholarship must be
engaged in or planning a program
of undergraduate study in science.
Scholarship awards are meant
to contribute toward the costs of
tuition and fees and recipients
are required to reapply each
academic year. Support beyond
the initial award year requires
continuing strong academic performance as a full-time student.

In 2003, Sigma-Aldrich
gave $105,000 to replenish
the Broida Scholarship fund. In
2004, the Company donated a
further $100,000 to the fund.
The scholarship fund's operation
is independent of Sigma-Aldrich.

## Cast of Characters:

Beauty — Roma Broida (1924), wife of Dan Broida

The Beast — Dan Broida (1913-1981), former President of Sigma
Chemical Company and Chairman of Sigma-Aldrich Corporation.

Young/Middle-aged/Old Man — David Harvey (1939), Chairman,
President and Chief Executive Officer, Sigma-Aldrich

This story was written by David Harvey for inclusion in a book presente
to Roma Broida on the occasion of her 80th birthday, February 8, 200

This is a fairy tale! Children, are you listening carefully
and sitting comfortably? If so, I'll begin.

PLATE 5: "Beauty and the Beast," the story written by
David Harvey for Roma Broida's eightieth birthday.

Once upon a time (it was more accurately in the mid-1970's), a young Englishman sat dispiritedly on the stairs in a tiny house in Munich that served as the overseas German location of a very small American company. The Big Boss, the unkempt Beast, had been particularly demanding that day and his favorite word "stoopid" had been, kindly said, somewhat overused. Even so, the aspiring employee had to admit the Beast was usually right. However, it had indeed been a tough day. But suddenly, and almost magically, the young man's mood changed. Out of a mirage appeared a Beauty — real Beauty! What an elegant, well-dressed, good looking woman, surely a film star! Furthermore, she was also very charming and considerate. It was hard to comprehend that this was indeed the wife of the Beast. What did she see in him? It became apparent later when she sat down on the crooked stairs and confided to the young man. "Don't be upset — he's really such a friendly, entertaining Beast." How right she proved to be! The Beast, in fact, became "almost" human (you must note he was an exceptional creature) now in Beauty's company. And their mutual affection could be observed by the young man in many future occasions.

Just a few years later, Beauty and the Beast were out to dinner in rural southern England. Now Beauty did not eat a lot, surely one of her well-kept secrets for that trim figure. The Beast was also not a big eater — in fact, he really did not have sufficient time for eating as talking was far more important. But certainly they both liked ice cream. Unfortunately there was a very limited choice on the menu which resulted in

the Beast giving the whole restaurant a lecture on the virtues of America — apparently one could get 39 flavors at certain very upscale ice cream parlors back home. The young man who listened attentively did not dare to admit that he preferred plain vanilla.

At the end of the 1970's, Beauty and the Beast were entertaining friends at their home. While Beauty served lots of exquisite food and the Beast poured good chilled white wine, this unusual pair regaled everyone with stories. Beauty seemed more than somewhat preoccupied with the state of her kitchen that the Beast had been, was, and would be working on well into the future. The Beast, however, was far more concerned about the condition of his back than the chaos in the kitchen — maybe they were connected! Apparently he had been in such pain that he could not go to bed. The Beast had received little sympathy from his doctor. He was told "it's simply mind over matter. You must just go to bed." So one night he decided the time had come to try to follow the doctor's instructions. He manfully (well, Beasts are by definition brave) got out of his chair, and even boasted that he removed his socks. It was a long, arduous process. However, finally success — he was again in bed. What bliss! But not for long, as suddenly there was the call of human nature — he had to get up! So just two hours after deciding to go to bed (do Beasts exaggerate? Well, maybe), he was back in his chair. The young man particularly empathized with these tales for he, himself, was rather hopeless in doing jobs around the house and was at that time also suffering with a very bad back. But he kept his thoughts to himself and

just sat back and enjoyed the delightful evening.

The beginning of the 1980's was the last time the now middle-aged "young" man saw Beauty and the Beast together. On this occasion, the Beast was particularly friendly and supportive and not a single "stoopid" crossed his lips. And Beauty protectively hovered around her now fragile Beast who was unfortunately to leave the real world very shortly thereafter.

In the interim years, the young man himself has grown old. His mane became grey just like the Beast. Now the Big Boss himself, he often reflects appreciatively on the Beast's mentoring that started decades ago in that tiny house in Munich.

His path continued to cross with Beauty (most recently just before her approaching 80th birthday) who seemed, unlike most mortals, to be able to defy the ravages of time. That's the essence of real beauty. And her natural charm has not faded with the passing years.

So, children, there is a real Beauty, who lived with a Beast whose endeavors started a small company that turned into a world leader in its industry.

Yes, this is a fairy tale, but let me assure you, it's absolutely true!

*David R. Harvey*

David R. Harvey
CEO, Chairman and President
Sigma-Aldrich Corporation

**P.S.** We would also like to take this opportunity to honor another octogenarian, **Alfred Bader,** the Founder and former President of Aldrich Chemical Company and former President and Chairman of Sigma-Aldrich Corporation. We wish him all the best on his 80th birthday.

PLATE 6: Jai Nagarkatti.

ALDRICH CONGRATULATES THE 2007 ACS AWARD WINNERS

# Aldrichimica ACTA

VOL. 40, NO. 2 • 2007

Recent Advances in Intermolecular
Direct Arylation Reactions

Evolution and Applications of Second-Generation
Ruthenium Olefin Metathesis Catalysts

**ALDRICH**
Advancing Science

sigma-aldrich.com

PLATE 7: Under Jai's tenure, I was asked to be the company's "chemist collector" of paintings for the *Aldrichimica Acta* covers again.

PLATE 8: Marvin Klitsner.

Isabel and me to write our wills, with the same aim. My greatest sorrow has been his death in 2001 and the deep loss that I feel in so many aspects of my life.

How can I say thank you to such a man? Only by working hard for Alfred Bader Fine Arts, with half of its profits going to Marvin's grandchildren. For with his son, Steven, I can say that every significant action or decision of mine is consciously or subconsciously driven or measured by "What would Marvin say? What would he think? What would he do?" But I cannot be clearer than the eulogy given by Steven in Jerusalem on August 12, 2001.

### Steve's *Hesped* (Eulogy) for Dad[1]

*Abba*, *Saba*, how can I begin to paint a portrait of your magnificent life? I can't. I already apologized to Mom, that neither I, nor anyone else, could do justice to the work of art that has been your life.
PURE GOODNESS AND KINDNESS WRAPPED IN GREAT WISDOM.
EMANATING LOVE AND SURROUNDED BY LOVE.

All this accompanied by the power and determination to translate all that goodness and wisdom and love into *maasim tovim*, not just individual *maasim tovim*, but a well-woven tapestry, a life strategy to transform yours and *Savta*'s lives, the lives of your children, and their children, your *kehilla*, and even *klal Yisrael*. You had such great dreams, such great plans, and you quietly and humbly set about realizing them, while attributing everything ultimately to *Hashem*— and to *Savta*.

We love you, Mom. I won't even try to describe the great love story of your life together. Francie once confided to me that sometimes it was even embarrassing to witness the intimacy and love in the look

---

1 A glossary of Hebrew terms that have been used here can be found at the end of this chapter.

of his eyes for you and in yours for him, and this, as an unwavering constant for more than fifty-two years.

Many of your wonderful friends who are here, who love you so dearly, are relatively new friends, over the last decade since your *aliya*. They grew to love you, Dad, while mainly knowing you as a kind, intelligent, and giving friend, a quiet man in his retirement years, still making the most of each hour, of each day. But how can I convey to your friends the totality of your life as a *tour de force*, as a powerful influence on whole communities, and upon countless individuals?

Dad, the end of your life was exquisite, as was your life, and your struggle to stay alive one more hour until *Shabbat*, and to share the same *Yahrtzeit* as Rabbi Shapiro zt'l, whose life was so influential upon and influenced by yours. This somehow conformed to the same spiritual logic that guided your life. The story is an amazing one, almost impossible, yet entirely consistent with a divine *hashgacha* that defies rational explanation, but absolutely conforms to the metaphysical coherence of your life.

Our father, *Saba*, was born in Augusta, Wisconsin, nearly eighty-three years ago to the only Jewish family in town. How does one begin life in a small town, a marginally affiliated Jew, and manage to come home to *Torah*, to come home to *Yerushalayim*, and to lead countless others on the journey?

It's as if you had an inborn homing device tuned to the frequency of truth, of *chesed*, of *Torah*, of Jerusalem, of *Hashem*.

*Saba* grew up in the context of a typical middle-America life. The works. Including playing on the high-school football team, working in his father's store, and selling encyclopedias to farmers off country roads. He made history at the University of Wisconsin. The last time anyone checked, he still had the record for achievement and honors at the law school there.

One of his professors once said, "If Marvin Klitsner told me the sun was rising in the west, I'd go look."

In the navy, in the Pacific, as an officer, he was one of the first to be trained in the new radar technology. I later understood that Dad was never afraid to learn anything new. In a major trial on behalf of a pharmaceutical company involving neo-natology, he became expert enough in the field to cross examine world-class medical experts. It's one of the things he loved about law—constant challenge and exposure to new worlds.

You always told us, Dad, that the most important and best decision you ever made was marrying Mom. We agree. But in your own words, the event that changed the course of our family history took place in August of 1955. Dad, allow me to quote from your letter to us that we received from Mom only last night.

"It is interesting . . . to speculate about what would have happened had we at any fork in the road, taken another path . . . It is true that we were searching for something meaningful at the time of the Bnai Brith Institute in the summer of 1955. There we first met Rabbi Abraham Joshua Heschel . . . I had taken that midnight walk in the woods of northern Wisconsin with Rabbi Heschel on that *motzaei Shabbat* (while Jane, pregnant with Steve, took Francie and Betsy back to the cabin to put them to sleep); he had suggested that we take on one *mitzvah* until it became a part of our lives, and then add another, and another. There [had] been the feeling that I was seized by both shoulders and urged to sit at the feet of Milwaukee's greatest treasure, Rabbi David Shapiro . . . [Without this there would never have been the] thought of becoming involved in building and sending Steve to a day school. That and more was attributable to Rabbi Shapiro.

"There followed step by step, as suggested by Rabbi Heschel, the process of our becoming *dati*; to begin with, *kashering* the house, no longer going to the office on *Shabbat*, no longer eating out . . . the establishment of Hillel Academy and the decision a year later to send Steve there, the purchase by Grandma and Grandpa of the 55th Street house, and the establishment of our *Shabbat* home in their upstairs space, ceasing to use the telephone or car on *Shabbat* . . . In the midst of it all there was the process of limiting our social and family engagements to avoid conflict with *halacha*, and getting clients, courts, partners, and associates, as well as the school

25

authorities, to understand that we were unavailable for business or office matters from some hour on Friday until Saturday night, as well as on *Yom Tov*. All of that process occurred with the participation and encouragement of our children. Rabbi Shapiro never pushed, but was there to answer questions and to provide an inspiring example. We cannot recall any other examples or even company from our generation and social friends [in this journey]."

Very early on, Dad underlined a line from Heschel, saying that the infinite God is of such a nature that He is either of prime significance or of none. The road to *shmirat mitzvoth* was clear to you, Dad. And it intimately involved the great inspiration of Rabbi David S. Shapiro. Dad, you were one of the only people in Milwaukee at the time capable of appreciating this saintly man of giant intellect and great humility. This is because you were cut from the same cloth. The love was mutual, and the influence which we speak of at every family *simcha* was also mutual. We always emphasized the rabbi's influence on you. But now, Dad, I can relate, but because of your modesty only a small part, of how you impacted upon his life and his ability to contribute to *klal Yisrael*.

Career and professional decisions made together with Mom (everything was always together with Mom), such as not to accept a law professorship, or not to accept chief counsel of Wisconsin Telephone, or not to accept the presidency of Aldrich—each decision was guided by a value system that emphasized family, community, *and* the road already embarked upon towards *shmirat mitzvoth*.

I want to read to all of you one small section of Dad's letter to the three children, much of which reads like an ethical will. This may give you some small idea of the kind of thinking and values that he and Mom tried to teach us:

"Material things can be ugly or beautiful, depending on how they are acquired and how they are utilized; depending upon whether their acquisition becomes an end in and of itself, or a means of achieving worthwhile objectives ... whether they are acquired and utilized ethically or by questionable means or with questionable objectives. One might even say that it is in connection with material matters that most ethical dilemmas present themselves. Whether one accepts a position for which he lacks qualifications, or enters into a transaction without full disclosure of all known relevant facts, or accepts a full day's pay for less than a full day's work, or undertakes to counsel someone without full preparation or ability to do so, or performs an act of kindness without disclosing a selfish motive, or engages in any act with his fellow man with less than complete integrity—all of these situations or temptations involve ethical or moral dilemmas which constantly put us to the test. And any deviation from total self-integrity, no matter how insignificant it seems at the time, can chip away at the soul. Thank *Hashem*, we do not have to talk to our children about outright dishonesty or about ethics as such; however, none of us are totally immune from the ever-present daily pitfalls unless we constantly keep on the alert for them."

Clients knew that despite the most scrupulous legal and moral constraints of your counsel, Dad, that your genius, your incisive mind, your creative thinking, in short, your wisdom, would lead them to the shores of success as well as to the moral high ground. So many wealthy clients attributed their success to you, Dad, and because of their love and admiration for you, they would also follow your advice and guidance to ever-greater and wisely chosen acts of philanthropy.

I know that one of your great feelings of accomplishment, *Abba*, came from suggesting, planning, and setting up the Helen Bader Foundation, with all of the important work it does for thousands, in Milwaukee and here in Israel—for Alzheimer's research and care, for Russian and Ethiopian *olim*, and for so many institutions of learning and *chesed*.

Dad, none of your values remained in the realm of the abstract or theoretical. Through your wisdom, your goodness, and the power of your God-given gifts, you always managed to translate these values into action:

• Your love of *Zion* became crucial help to the State of Israel, leading the middle-sized Jewish community of Milwaukee to what at the time, under your leadership, as president of the Milwaukee Jewish Federation, led the world's communities in the highest per-capita monetary contributions to Israel. The methods you devised with Mel Zaret in our den on Circle Drive then became a model for other communities and federations. It was inevitable that your love of *Zion* would also translate into *aliya* for yourselves and for all of your children.

• Your dedication to Jewish education translated into creating the first Jewish day school in Milwaukee—you and Rabbi Shapiro. There was no Orthodox community to speak of, so you created American Jewish history by creating the first Jewish-Federation-sponsored day school. *Torah Umesorah* told you it couldn't be done. The school would not long remain Orthodox. But you knew better. It's still Federation sponsored forty years later, and it's still Orthodox. You were so certain that you were also willing to stake your own son's education on an experiment that others of less vision tried to discourage you from.

Thank you, Dad, for not listening to them.

• Your love and appreciation for *Torah* didn't remain in the realm of abstract emotion. It translated into the adoption of your soul-mate, Rabbi Shapiro, into seeing his books published, and in sponsoring other works of *Torah* including the important commentary on Exodus of Benno Jacob. It also led you to offer your skills and time in helping edit Rabbi Quint's many volumes of *The Restatement of Jewish Law*. And in your later years, after founding schools and sponsoring *yeshivot*, you finally joined one. Rabbi Quint, learning with you and your group of men in their sixties, seventies, and eighties, many, like Dad, learning *Talmud* seriously for the first time—it meant so much to him. Mom told us yesterday of how fond Dad was of quoting Rabbi Steinzaltz, who asked why Jews talk about 120-year life spans, and answered, "So that we will have the gumption to start new things in our seventies and eighties."

• Dad, your *hakarat hatov*, your gratitude to *Hashem*, which was always on your lips and in your heart for all of these beautiful and healthy grandchildren and great-grandchildren, translated directly into your desire to help Udi found and develop Tsaad Kadima, a revolutionary system of care and advancement for children with CP.

Some people hold wonderful value systems; few make them a reality with such consistency and brilliance.

Dad, even more difficult than giving a hint of who you were for *klal Yisrael*, is to speak as a son, to speak on behalf of Francie and Betsy. Dad, everything we have and everything we are starts with you—you and Mom. You have been our loving *Abba*, whose hugs warmed us on cold Wisconsin mornings. "Dad is home from work!" And we would run to your arms, the highlight of our day. You are our compass, our counselor, our teacher, our moral guide. Every significant action or decision is consciously or subconsciously driven or measured by, "What would Dad say? What would he think? What would he do?"

Until now, we would come to you, and now we are bereft. Questions will arise—life questions, moral issues, the need for practical advice. Your *kol*, your voice, will be thunderously silent for us. But I believe we carry within us a *bat kol* from you. I think I know what the *midrash* was talking about when it described *Yosef* as always having *dmut d'yukno shel aviv lefanav*—a graphic image of his father's presence before him. We will always have that to guide us. To paraphrase the poet, "You are our north, our south, our east, our west, our working week, our *Shabbos* rest."

I began by talking of pure goodness and kindness, wrapped in great wisdom, emanating love. Dad, I now have to speak about your endless capacity for love. I've spoken of your love for Mom, of your love for *Torah* and for *klal Yisrael*, but I must turn for a moment to the other great loves of your life. Your children: only three biologically, but you always said you had six children, including Denny, Mendel, and Judy. As son to father, I've chosen an almost humorous anecdote to reflect the extent of your devotion. Sending me to the

29

fledgling day school you founded resulted in my being the only kid in the school from our side of town, with a rather lonely after-school social life. You and Mom tried to compensate by spending time with me in ways that included Mom pitching baseball to me in the back yard, and Dad shooting baskets with me in the driveway. Perhaps the most extreme act of devotion, Dad, was your joining a boy-scout-like father-and-son organization called Indian Guides, where grown men and their sons sat on floors of various living rooms each week, exchanging platitudes of friendship ("Pals forever, dad—pals forever, son"), and building teepees and going camping. I knew it was ridiculous, you knew it was stupid—but nothing was beneath your dignity in your school of devoted parenting. You stayed because you wanted me to have friends. I stayed because I loved being with you. Later we would find our time more wisely spent learning together, but those hours as Big and Little Osceola are no less precious than our hours with *masechet Yoma*.

Your next great love, *Saba*, is as a *Saba*—and I can't just mention them as "the grandchildren and great-grandchildren," because for you, *Saba* and *Savta*, they aren't just a group or category. Each one is special to you. You know their idiosyncrasies, their special traits, and strengths. You delight in their successes and share in their struggles. Your love for the Wolff children: Ephraim and Tamar, Naomi and David, Yoni and Chagit, Michael and Tamar, Rachel and Miriam, Sara and Yael. And for the Shapiro children: Adina and Zvi, Dani and Yitzchak, Avi and Tamar. And for our children: Akiva and Noam, Nechama, Yisrael and Amitai. You and Mom love each one uniquely. The incredible *bar* and *bat mitzvah* trips you and they treasured as bonding time without the parents. To see you, *Saba*, with the great-grandchildren—Yishai, Chana, Re"ut, Shalom, Shira, Mordechai Aviad, and Hallel—was to see a man experiencing the paradise of the world to come.

Your love and devotion for your parents, Grandpa Harry and Grandma Sara, extended to Mom's mother, whom you could never refer to as "mother-in-law," only as "Mother." You were always in her prayers, and she in yours. She is experiencing mourning now in

Milwaukee, as are your loving siblings, Uncles Sid, Irv, and Stu, and Aunt Miriam on the West Coast.

Dad, you so loved *Shabbat*. Heschel's book, *The Sabbath*, inspired us, but it was the real experience of *Shabbat* that captivated you. So many people discovered *Shabbat* at our table, and those who thought they knew *Shabbat* experienced a new level of experience at your table.

The last hours, Dad, surrounded by family, with Francie already traveling towards us and connected to you by telepathy and heart-strings—you waited till *Shabbat*. Just one more *Lechu neranena*, which we said together. Just one more *Lecha dodi*, which we sang at your side. At the very end, you seemed to be gasping for just one more breath, and then another. I believe you did this in order to depart this world on your beloved *Shabbos*, as well as on the very *Yahrtzeit* of your beloved Rabbi Shapiro, twelve years ago to the day.

You left us at the very moment we recited *shema Yisrael* with you, all of us together—in Mom's embrace. All your great loves—Mom, family, Rabbi Shapiro, Shabbos, Yerushalayim—all coming together in the final notes of a symphonic masterpiece that was your entire life. Did you merit this exquisite moment of departure because of all the *chesed*? All the *tzedaka*? All the love? Or because, old and frail, you flew across the world to bury your cousin Leajean and speak at her grave? Or because you once flew across the US to bury a fellow Jew whom you had met only once in your office years before—a man without any family (a *met mitzvah*)? Or was it because you so graciously agreed and encouraged me to say *kaddish* for Judy's father?

Dad, we tried our best. On *Shabbat*, David and his father, Eliezer Ansbacher, were your *shomrim* (guardians), insisting on dividing the twenty-one hours of *Shabbat* between them, *tzaddikim* accompanying a *tzaddik*. And from *motzaei Shabbat*, your grandchildren wanted to be your *shomrim*—how fitting, how beautiful.

But if in your life and if in your afterlife, we have been remiss or negligent, or if there were times we showed less than the infinite respect and love we feel for you, please grant us forgiveness.

Finally, Dad, while God miraculously spared you most of the pain of cancer, you so deeply felt the pain of *am Yisrael* in these difficult times. Only hours before you left us, you were aware that Judy and I and Sara were in this very hall at the funeral of fifteen-year-old Malki Roth, the victim of savage terrorism. We know that now, as you approach the heavenly bench, the *kise hakavod*, the Divine throne, you will be the most effective defense attorney, defending *am Yisrael*, arguing passionately on behalf of your greatest desire and wish, peace for your nation, Israel.

May your soul be bound with the bonds of eternal life, and your memory a blessing.

GLOSSARY OF HEBREW TERMS:

*Abba* father

*aliya* (lit.) ascent to Israel, emigration

*am Yisrael* the nation of Israel or Jewish people

*bar mitzvah* Jewish boys are deemed to have reached the age of maturity and responsibility for the fulfillment of religious obligations *(mitzvah* or plural *mitzvot)* at age thirteen. At this point they become *bar mitzvah*

*bat kol* an inner resonance, a voice's echo

*bat mitzvah* same as *bar mitzvah* (see above) for girls, who reach *bar mitzvah* earlier at age twelve

*chesed* acts of loving kindness

*dati* religiously observant of the commandments of the *Torah*

*hakarat hatov* gratitude (lit. "recognizing the good")

*halacha* the system of Jewish law that goes back to ancient times and is still practiced meticulously today by many Jews—mostly by those who consider themselves Orthodox

*Hashem* God

*hashgacha* divine providence

*hesped* eulogy

*kaddish* the prayer for the deceased

*kasher (the house)* the painstaking process by which a kitchen and serviceware is made fit for use by those who observe the Kosher laws that define dietary restrictions and prescriptions for the kosher preparation of food—e.g. the separation of utensils used for dairy or meat meals

*kehilla* community

*kise hakavod* lit. "the throne of glory"—a metaphor used to describe the immediate presence of the Divine

*klal Yisrael* the entire community of Israel, the world over *kol* voice

*Lecha dodi* "Come, my beloved Sabbath queen," central hymn of the Friday evening Sabbath service

*Lechu neranena* lit. "let us sing"—the first words of the Friday evening Sabbath service

*maasim tovim* good deeds

*masechet Yoma* a tractate of the *Talmud*

*met mitzvah* a dead person with no family to bury him

*midrash* ancient Bible commentary

*mitzvah* Jewish religious obligations as prescribed in the Five Books of Moses and later interpretations. (see *bar* and *bat mitzvah* above)

*motzaei Shabbat* the period of time immediately following the end of the Sabbath (Saturday night)

*olim* immigrants to Israel

*Saba* grandfather (Marvin)

*Savta* grandmother (Jane)

*Shabbat (Shabbos)* the Sabbath

*shema Yisrael* the most famous Jewish prayer, recited twice daily (Hear O Israel—the Lord our God—the Lord is One), which appears in Deuteronomy 6:4

*shmirat mitzvoth* observance of Jewish law

*shomrim* lit. guardians, people who volunteer to remain vigilant near the body of the deceased (usually reciting psalms) until the burial

*simcha* joyous occasion

*Talmud* the body of Jewish civil and ceremonial law and legend comprising the *mishna* (200 CE) and the *Gemara* (500 CE)

*Torah* the Five Books of Moses (the holiest section of the Hebrew Bible)

*Torah Umesorah* the national organization of Jewish day schools

*tzaddik* righteous person (plural—tzaddikim)

*tzedaka* charity, philanthropy

*Yahrtzeit* Yiddish for the anniversary of one's death (Dad's is the 22nd of the month Av)

*Yerushalayim* Jerusalem

*yeshivot* Jewish institutions of higher learning, Talmudic academies

*Yom Tov* general name for major Jewish festivals that include Rosh Hashana, Yom Kippur, Passover etc.

*Yosef* the biblical figure Joseph, son of Jacob

*Zion* the land of Israel

# 3

# Great Paintings by Old Masters

After my expulsion from Sigma-Aldrich, my efforts as a dealer changed dramatically. I teamed up first with two international dealers, Otto Naumann in New York and Clovis Whitfield in London, and later with another dealer in London, Philip Mould, and the Galerie Arnoldi-Livie, owned by Angelika and Bruce Livie, in Munich, to buy truly major paintings.

My first major purchase with Otto was Rembrandt's *Portrait of Johannes Uyttenbogaert*, bought at Sotheby's in London in July 1992 and sold in the same year to the Rijksmuseum. This was followed by our purchase of Rubens' *Entombment* at Christie's in London in December 1992 and quick sale to the J. Paul Getty Museum. Rembrandt's paintings have always moved me most, as even his portraits of rather boring people are first-class paintings. And so we purchased the *Portrait of a Young Man*, fully accepted by the Rembrandt Research Project (RRP) as A-60, from a bank in Geneva, and Otto sold this to Peter Ludwig, whose widow recently gave it to the museum in Aachen. Rembrandt's *Man in a Red Coat* is a far more interesting subject, and we purchased this with a fine Rubens of a ghastly subject, *The Head of John the Baptist Presented to Salome*, at the same sale at Sotheby's in New York in January 1998. Otto sold both quite quickly to Stephen Wynn, the Las Vegas casino operator, but Wynn didn't keep them long. The Rubens was transferred to the MGM Grand Hotel when Wynn sold the Bellagio Hotel, and was later sold to a private collector in New Jersey. The *Man in a Red Coat* was sold at Christie's in New York in January 2001, bought there by Robert Noortman, a dealer who was our major competitor for Rembrandts.

We purchased our finest Rembrandt, the last great historical Rembrandt ever likely to come on the market, the *Minerva* of 1635 (Plate 9), from owners in Japan in 2001. Its beauty and great condition had been obscured by layers of dirty varnish. It was one of the masterpieces in the Amsterdam and Berlin exhibitions of 2006, which celebrated the 400th anniversary of Rembrandt's birth.

The *Minerva* and one of the finest van de Cappelle seascapes (Plate 10) I have ever seen, purchased from the Earl of Northbrook's family in 2001, have only just been sold. You would think that the better the painting, the faster it would sell, but that just isn't so. But as we don't owe any money to a bank, keeping great works in inventory is no great concern, and such great masterpieces steadily increase in value.

My collaboration with Otto has not been limited to only Rembrandt and Rubens. A beautiful Aert de Gelder of *Tobias*, bought in 1994 from a Dutch dealer, was sold to a collector in New York; one of Ter Borch's finest works bought from Sotheby's New York in a private sale also went to a private collector; and a great Paulus Potter, from Sotheby's in London, went to the Art Institute of Chicago. And so on—great works by van der Heyden, Aert van der Neer, Jacob van Ruisdael, and Frans Hals. The last, bought in Christie's in New York in January 1999 for less than a million dollars, gave us particular pleasure. It was offered at auction ill-framed and ill-restored and looked so much better after conservation by our good friend and conservator Charles Munch that Otto was able to sell it to a knowledgeable private collector for well over twice our cost. Otto published his reasons for this "high" price, and in retrospect, in comparison with similar works by Hals sold since then, $2 million plus seems low.

Another painting bought with Otto and Konrad Bernheimer of Munich and now Colnaghi's in London, gave me immense pleasure for a different reason, best explained by quoting from Konrad's booklet prepared for this painting:

The focal point of our display is a magnificent work of early German art and the present catalog is indeed dedicated exclusively to the presentation of this masterpiece (Plate 11). It is a large-format Calvary of unique beauty and quality. This impressive depiction is without doubt one of the most significant of its kind within German post-war art trade.

The recent history of this masterpiece is also most poignant. Following expropriation from the Seligmann family in Paris by the Nazis, after the war it was in the Louvre. It was not until last year that it was returned to the heirs of Seligmann, namely the two daughters now living in the United States. The two ladies had their recovered family treasure auctioned in New York, and my colleagues Alfred Bader and Otto Naumann and I were fortunate enough to jointly purchase the painting. The most impressive elderly ladies were quite obviously deeply moved when we were introduced to them as the new owners of "their" painting.

It is with the greatest of pleasure that I am now able to present this masterpiece of early German painting. I would like to thank my colleagues Alfred Bader, Milwaukee, and Otto Naumann, New York, for their unceasingly pleasurable (and hitherto without exception successful!) cooperation.

The Christie's New York estimate in January 2000 had been only $800,000–$1,200,000, and the owners of the painting were of course really happy that the hammer price was $3,200,000. Eventually, Konrad was able to sell this masterpiece to the National Gallery in Washington.

With Clovis, I have worked mainly with Italian paintings, one of which, the Caravaggio with full details in Chapter 5, may be the most valuable painting I have ever acquired. Another truly interesting puzzle was a self-portrait of Guido Reni offered with a most intriguing period letter affixed to the unlined canvas at Sotheby's London in October 1999. Sotheby's described it as Bolognese School, first half of the seventeenth century, portrait of Guido Reni, and estimated it modestly at £6,000–£8,000. Clovis has now proven beyond a doubt that it really is a Reni self-portrait (Plate 12).

Philip Mould is the ablest expert of British portraits I have ever met. Our unsuccessful effort to buy a John Singer Sargent portrait of Balfour is described in Chapter 5. Our happiest collaboration was the purchase at Phillips in London in July 2001 of a portrait of Lady Mary Villiers by Van Dyck (Plate 13). Cleaning improved it greatly and, more important, removal of the relining showed King Charles I's royal cipher. The King had adopted Mary Villiers after her father, the first Duke of Buckingham, had been murdered, and Van Dyck had painted this portrait for the King. This is now one of the masterpieces in the Timken Museum of Art.

My happiest and most challenging collaboration with the Arnoldi-Livies was the purchase of the Menzel, also described in Chapter 5.

## An Old Woman by Rembrandt

One of the most interesting auctions I ever attended was at Christie's in London on December 13, 2000, where a genuine Rembrandt in wonderful condition, RRP A-63, an oval portrait of a sixty-two-year-old woman, from the estate of Baroness Bathsheva de Rothschild in Israel, was offered with a very low estimate, £4–£6 million. Just before the sale, Rob Noortman asked me whether I liked this painting, and I replied that I loved it and would bid on it. He said that his greatest teacher, many years ago, had taught him two principles that

Rob would pass on as his advice to me: "One, never buy an oval, and two, never buy a portrait of an old woman."

But the painting is so beautiful and was in such fine condition that I was determined to try to buy it anyway. Otto Naumann, Johnny van Haeften, a major dealer in London, and I had decided to bid together to £11 million. Johnny, sitting in the second row, was to bid for us, and Otto and I, sitting right behind him, were surprised when Johnny got carried away and bid £12 million. At £13 million, he stopped, and I decided to carry on, now alone with Otto, who told me later that he was worried when I bid up to £16 million. But that was my limit, and the auctioneer knocked it down to Rob Noortman for £17 million, a world auction record for a work by Rembrandt. With commission the total cost was £19,803,750.

After the sale, Rob came up to me and inquired whether I might like a share. I said I thought the price was too high but asked him about the two principles his master had taught him. He said, "Ah, I forgot to tell you the third principle: times have changed." We both smiled. My dealings with Rob have been varied, almost always pleasant, and always instructive. He even came to my gallery in Milwaukee and purchased two paintings. Well, the oval portrait is a beautiful painting, but Rob paid close to $30 million and it took quite a while for him to sell it. Perhaps I was lucky not to acquire it for a hammer price of £16 million.

Sadly, Rob Noortman died of a heart attack, though he was only sixty, in January 2007. The previous spring he had sold his company to Sotheby's. In the autumn of 2006, he had been diagnosed with cancer but was responding well to treatment, and so his death came as a tremendous shock. His son William wrote to me, "His determination never faltered and his vision never dimmed. As you know, he was indefatigable." Of course, this reminded me of what was said of Moses, "... his eye was not dim, nor his natural strength abated." But Moses was 120, Rob only sixty.

The most important old master in the last few years was offered at Sotheby's in London on July 10, 2002. *The Massacre of the Innocents* was painted by Rubens around 1610, a time when he still worked alone, without a workshop, and was at the height of his powers. For the previous three decades, it had hung in a covered courtyard in the Stift Reichersberg monastery in Upper Austria. The eighty-eight-year-old owner who had loaned it thoroughly disliked the violent subject of the painting, which she had inherited in 1923. Before that, in 1920, a small auction house in Vienna, Glückselig & Co., had sold it to her father as a work by Jan van den Hoecke, apparently acting as a broker for the Prince of Liechtenstein. It had been in the Liechtenstein collection since 1702 when it was bought as an early Rubens, but was misattributed to Frans de Neve in 1767, and to Jan van den Hoecke in 1780. In October 2001, a relative of the owner had brought a photograph to Sotheby's in Amsterdam, where Judith Niessen, thinking of Rubens, passed it on to George Gordon, their great old master expert. They immediately flew to Austria and were most excited by what they saw with the aid of a flashlight. George had seen only one similar painting, Rubens' *Samson and Delilah*, in the National Gallery in London, and it, too, had belonged to the Princes of Liechtenstein.

George showed me the *Massacre* a month before the sale, telling me that the estimate was £4–£6 million. My first question was whether I might be able to purchase it privately at a higher price. The answer was no. Otto Naumann and I discussed buying it together. Knowing that Rob Noortman was also interested, we met with him at 4 p.m. the afternoon of the sale and agreed that the three of us would bid together to £34 million, with Rob bidding for us. Rob and I were sitting in front, to the left of Henry Wyndham, the auctioneer, whom Rob had told minutes before the sale started at 7 p.m. that we would bid together. Bidding opened at £3 million with Ben Hall from Sotheby's New York shouting, "£6 million," to which Wyndham replied coolly, "Now I"ll take £12 million!"

Bidding continued briskly, in million pound increments, from 7 to 34 million, with Rob bidding two or three times. At £34 million, he turned to me and asked "One more?" I said yes, but even with that we were not the underbidder; that was a telephone bidder for the Getty. The climax came a minute later, with Wyndham calling, "£45 million—last chance at £45 million," and down the hammer came amidst a burst of applause and Wyndham's reminding us that "We have many more pictures to sell"—this was only lot 6 of 83. The successful bidder was Sam Fogg, acting for Ken Thomson, the richest man in Canada. The total cost was £49,506,650, a world record for a Rubens and a world record for a painting sold at auction in London. What a painting, and it went to Canada!

### Rembrandt A-84, *Portrait of a Woman*

In 2001, Otto and I made an offer to a very likable elderly couple in New York who owned a great early Rembrandt portrait of a woman. Signed and dated 1633, it had been in the family since 1954 and was accepted by the Rembrandt Research Project (RRP) as A-84. The comment in Volume I of the RRP *Corpus* states that it "shows an uncommonly subtle treatment of the face, which is modelled softly against a dark background, yet the execution and the handling of light and plasticity achieved are so characteristic of Rembrandt's style that there can be no doubt as to its authenticity."

Neither Otto nor I had any doubt, although we thought that it needed a gentle cleaning. Our offer to the couple was fair, with payment at once. But Sotheby's suggested that the owners would do better if they sold it at auction, and that is what they decided to do. For their part, Sotheby's tried very hard to ensure that the couple got a good price. The painting was on the catalog cover of the great auction that also included the magnificent Rubens, *The Massacre of the Innocents*. Thirteen pages of the catalog dealt with the Rembrandt, lot 35. For comparison, five other Rembrandt portraits were illustrated, one of which was the first undoubted Rembrandt Otto and I had purchased at Sotheby's and sold to the Rijksmuseum. Another was the oval of a sixty-two-year-old woman that Rob Noortman had bought.

Before the auction on July 10, I had a long discussion with George Gordon and Henry Wyndham, who conducted the sale. We talked mainly about the Rubens, but Wyndham asked me what I thought of the Rembrandt A-84. He saw no reason why it should not bring as much as Noortman's oval. The reason seemed simple to me. I had been the underbidder on the oval, from around £12 million to £17 million. Otto and I had already made an offer to the owners for this painting, A-84, and did not intend to bid at auction. The estimate of £10–£15 million, presumably with a reserve of £10 million, well over $14 million at the time, seemed high. Would there be at least two bidders to send it up to that price? Perhaps some buyers were put off by the alleged similarity of the sitter's face with that of Dede Brooks, the dethroned head of Sotheby's New York. Newspapers like to stress such foolishness. But bottom line: there was no bid at all, and the painting was returned to its owners who, I'm sure, were not at all happy.

Even before our trip to New York for the sales in January 2003, I had asked Otto whether we might talk to the owners once again and make a new offer without being hurtful. So Otto called, and we were invited to their apartment. To my surprise, I learned that the husband had been in the chemical industry and knew a good deal about me. We had a lot to talk about before we got to the painting, and it was no surprise that Isabel and Otto had a good rapport with his wife, whose father had bought the painting. Over a cup of tea, I made my offer, again with immediate payment, and was told that they would think about it and let us know. The next day, Isabel and

I were invited to their apartment at 2 p.m. on Sunday—it had to be early because we were flying back to Milwaukee from LaGuardia at 5:30 p.m. But, of course, we knew that the offer would be accepted—a phone call would have sufficed for a "no." As luck would have it, their lawyer, Ralph Lerner, knew about us, since he had handled the Japanese owners' sale of the *Minerva*. There were no problems, the money was wire transferred as soon as we returned to Milwaukee, and that same day Otto took the painting to Nancy Krieg, one of the country's great restorers who lives in New York, for the gentle cleaning that would greatly improve the sensitive portrait (Plate 14).

Shortly afterwards, Otto called with the exciting news that cleaning revealed a line of swirling brush strokes conforming to the oval shape of the painting. This was very important information, since there was much speculation about the original shape when it had been offered at Sotheby's. Like the *Man in a Red Coat* that Otto and I purchased a few years ago, Rembrandt painted an oval-shaped painting on a rectangular panel that was subsequently cut down to the inner oval. Although the spandrels in the corners are gone, we are not missing much. In Rembrandt's *Self-portrait*, offered at Sotheby's London on July 10, 2003, for instance, the spandrels are more or less roughly indicated. Clearly Rembrandt meant them to be covered by a frame. About a year later, the museum in Houston decided to purchase our fine painting at a price considerably less than they would have had to pay to Sotheby's in London in July 2002 if they had bid for it in the auction. All's well that ends well.

## Bredius 112, Barent Fabritius, Preti, Mantegna, and others

I don't think I have ever been offered as many very interesting paintings in the short period of six days as I was between January 21 and 26, 2003. Isabel and I flew to New York specifically to bid on two works at Sotheby's. One was the last Mantegna not in a museum. Eighteen pages of the Sotheby's catalog were devoted to the life and work of the artist; to the beautifully rendered ghastliness of the subject of Jesus descending into limbo, the waiting room at the entrance of hell, before his resurrection; and to Mantegna's sources and the history of this painting. Barbara Piasecka Johnson, who had bought this powerful painting in Paris in 1988, had decided to send it to auction, even though she was reported to have said at one time, "It's my greatest painting and I'll never sell it!" The reserve now was $20 million. Otto Naumann and I tried to persuade George Wachter, head of Sotheby's old masters, to lower the reserve because we thought the subject almost unsaleable. He assured us this would not be necessary and bet me $100 that the hammer price would be $30 million or more. It sold at $25 million, not to me, and George's $100 paid for many of the taxi rides around the city.

The second painting we bid on was a fine portrait of a man by Frans Hals on which Otto and I had been the underbidders at Christie's London in July 1999. The Nazis had stolen many paintings, including this and two other portraits by Hals, from the Austrian branch of the Rothschilds. Recovered after the war, they were taken to the Kunsthistorisches Museum in Vienna but were not returned to the Rothschilds until 1998. The California collector who bought this portrait in 1999 paid £2,201,500 for it. In January 2003, it had a reserve of only $2 million and brought a hammer price of $2.6 million, paid by the Prince of Liechtenstein. The Prince sold several great masterpieces after the last war, but has been rebuilding his collection in recent years. Otto and I were rather concerned by the attribution—Claus Grimm, the expert on Frans Hals, had labeled it "workshop"—but we were even more concerned by the condition. The blacks in the lower left looked very flat, so although the face was beautiful, we were not disappointed at being unsuccessful.

After the Sotheby's sale, Isabel and I visited several art dealers, one of whom, Budi Lilian, had a very interesting Rembrandt School work that I had seen at auctions over the years. Painted in 1660, it was said to be a self-portrait of Barent Fabritius as a shepherd. There is no Barent Fabritius in my collection, but the price the New York collector had paid at a small auction in 1979 seemed outlandishly high. Budi had bought it from that collector much more reasonably, and, true, it was signed, dated, and colorful, yet unlike his brother Carel, Barent was a minor master. I was tempted but undecided.

Budi then offered me two other Rembrandt School paintings of great interest. One, which he attributed to Willem Drost, had previously been called Rembrandt, Bredius 260 and is one of two versions; the other, at the National Gallery in Washington, is superior. The author of the excellent book on Drost, a Canadian, Jonathan Bikker, does not think that either version is by Drost, and I asked myself, "Was he really an artist to repeat himself?" Budi was asking $500,000, perhaps excessive for a work with a questionable attribution, and I decided to pass. He had acquired it very inexpensively at an auction in California and did eventually sell it for $225,000 to the Marquette University Museum in Milwaukee. Years ago, it had belonged to a collector in Milwaukee, Harry John. What is there about Milwaukee that attracts paintings by Rembrandt and his students?

The other painting Budi was offering was of much greater interest to me. All the Rembrandt experts, including the great naysayer Horst Gerson, had accepted Bredius 112, a portrait said to be of Hendrickje Stoffels (Plate 15) as a Rembrandt of the 1650s. Jakob Rosenberg, from whom I first learned about Rembrandt, had written glowingly about it. Norton Simon had purchased it in 1957 from Joseph Duveen, the greatest dealer of his time, who sold it for $133,500, as a Rembrandt, of course. It was his wife Lucille's favorite painting, and hung in their living room. When they divorced, she took the painting.

I had admired it in the great Rembrandt exhibition in Chicago in 1969, where it was the frontispiece in color in the catalog. Since then the experts of the Rembrandt Research Project have turned it down. Lucille Simon's estate sent it to Christie's New York in June 2002, where it was offered with an estimate of $300,000–$400,000, but without a reserve, and was bought by a consortium of four dealers, which included Budi and Johnny van Haeften. The hammer price was only $130,000. Had I known there was no reserve or had I been at the auction, I would certainly have bid higher.

Since that sale, I had seen it several times at Johnny van Haeften's gallery, really liked it, and had countered Johnny's offer to sell it at $300,000 with my offer of $200,000, which he politely declined. Now Budi was offering me both this beautiful portrait and the Barent Fabritius at what I considered a reasonable price, and I accepted without further bargaining. I am getting old. Isabel was with me, and she has always looked askance at my bargaining. Perhaps she doesn't fully realize that if I had not bargained hard years ago, I would have many fewer paintings, and, after all, the seller can always say no.

On the first day of our stay in New York that January, we had viewed an enormous canvas without a stretcher at the home of a very likable dealer, Larry Steigrad. This *Jacob Blessing His Grandchildren* by the Neapolitan Mattia Preti, of about 1680, was too big to be taken into Larry's gallery! Clovis Whitfield, who knows a great deal about such paintings, had liked it when he saw it and brought it to my attention. These days our worries are whether such paintings might have been stolen during the war, but the Preti had come to this country from Cuba before the war and been in storage all these years. I liked the painting and loved the subject. One of my favorite paintings in Kassel is Rembrandt's depiction. In the *Festschrift* for Ulrich Middeldorf, published in 1968, Wolf Stechow wrote a moving article, "'Jacob Blessing the Sons of Joseph' from

Rembrandt to Cornelius." He pointed out that the subject is quite rare. Rembrandt, Jan Victors, Guercino, and Johann Carl Loth were the only artists I knew who had painted the subject in the seventeenth century. When I was the curator of the exhibition The Bible Through Dutch Eyes at the Milwaukee Art Museum in 1976, Oberlin College had loaned us its Adriaen van der Werff, but it contains Prussian blue, so it must be eighteenth century.

I had never owned a painting of the subject, and this one was certainly striking, but the asking price was high. I offered Larry a third less, plus his commission, and my offer was accepted. Clovis and his associate, Edward Clark, who had come to New York, rolled it around a big tube to ship to London and then to Naples for restoration. When I saw it later in the year, carefully restored (Plate 16) and well framed, I realized how right I had been to acquire it. Here was another quite unknown seventeenth-century work! Art historians will always compare paintings of that subject with Rembrandt's masterpiece painted in 1656. As Stechow wrote, "Its beatific calm, its restraint in referring to the quarrel between Jacob and Joseph, its suggestion of a spirit of accord between the children, its emphasis upon their mother, Asenath—all these features are without parallel in seventeenth-century painting." Now we have one more comparison. Clovis sold the Preti to a collector in Hong Kong in January 2007.

Here was yet another link with Wolf Stechow, that human masterpiece, as I think of him. Wolf transformed the Allen Memorial Art Museum at Oberlin from a minor into a major museum, one of the best in the country. Isabel and I have always looked forward to going to Ohio and talking over old times and memories of Wolf with his widow. Intelligent and witty, Ursula shared Wolf's love of art and music, and was then still living in Oberlin. Sadly, she died in January 2008. On one such visit, she showed us one of his essays, "Rembrandt and the Old Testament," which had never been published. It was of great interest to me! Another, "The Crisis in Rembrandt Research," had been published in 1975 but was not well known, yet so succinct in its criticism of the then-current state of Rembrandt research.

Surprisingly, some young art historians have never heard of Stechow. I very much want to remind them of this great man but have only partly succeeded. Luckily, Betsy Wieseman, the acting director of the museum in 1998, knew a great deal about Wolf and really admired his work. I suggested to her that we honor Wolf's memory, first by dedicating a volume of the Oberlin Art Museum's *Bulletin* to him, and then by preparing an exhibition of the masterpieces he acquired for the museum. Betsy arranged for a beautiful publication. Volume L I, Number 2, and L II, Number 1, both of 1998, were combined into one and included Wolf's two essays, and also one by David Levine and Nicola Courtright titled "Wolfgang Stechow and the Art of Iconography, and an Appendix: Table of Contents and Addenda for Stechow's 'Gesammelte Aufsätze'." Betsy ended her introduction to this volume with, "Finally, I am pleased to dedicate this publication to two very special people, who have enriched my appreciation of Stechow the scholar with an understanding of the man: Wolf's widow, Ursula Stechow, who continues to be a devoted supporter and beloved friend of this museum; and Dr. Alfred Bader, who not only underwrote the cost of this publication, but whose continued generosity to this museum and to the Department of Art is a powerful and lasting memorial to the intellect and character of Wolfgang Stechow."

The plans were to follow this publication with an exhibition of the Stechow masterpieces, all at Oberlin. This should have been done quickly while Ursula, who was in her nineties, and I, in my eighties, were still alive. Sadly for the project, Betsy Wieseman moved to the Cincinnati Museum of Art and then on to the National Gallery in London. Her successor, Dr. Sharon Patton, had no interest in preparing what could have been a wonderful exhibition of the truly exceptional paintings Wolf had been able to collect for Oberlin.

I learned so much from Wolf about the quality of paintings and was so impressed with his contributions to Oberlin that I was inspired to try to build up a collection at my own university, Queen's, that might some day be the "Oberlin" of Canada. When I am considering buying a painting, I often ask myself whether he would approve of my choice. He certainly would have approved of the Mattia Preti and of the portrait, perhaps of Hendrickje Stoffels, that I bought in January 2003.

## Teniers, Drost

The second week of July 2003 was a very interesting auction week in London. On Wednesday the ninth, Christie's had two paintings of great interest to me; lot 18 was a David Teniers interior of an inn that, but for its history, would have been fairly estimated at £150,000. Since about 1700, it had belonged to the Wittelsbach Princes and Electors of Bavaria, then by inheritance to the King of Bavaria. In 1836, King Ludwig I transferred it to the newly built (Alte) Pinakothek where it remained until August 1938. Perhaps directed by Hitler, who preferred early German paintings, the museum decided to deaccession it. Fritz Nathan, a dealer in Zurich, bought it directly from the Pinakothek and sold it to his friend, Walther Bernt, in Munich. I first met Walther and Ellen Bernt in 1954 and visited their home every June for almost fifty years. Each time I had the great pleasure of looking at their fine collection, including this Teniers, so I knew the painting well. When Walther died, his widow Ellen remained in their beautiful home in the Mottlstrasse until her death in September 2002.

Their two daughters decided to divide the family home into two apartments so that they and their families could move into the house they love. Such renovations are costly, and both

Walther and Ellen had recommended that if the daughters had to raise funds at any time, they should first sell the Teniers. Isabel and I knew this because when we visited the daughters on June 19, 2003, they told us of their plans and hopes that the Teniers would do well at auction. I assured them that I would be bidding on that painting and believed that there would be a great deal of interest. We would do our best to make sure that it would do well.

In discussions before the sales in July, it became clear that many dealers were anxious to buy the Teniers. I believed that the dealer most likely to be able to sell it easily was Konrad Bernheimer, who owns Colnaghi's in London as well as a splendid gallery in Munich. When Otto Naumann and I discussed this with Konrad the day before the sale, Konrad explained that he knew of several potential customers in Germany, and with the painting's Bavarian provenance, it would be most fitting for it to return there. Otto often bids with his good friend Johnny van Haeften, but we could not involve Johnny because he had agreed to bid with Richard Green, a very aggressive London dealer, who insisted on a half share. So the three of us, Otto, Konrad, and I decided to bid jointly. A delightful fight was in the offing, which would greatly help Walther Bernt's daughters.

When you are hoping to buy a painting it is always good to be able to see the other bidders—it heightens the excitement— and our seating made it possible to do just that. Otto and I were sitting two rows behind Konrad, who was bidding for us. Johnny sat just behind Konrad and directly in front of us. Richard Green was across the aisle, also easily observed by us. We all knew the Teniers would go much higher than the estimate, and we three knew how high we were prepared to go. When we reached our limit, all our eyes were on Johnny and Richard Green. Would they bid one more? Richard Green did, and the successful bid of £460,000 was over three times the low estimate: a very good result. I was so happy to be able to call one of Walther's daughters in Munich and relate the details. She and her sister were delighted with the outcome. They hoped that it would end up in a museum, and that may happen eventually.

The second painting of particular interest to me was lot 34 in Christie's sale, a splendid self-portrait by Willem Drost (Plate 17), one of Rembrandt's ablest students. Only some thirty-eight of Drost's paintings are known, and Professor Werner Sumowski (see Chapter 10) had told me that this was one of Drost's two best paintings, the other being the magnificent *Bathsheba* in the Louvre. Well, that's a matter of taste. I also like Drost's portraits of women in the Wallace Collection and in Budapest, and I was concerned about how high this self-portrait would go. Not long ago, a Drost portrait of a man, which I did not like as well, sold at Sotheby's in New York for over $2 million. Again, Johnny van Haeften was bidding with Richard Green, and I had to go to £400,000, over three times Christie's low estimate. A high price, but when again might I have a chance to acquire such a great Drost?

The next day, July 10, Sotheby's offered three paintings of interest to me. This was the same date on which I had failed, the year before, to acquire that great Rubens, *The Massacre of the Innocents*, that was bought for Lord Thomson. The July 10, 2002 catalog cover had featured the Rembrandt portrait that did not sell at auction but which Otto and I were able to buy in January 2003. The 2003 cover was of lot 19, a Rembrandt self-portrait, signed and dated 1634, with a very curious history, most of which I knew well before the sale. Shortly after Rembrandt finished this self-portrait, it was over-painted, perhaps by one of his students, with an imaginary portrait of a man with a high Russian hat, gold chains, and pearl earrings. Around 1640, such a "tronie" might have been easier to sell than a rather bland Rembrandt self-portrait of 1634. When a copy of this overpainted work was shown to Professor Sumowski in 1955, he suggested to the German owner that it was likely based on an original overpainted Rembrandt. And so it was. The original turned up at a sale in Paris in 1955 and since then has been cleaned in stages. The last restoration, by Martin Bijl, the chief restorer of the Rijksmuseum, took two years to complete, as Bijl had to use a fine scalpel under strong magnification to remove the last of the overpaint: truly painstaking work.

George Gordon first showed me the partially cleaned painting at Sotheby's in 2001. I was struck by the quality of the lower half and what seemed to me an authentic signature and date in the lower right. Since then, Professor Ernst van de Wetering has written a long article about this restoration saga for the publication of the Rembrandthuis that exhibited the self-portrait early in 2003. I was able to examine the original carefully several times in London at Sotheby's. It is undoubtedly a genuine Rembrandt, in remarkably good condition considering its history, yet it is one of Rembrandt's blandest self-portraits—and that was probably the reason for the "more exciting," though poorer, overpaint.

In December 2002, Rob Noortman asked Otto and me whether we should bid on this Rembrandt together, as we had tried to purchase the Rubens. But the more Otto and I thought about the painting, the less we liked it. The reserve was said to be £3 million, a high price, it seemed, for Rembrandt's most boring self-portrait. Then, the day before the sale, Noortman again talked to us—with my son David listening carefully—and forcefully made the argument that this was likely to be quite easily sold, particularly if we just put it away for a year or so. We all knew that together we had four far better Rembrandts that have not been easy to sell, but Noortman was a superb salesman, and we agreed to go to a hammer price of £4.2 million, with Noortman bidding. Just before the sale, I wished him luck, and he invited all of us for lunch—if he was successful. I was not really certain whether or not to look forward to lunch.

Noortman was sitting in the front row, close to Henry Wyndham, the auctioneer, whom he had advised that we would be bidding together. Next to Noortman were his two sons, and close by were Isabel, David, and our granddaughter Helena, a serious eight-year-old interested in auctions. Otto and I were on the other side of the aisle, where we were able to watch Noortman and also the bank of Sotheby's staff, including George Gordon and George Wachter, taking telephone bids. At 10:56, Wyndham opened the bidding on lot 19 with £3 million. Noortman went on to £4.2 million as agreed, but bidding continued rapidly by telephone, ending at £6.2 million on a bid from Stephen Wynn. Wynn has long been interested both in major old master and impressionist paintings, and in 1998, he had purchased a Rembrandt portrait of a man in a red coat and a Rubens from Otto and me. He has sold both since then, and the *Man in a Red Coat* now belongs to Noortman.

The only other paintings of real interest to me were a pair of great Vernets, sold together as lot 65, the last lot of the sale. Usually I am not interested in French paintings, but these are such beautiful works, a sunset and a shipwreck, ordered from the artist in the summer of 1772 by the King of Poland. When difficulties with payment arose, Lord Clive of India purchased the pair, in the frames chosen by Vernet, for 400 louis, the price quoted to the King of Poland. And the paintings had remained in the possession of Clive's family until 12:15 that Thursday noon.

Naturally this magnificent pair should go to a museum, but who could sell them? Certainly not I, from Milwaukee, and probably not Otto in New York. Loath not to have had any hand in the purchase of these beautiful paintings, I turned to Konrad. At first, we agreed that he would bid to £1.5 million, but when a higher bid was made, I quickly urged him to go to £2 million. But even that was not enough, and Konrad was the underbidder when the hammer fell at £2.2 million. Noortman and his sons had left, disappointed, right after the Rembrandt sale, and so Isabel and I invited Hubert van Baarle, an old friend from Rotterdam, to a simple lunch at Debenhams, just soup and salad, certainly less expensive and perhaps healthier than lunch would have been if we had bought the Rembrandt. And so the week ended with my buying only one great painting: the Drost. But the silver lining was that I enjoyed working with both these major dealers, and we may collaborate even more closely in the future.

## Lievens

It doesn't happen very often that I am really happy that a painting at auction "got away." Not often, but sometimes. So it was at 4:30 in the morning on Wednesday, October 1, 2003, when a very pleasant young lady from the Dorotheum in Vienna called me at home to bid on lot 85, a portrait of a man in profile, painted by Jan Lievens in Leiden around 1630. Isabel and I had examined the painting carefully at the Dorotheum in June, and Dr. Wolf, the director of the auction house, had explained that it came from an Austrian nobleman who had no idea what the painting was. But there was no question that it was a fine Lievens, and in the catalog, Dr. Wolf illustrated it with a photo of my painting of Rembrandt's mother by Lievens, painted at about the same time.

The young lady told me there were no less than thirteen bidders on the telephone. Bidding started modestly enough at €12,000 and climbed very rapidly to €120,000, where I stopped bidding, but then listened for what I thought was the final result, which was €650,000, a result that was accompanied by applause. I told the young lady that I presumed that Richard Green was the buyer, and she replied that she could not tell

Plate 9: Rembrandt, *Minerva*.

PLATE 10 (opposite top): The van de Cappelle seascape I
purchased from the Earl of Northbrook's family in 2001.

PLATE 11 (opposite below): The Calvary I bought with
Otto and Konrad Bernheimer in 2000.

PLATE 12 (above): The painting bought at Sotheby's in
1999, which Clovis Whitfield has now proven to be a Reni
self-portrait.

PLATE 14: Rembrandt A-84,
*Portrait of a Woman.*

PLATE 15: Rembrandt
School, Bredius 112,
*Portrait of a Woman.*

PLATE 16: Preti, *Jacob Blessing His Grandchildren.*

Plate 17: Willem Drost, *Self-portrait*.

PLATE 18: Rembrandt, *Abraham and the Three Angels*.

me that but that she could tell me that he was bidding and Johnny van Haeften was also.

I am a compulsive buyer, so in fact I was happy about the result, because at home we have three works by Lievens that I like very much better, and Queen's University has three better works that we have given them. After the telephone call, I was able to sleep soundly for another two hours after reflecting that this Lievens had cost about as much as I had to pay for the wonderful Drost self-portrait at Christie's on July 9, 2003, and, of course, there is really no comparison.

The next day I learned about an amazing sequel to the bidding. Among the telephone bidders were Richard Green, Luca Baroni, and Johnny van Haeften, all well-known dealers, and the hammer went down when Johnny bid €650,000. A few minutes later, unbeknownst to me at the time, the auctioneer reopened the bid. Luca Baroni had been bidding on his cell phone from Florence and the girl talking to him had misunderstood him, thinking that he would not go higher than Johnny's bid of €650,000. But Baroni called back, and the Dorotheum called both Richard Green and Johnny van Haeften to tell them that the bidding was being reopened. The painting was finally knocked down to Baroni for €760,000, which means that Baroni had to pay a total of €912,000, about $1 million, for this competent painting that is certainly not Lievens' best. Johnny was furious, but I think that he should really be happy not to have to pay that amount for a painting that might not be all that easy to sell.

## Bredius 515

From October 2003 to May 2004, the Museum of Fine Arts in Boston and the Art Institute of Chicago had an important exhibition titled Rembrandt's Journey showing many works by Rembrandt the painter, the draftsman, and the etcher.

Whenever I look at catalogs of Rembrandt exhibitions, I check who the lenders are. Museums are unlikely to sell their works of art; individual lenders might.

There were three privately owned paintings in this great exhibition. The first, No. 31, I knew well. It is the bust of an old man of 1633, a tiny oil on paper, laid down on panel, RRP A-74. Richard Feigen, the well-known New York dealer, had sold it to Saul Steinberg in New York in 1986 and then it came up at a Sotheby's New York sale in January 1997 where it was bought by a collector in Japan. It is a tiny painting, perfectly genuine, but I believe not as attractive as the painting of an old man, RRP C-22, that I had just given to Queen's University.

The second privately owned painting was a small masterpiece, only 16 cm x 21 cm, oil on panel, Bredius 515 (Plate 18), to be described in RRP Vol. V. That painting, owned by the Aurora Art Fund, was certainly of such beauty that it was worth considering carefully.

The third painting, owned, I believe, by a collector in Boston, was the last painting in the exhibition, No. 216, the Apostle James, signed and dated Rembrandt f. 1661. In the exhibition, it hung close to the second-to-last painting, a Rembrandt self-portrait of 1659, in the National Gallery of Art in Washington, perhaps the finest painting in the exhibition, and the comparison was very hard on the Apostle James. I had seen that painting several times before, and I simply do not like it. And, of course, I did not bid on it when it was bought by a Japanese collector at Sotheby's in New York in January 2007.

That left *Abraham and the Three Angels*, signed and dated 1646, for careful consideration.

I discussed this with Otto Naumann, who knows Gerald Stiebel of Stiebel Ltd., who had arranged for the loan. Otto said that Stiebel was both able and straightforward and that he would speak to him.

When he told me later that he had offered $6 million, I said that this seemed much too low and that he should go very much higher, subject to our examining the painting very carefully. Of course, we soon made the much higher offer and the answer came back very quickly: The painting is yours at the price offered plus 10 percent, provided we can work out all the delivery details, with handover after the exhibition ended in Chicago in May.

The provenance of the painting is most impressive. It was probably first mentioned in a transaction in March 1647 in which one merchant agrees to exchange diamonds, silverwork, and several paintings for a supply of ropes, masts, and iron. Among the paintings was an *Abraham and the Three Angels* by Rembrandt. Then, in 1669, it had belonged to Ferdinand Bol, Rembrandt's student, and to Jan Six, in whose sale in 1702 it was lot 40. It had then belonged to Benjamin West and several well-known English collectors, of which Sir Thomas Baring was the best known. In 1923, it was acquired by Walter and Catalina von Pannwitz. Around 1950, Catalina von Pannwitz established the Aurora Trust, and in 1986 the painting was placed into the Aurora Art Trust Fund. Thus, there was no concern whatever about where the painting had been during the last war. The Art Fund was owned by the Pannwitz descendants, one of them in Argentina and another in England. Barry Kessler, Trustee of the Aurora Art Fund in New York, confirmed that Gerald Stiebel, as art advisor to the trust, was authorized to sell the painting. Where to transfer the painting became a bit complicated, and finally we agreed that the invoice would be written "CIF Chicago," which would allow the painting to be picked up there on Monday, May 10, the day after the exhibition ended, and taken directly to restorer Nancy Krieg.

Otto called me the next day to tell me that Nancy Krieg had begun cleaning the *Abraham* and that it was clear that it would be much improved. By Friday, May 14, the cleaning was complete, Otto had acquired a fine little frame and was ready to offer it to interested customers; on May 27, 2004, Otto e-mailed me, "This is the most precious and beautiful object I have *ever* handled."

Isabel and I first saw the painting in Chicago, together with David de Witt, the Bader Curator, and Janet Brooke, the director of the Agnes Etherington Art Centre, on Sunday, March 14. Before that, I had, of course, discussed the quality of the painting with Otto Naumann and Bill Robinson (at Harvard), both of whom liked it immensely. So did I, realizing how much improved the painting was likely to be when cleaned and placed in a fitting frame.

Rembrandt's vision of the visit to Abraham was very different from mine. I always thought of the three angels as being messengers from God, but Rembrandt depicted the central angel, from whom light emanates so wonderfully, as God himself. While the painting is tiny in scale, it is executed very freely and really looks like a finished work. Traditionally the scene has always been placed during the middle of the day, but surprisingly, here it is just at sunset, almost in darkness. That makes the light from the central figure appear all the more stunning.

The Rembrandt Research Project had examined the painting in August 1971 and then again in May 1992. On January 15, 1999, Professor Ernst van de Wetering, the remaining member of the original RRP, sent Gerald Stiebel a twenty-two-page report, which was to become the entry for RRP *Corpus*, Vol. V. In that letter, Professor van de Wetering wrote, "This is to enable them [the owners] to propose corrections or additions for which we will be grateful and to react on our opinions." In the report, Ernst van de Wetering had some reservations, particularly about the condition, stating "Condition: good insofar as can be assessed through the thick varnish layer. No clear paint loss can be observed." Now, of course, with the painting cleaned, we could see so clearly how excellent the condition is.

When Otto showed this painting to Professor Ernst van de

Wetering in Amsterdam in November 2004, he had no doubt about the authenticity and condition of the painting, and revised the entry for *Corpus* Vol. V and the catalog of the great 2006 Rembrandt exhibition in Amsterdam and Berlin, celebrating 400 years since Rembrandt's birth.

Two dealers, Konrad Bernheimer in Munich and Richard Feigen in London, decided to exhibit this painting in their galleries. Eventually, in April 2005, an old customer and friend of Otto's, Mark Fisch, decided to purchase a three-year option, which I have little doubt that he will exercise. In the meantime, the painting was being admired in the Metropolitan Museum and was in the great Rembrandt exhibitions in Amsterdam and Berlin. Mark Fisch has purchased many great old masters from Otto before, and this will, I believe, be the jewel of his collection.

# 4

# *Rembrandt/Not Rembrandt*[1]

E ver since listening to Jakob Rosenberg's lecture on Rembrandt at Harvard in 1948, I hoped that some day I would be able to acquire one of Rembrandt's paintings. The first opportunity arose when the Viennese owner of a small work on copper depicting *A Scholar by Candlelight* (Plate 19) sold this to me in 1959. I bought it subject to Jakob Rosenberg's accepting it as a Rembrandt, which he did after close inspection at Harvard during a week I left it with him.

Two members of the Rembrandt Research Project (RRP), S.H. Levie and Ernst van de Wetering, examined this painting in my house in September 1972 and told me during their visit that they believed it to be an early work by Rembrandt, in paint handling very similar to that of Rembrandt's *Flight into Egypt* in Tours. The RRP then asked me to bring it to Amsterdam in 1973, and in Volume 1 of the *Corpus* that appeared in 1982, gave both my painting and that in Tours C numbers (not by Rembrandt), C-18 and C-5, probably by the same artist from Rembrandt's immediate circle.

From November 2001 to May 2002, the museum in Kassel and the Rembrandthuis in Amsterdam held an exhibition, The Mystery of the Young Rembrandt, which included the *Flight into Egypt* as a Rembrandt and my painting hanging next to the *Flight* as a Rembrandt or Circle of Rembrandt.

The history of this painting and the question of attribution have been described clearly in David de Witt's 2008 catalog *The Bader Collection*.

My next Rembrandt acquisition, again initially a C, C-22 in the *Corpus*, was the *Head of an Old Man in a Cap* (Plate 20), which I was able to purchase very inexpensively at Christie's in London in March 1979. I was convinced of its authenticity, but as the Christie's catalog stated that the RRP did not accept it, there was little competition. Volume I of the *Corpus*, published in 1982, gives a three-page discussion of the painting, beginning with the summarized opinion that describes C-22 as "a well preserved painting from Rembrandt's immediate circle, reproduced in 1634 as his invention in an etching by J.G. Van Vliet." Following Section 4. Comments is a note, "December 1979: one of the authors (Ernst van de Wetering) does not rule out the possibility of no. C-22 being an autograph work by Rembrandt."

As David de Witt has pointed out in the catalog *The Bader Collection*:

> The turning point came with the 1996 exhibition on Rembrandt and Van Vliet in the Rembrandthuis in Amsterdam, where it was proven that Van Vliet and Rembrandt collaborated on some prints, and that the watermarks appearing in the paper on some examples also appeared in impressions of Van Vliet's print after the present painting. Evidently, Rembrandt returned regularly to Leiden to direct the work of Van Vliet, and so there would not have been a mistake about the right in authorship of the present painting. Since the 1996 exhibition, scholars have generally voiced approval of the attribution to Rembrandt.

Isabel and I gave this painting to Queen's University in 2003, the first of several Rembrandts to go to Queen's.

In his two-volume work on Rembrandt published in 1949, Jakob Rosenberg illustrated two heads of old men (Plates 21 & 22) side by side on one page. Both of these subsequently came up at auction. The one I liked particularly (fig. 100 in Rosenberg's book) was offered in the sale of the famous Alfred W. Erickson collection at Parke-Bernet in New York in November 1961. There it was one of three Rembrandts, the most famous of which, *Aristotle Contemplating the Bust of Homer*, was purchased by the Metropolitan Museum for $2.3 million. The other two Rembrandts were estimated very reasonably, and so I flew to New York to bid for the *Old Man*, signed and dated Rembrandt f. 1659 (Plate 21). I was not the only one to love this work, however, and Derek Cotton, a collector in Birmingham, England, bought it for $180,000. This was far more than I was able to pay. My salary was very modest; Aldrich was still a small company, and had not yet gone public. In the 1970s, the Rembrandt Research Project must have indicated that they did not accept it as genuine, and when Derek Cotton's son offered it at Christie's London in April 1993, it was described as Circle of Rembrandt, with an estimate of £60,000–£80,000. I was at the sale, once again hoping to buy it, but when I noted that no one was bidding, I decided not to bid either. I made a much lower bid after the sale, and that was accepted.

Both of my sons, David and Daniel, are serious collectors of paintings, and each will have two of my best paintings. Daniel has really loved this *Old Man*, and so I gave it to him. The painting has again been carefully examined by van de Wetering, who has told us that he is now certain of its authenticity. He borrowed it with three other works for a small exhibition in Amsterdam in 2005 titled Rembrandt's Studies: New Light on an Old Problem. In 2006, it was included in the great Rembrandt exhibitions in the Rembrandthuis and in Berlin in celebration of 400 years since Rembrandt's birth. Is it by Rembrandt? I am not totally certain, as I am not certain of some of van de Wetering's other new attributions, but I love it, as does Daniel. Again, this painting is carefully described in David de Witt's *Bader* catalog, although it will not come to Queen's because it is Daniel's. The catalog also contains a description of a second painting that will not go to Queen's: a

*Joseph and the Baker* by a Delft Rembrandt student, which will go to David.

The second of the two paintings illustrated by Jakob Rosenberg (fig. 99) is *Head of a Bearded Man: Study for St. Matthew* (Plate 22), which I bought as Circle of Rembrandt at Christie's London in February 1995. David de Witt (Plate 25) has described this painting in the *Bader* catalog clearly:

> This little panel displays the moving visage of a man in robust middle age, with a heavy, thick beard. He turns to the right and looks off to the side. His lowered eyelids, furrowed brow, pursed lips, and empty gaze suggest that he is absorbed in thought. His expression connects him directly to Rembrandt's well-known depiction of *St. Matthew Inspired by the Angel* in the Louvre, as do his features, such as his prominent brow and cheekbones, and the pronounced *levator labii* muscles flanking the nose. This painting does not appear to be derived from the St. Matthew, however. In the Paris painting, the figure is seen more on a level, draws his hand to his chin, and wears a turban-like headdress. Here the figure wears a simple soft cap and a heavy smock. The differences between the two could reflect the transformation of a head study from a model into a finished history painting. The simple costume in the small panel is derived from contemporary dress, bereft of any historical allusions. The lack of any sign of Rembrandt's inventive elaboration of St. Matthew's figure again indicates that it is not a copy after it. It is nearly certain that the present work reflects Rembrandt's study of a figure in preparation for the St. Matthew. The question remains whether it is an original sketch, or a copy after one, by Rembrandt. Depictions by him of Jeremiah and of Jesus seem to have been preceded by painted studies in a similar fashion.

Bredius identifies it as autograph, but groups it with three other small panels showing the same model in slightly varying views. However, none of these other works approaches its decisive handling and structure. One of them, a panel in Washington, is an exercise in direct impasto strokes, but does not yield a strong impression.

Isabel and I took this painting to the National Gallery in Washington, where the curator Arthur Wheelock allowed us to compare it with their version (Bredius 302). His comments were, "I cannot tell you whether your version is by Rembrandt, but I can tell you that yours is much better than ours." Rembrandt/Not Rembrandt: clearly the jury is still out, but whether by the master or one of his students, it has given us a good deal of pleasure.

Perhaps my happiest acquisition was that of a *Small Head of an Old Man in Profile* (Plate 23) on panel, offered from the John Hay Whitney collection at Sotheby's in New York in May 2000. Described as Circle of Rembrandt, it was estimated at only $40,000–£60,000. Bidding by telephone, I was prepared to go very high, as I believed that there was a good chance that it was an original Rembrandt, and I was very happy when the auctioneer, George Gordon, knocked it down to me for $125,000. Our good friend George hand-delivered it when he came to Milwaukee on a visit to the Midwest after the sales.

Removing the dirty old varnish was very easy; conservator Charles Munch told me that he had seldom worked on a seventeenth-century panel in such good condition. I was eager to show it to Ernst van de Wetering and offered to take it with us when we went to Amsterdam in November. He spent a long time with the little panel when we showed it to him, and Peter Klein from Hamburg, who happened to be visiting him at the time, took a small sample of the wood and was able to determine by dendrochronology that a date around 1661 was likely. Ernst asked us to bring the panel to the Rijksmuseum the next day so that he could compare it with Rembrandt's *Self-Portrait as the Apostle Paul*, which is signed and dated 1661.

In *Rembrandt: Quest of a Genius*, the catalog of the Rembrandthuis exhibition of 2006 where our paintings were exhibited, Ernst wrote:

This small painting, which is evidently related to Rembrandt's *Circumcision of Christ in the Stable* in 1661 in Washington, originated rather late in Rembrandt's career. In the *Circumcision*, several old men—including the Mohel who carries out the circumcision and a man who writes in a book—are depicted in roughly the same way as the man in this study ... Now that the painting has been freed of its thick layer of varnish, it can be seen as a small masterpiece, both as regards colour and *peinture*. It has been executed at a high tempo, wet in wet. With all its dynamism, it betrays such an astonishing control of the pictorial means available and, as a result, such a supreme sense of form on the part of its author, that one can scarcely imagine it could have been painted by a pupil. Nor could it be a copy, executed by a pupil, after one of the figures in the Washington *Circumcision*: the visual "information" in the *Circumcision* is simply too scant for that. In its execution and color scheme, the *Lighting Study of an Old Man in Profile* shows a striking resemblance to Rembrandt's *Self-Portrait as Paul* from 1661 in the Amsterdam Rijksmuseum. Confrontation between these two paintings leaves no room for doubt as to the study's authenticity. On this basis alone, it may be assumed that the study originated around 1661, the year in which the Washington *Circumcision* originated according to the date applied to that painting. We can safely accept, therefore, that the small painting from the Bader collection was a preparatory study for the *Circumcision*.

This painting was also in van de Wetering's small 2005 exhibition and in the major Rembrandt exhibitions in Amsterdam and Berlin in 2006, and I have now given it to Queen's University.

One of the best dealers in old master paintings I have ever known was Neville Orgel in London. Despite his great knowledge, he was pessimistic and so self-effacing that he asked me not to mention his name in my first autobiography. I bought many paintings from him before he moved from London to Israel, where he died in 2003. In 1977, on one of my rare visits to his home in Golders Green, I saw a fine portrait of *Rembrandt Sketching* (Plate 24), much like Bredius 46 in Dresden and Bredius 47 in San Francisco. In 1970, Neville had sent a photograph of his painting to Dr. Kurt Bauch, the great Rembrandt expert in Germany, who had replied that he preferred Neville's portrait to those in Dresden and San Francisco, but did not believe that Neville's was by Rembrandt. I loved the portrait. Neville was not keen to sell it (he had never taken it to his gallery), but he said he would sell to me if I paid him enough to buy an apartment he wanted in Israel—£40,000.

Since then, it has hung over my desk at home and given me a great deal of pleasure. It has graced the cover of an Aldrich catalog and has been in two exhibitions at Purdue, two at Queen's University, and one titled The Detective's Eye at the Milwaukee Art Museum.

There are six versions of this portrait of Rembrandt, and at first I had hoped that mine might be the original. It is not. Volume IV of the Rembrandt Research Project deals only with Rembrandt self-portraits. In this volume, van de Wetering has written about all six versions, including mine, which he has illustrated extensively giving one full color illustration and one black/white and two color illustrations of details of my painting, coming to the conclusion that it is a period portrait of Rembrandt, but not even painted in Rembrandt's workshop.

Over the years, I kept Neville informed about my findings, and shortly before he died, he offered to repurchase the picture for $100,000. I declined. I just like it too much, no matter who painted it.

The last Rembrandt/Not Rembrandt painting I acquired was the *Portrait of a Woman*, perhaps Hendrickje Stoffels, Bredius 112, the purchase of which I have described in Chapter 3.

Who painted Lucille Simon's favorite portrait? In 1979, when I purchased *Head of an Old Man in a Cap*, RRP C-22, at an auction at Christie's London, I was convinced that it was by Rembrandt, although the RRP was not. Now it is universally accepted as by Rembrandt. With Bredius 112, however, I am not convinced, but I love it and, like the four dealers who owned it until February 2003, I have been searching for a name. It is certainly period. Drost has been suggested, but it is not like any of the thirty-eight works accepted by Jonathan Bikker. David de Witt, the Bader Curator at Queen's, thought briefly of Abraham van Dyck, and that is close. But I have two of his signed works at home, and the paint handling is not quite the same. Now David has considered the possibility that it might be by Jacobus Leveck, working in Rembrandt's studio in the 1650s. Again, a detailed history and description of this painting is given in David's *Bader Collection* catalog.

Ernst van de Wetering has told me that he hates the painting. What a strange reaction to a painting, which Jakob Rosenberg had loved and considered a great Rembrandt, and which was the frontispiece in color of the catalog of the Rembrandt exhibition in Chicago in 1969. Paintings do cause strong emotions, and I buy only paintings I really love for my own collection. This is one of them.

REFERENCES:
1. I want to thank Walter Liedtke for allowing me to use the title of his great exhibition in the Metropolitan Museum in 1995–6 for the title of this chapter.

5

# More Great Paintings by Old Masters

## Caravaggio

Perhaps the most exciting painting I ever acquired was the *Lute Player* sold by Sotheby's in New York, in January 2001, for $110,000. That was not the reason Isabel and I were there, for we had gone specifically to buy a lovely but very dirty and unpublished painting of Tobit by Eeckhout (Plate 26), signed and dated 1652. Eeckhout may have seen his friend Rembrandt's 1626 treatment of almost the same subject (RRP A-3). In Eeckhout's painting, the old, blind Tobit is clearly fearful that his wife may have stolen the kid. In Rembrandt's version, Tobit regrets having accused his wife of theft. During the preview, I was bothered when Ben Hall of Sotheby's offered to take the painting down from the high spot where it was hard to see, to show me its real beauty with the help of mineral spirits. I already knew how much I liked the painting and feared that he would do the same for others. Whether others had a good look at it or not I do not know, but I was able to buy it for the bargain hammer price of $30,000.

Of course, we looked at all the other paintings in the preview and really liked one other, lot 179, the large *Lute Player*, cataloged as Circle of Caravaggio and estimated at $100,000 to $150,000. Its appearance was deceptive, because the thick, yellowed varnish gave it the impression of a later work, even nineteenth century—but it had been in an English country house since 1726. I am no expert on Caravaggio, or on Italian baroque paintings, but as luck would have it, our friend Clovis Whitfield, who certainly is an expert in these things, was at the preview at the same time. And so I asked him to look at lot 179. He was as intrigued as I was, only armed with more knowledge. We agreed that I would bid on the painting, and if I was successful, he would research the picture.

Since then, Clovis has worked hard to trace the history of the *Lute Player*, to show that it is not only a work by Caravaggio, but the prime original and the work that the artist himself recalled as his finest production. Tracing its history back to the eighteenth century was easy. The nineteen-year-old Henry Somerset, 3rd Duke of Beaufort, had acquired it on his Grand Tour as a Caravaggio. In Rome, where he was a supporter of the Old Pretender, he spent the enormous sum of 30,000 scudi on art, 200 of which on the *Lute Player*, which was then sent to England to hang at the family seat in Gloucestershire, Badminton House. Never visited by connoisseurs like George Vertue, Horace Walpole, or Waagen, the collection had many great works, but the *Lute Player* came to be regarded as a copy, and it was sent for sale at Sotheby's in 1969, where it brought £750. Marshall Spink, a dealer in London, bought it, and then sold it to a family in Athens, Greece, who were looking for decorations for their home. On their deaths, the contents of the home were sold to a dealer in London, who consigned the *Lute Player* to Sotheby's auction in New York in 2001. He must have been happy that I paid $110,000 for it. So was I.

To discover the path of the *Lute Player* from 1726 back to the time Caravaggio painted it, around 1596–8, was more difficult. It is not clear whether the Duke of Beaufort bought it in Rome, or on the way back from the Grand Tour through the Marches and Venice, but at Badminton, it was admired as Caravaggio's "Venetian courtesan," and its fame in Rome in Cardinal Del Monte's collection forgotten. The situation is complicated by the fame of the more famous *Lute Player* that has hung at the Hermitage in St. Petersburg since the early nineteenth century. This work (Plate 27) came from the collection of Marchese Vincenzo Giustiniani, Caravaggio's other main patron in Rome, and is first described in the inventory of his collection drawn up in 1638.

It had already been noticed that this famous work was lacking some of the elements described by Baglione, the earliest of Caravaggio's biographers. Giovanni Baglione famously brought a libel case against Caravaggio and friends for defamation, and bore him a grudge, but he did devote a fascinating biography to him, and described the *Lute Player* in the collection of Cardinal Del Monte with more detail than any other of his works in his 1642 *Vite de" pittori, scultori et architetti* (p.136): "He also painted for the Cardinal [Del Monte] a young man, playing the Lute, who seemed altogether alive and real with a carafe of flowers full of water, in which you could see perfectly the reflection of a window and other features of that room inside the water, and on those flowers there was a lively dew depicted with every exquisite care. And this (he said) was the best piece he ever painted." Only our version (Plate 28) fits this description, for the carafe with the reflections, and the dewdrops on the flowers and fruit (Plate 29), are absent from the Hermitage picture—and it used to be said, by way of explanation, that these features must have been cleaned away at some point, which is not the case.

Two other *Lute Players* have come to light, but with musical instruments (including a significant spinet) in place of the flowers and fruit, one on loan to the Metropolitan Museum (Plate 30) that has been traced back to Cardinal Antonio Barberini's purchase from the Del Monte heirs in 1628 of a picture of "young man playing the spinet." But then, the vendors did not describe the work as by Caravaggio when they sold it, unlike the two others in the group he bought, which included the *St. Catherine* now in the Thyssen-Bornemisza Collection, Madrid, and the *Cardsharps* in the Kimbell Museum, Fort

71

Worth. There, the "bird's eye" perspective that affects the table, each musical instrument, and the birdcage, as well as the inconsistent lighting, look unlike Caravaggio's. A fourth version, now in the Salini collection in Paris (Plate 31), also has musical instruments instead of the flowers, and seems to correspond with the copy Antonio Barberini had made of *his* version in 1642. So the painting from the New York sale is the only one to correspond to Baglione's description, and it must be the work listed among Del Monte's possessions in 1627 as a "young man, playing the lute, by Caravaggio" and distinct from the picture with a spinet sold to Cardinal Barberini.

To summarize: Clovis argues, I believe convincingly, that our painting is the *Lute Player* mentioned by Baglione in the Del Monte Collection, while on the other hand the *Lute Player* in the Metropolitan Museum was sold by the Del Monte heirs in 1628 to Antonio Barberini. Therefore we have to assume that Del Monte actually possessed two versions of the *Lute Player*, one autograph version (our painting) which was sold at an unknown date (but after 1627 when it is listed in the inventory drawn up for his heir Alessandro Del Monte) to an unknown collector, and an early pastiche (with spinet instead of flowers), now on loan to the Metropolitan Museum. This pastiche was sold in 1628 to Antonio Barberini. There is a copy of this in the Salini collection in Paris. Caravaggio painted a second, very beautiful version of the *Lute Player* (without the reflections in the carafe described by Baglione) for Giustiniani, now at the Hermitage.

How did Caravaggio paint our painting? Clovis enlisted the help of Professor Martin Kemp at Oxford, author of *The Science of Art*, a work that traces the connection between art and science. Kemp published his conclusions in *Nature* (in the November 28, 2002 issue of Vol. 420, p.364); Caravaggio probably used a concave mirror and the result evidently greatly impressed the painting's first owner, Cardinal Del Monte, who gave the artist space to live in and work, probably at Palazzo Firenze, one of the buildings he looked after in Rome for his great friend, the Granduke Ferdinando de' Medici. Cardinal Del Monte lived in the Palazzo Firenze and the Palazzo Madama in Rome (both Medici properties) in his official role as representative of the Florentine Court in Rome. He was of course chosen for this role because of his long-standing relation with Ferdinando and the Medici court.

Clovis, of course, has invited many experts to examine the painting, and also sent it to the Museum in Berlin, for the comparison with the Hermitage version then on view there. Sir Denis Mahon, the doyen of English experts on the Italian Baroque, agreed that our painting is by Caravaggio, and while at first he regarded the Hermitage picture as earlier, he subsequently came to see that since Baglione's description only fits our version, it must therefore be the first.

One of Italy's greatest Caravaggio experts, Professor Mina Gregori, agreed, and wrote the entry for the catalog of the exhibition at which our picture was first publicly exhibited, a beautiful show of Italian still life titled *Stille Welt, Natura Morta Italiana*, that was presented in Munich at the Kunsthalle der Hypo-Kulturstiftung, and then in Palazzo Strozzi, Florence, from 2002–3.

An even more instructive exhibition titled *Caravaggio: Originale und Kopien im Spiegel der Forschung* (Caravaggio, Originals and Copies in the Mirror of Research) opened in the Düsseldorf Museum Kunst Palast in September 2006. The extensive catalog illustrates all four *Lute Players*, each also with details and, most tellingly, on p.95, the detail of the carafe with flowers exactly as described by Baglione, present only in our version (catalog no. 33). The other version brought to Düsseldorf, from the Salini collection in Paris (catalog no. 32), is close to the picture now on loan to the Metropolitan Museum; in both, a spinet replaces the flowers present in the Hermitage picture and our painting. The prominent pentiments visible in this area of our painting are another indication of its originality, and the presence of light incisions in the ground that have been found by the EMMEBICI laboratory in Rome are further indications of its status as the first version. It is hard to believe that the Salini collection work could be from the period when Caravaggio was working, even though Maurizio Marini claims in an essay (pp.241–242), in the catalog, that it is the first one. Clovis' essay (pp.242–244) contradicting this idea, is very convincing. Of course, owners tend to be optimists, yet to me it seems clear that ours and the Hermitage versions are by Caravaggio, painted in that order, while the version in the Metropolitan Museum is a competent pastiche, and the Salini version a copy, in turn, of that picture.

The next step Clovis is hoping to take is to publish an essay on Cardinal Del Monte's *studiolo* in what became the Villa Ludovisi, where he argues the painting originally hung, and to have the work included in the major retrospective in Rome that will mark the quarter centenary of the artist's death in 2010.

## Velázquez

One of the most interesting and in some ways most difficult dealers I have ever known is Christophe Janet. Born into a wealthy French family, and educated at the Institute of Fine Arts in New York, he has a fine eye for old masters and has led me to some beautiful works. He has also bought several paintings from me but was sometimes unreliable businesswise. Some of his checks bounced, although eventually he always made good on them, and once gave me a beautiful painting by Aert de Gelder in lieu. Life for his second wife, Roxane, a New Zealander, may have been difficult, since Christophe seemed to have no idea of how to manage his financial affairs and make regular, adequate provisions for his home life. However, Roxane was always charming, and they were a fun couple to be with. Eventually, in 1985, they left New York; Christophe undoubtedly hoped to do better in Paris.

Once they moved to France, we saw each other less frequently. However, early in December 1996, I met him in London, viewing the old master sales. He urged me to look at and bid on lot 36 in the Phillips sale on December 10, a charming study of a Chihuahua, a Mexican dwarf dog in a mountainous landscape, from the studio of Velázquez. Interestingly the painting was on the catalog cover (Plate 32) of the Phillips sale on December 10, 1985, and the American collector who bought it then was now offering it eleven years later. The date December 10 has been an important one in my life—it was my last day in Vienna in 1938, and somehow, I have always been sadly alert on December 10. I really liked that little oil on canvas, just 47 cm x 37 cm, but so did several others, including Rob Noortman, and I had to go to a hammer price of £30,000, way above the estimate of £6,000–£8,000.

If Christophe had not brought the painting to my attention, I would not have noticed the little gem, and so I promised him that if I could sell it profitably, we would share the profit equally. The painting was in very good condition. It just needed a simple cleaning by my friends Charles Munch and Jane Furchgott, and Charles found a decent frame for me.

Naturally I sent photographs to many art historians and received very diverse opinions. Werner Sumowski wrote that he had no doubt whatever that this was painted by Velázquez. He believed that the animal must come from the same hand as the dog in the portrait of the *Infante* Don Fernando, painted around 1632–6. And not just the dog but the landscape! But he concluded that, sadly, he was just Sumowski and not a Velázquez-dictator.

William Jordan, one of the great experts of Spanish

seventeenth-century paintings, thought differently. He remembered the little painting of a dog that he had seen at both Phillips sales:

> It is a very beautiful painting, and one filled with charm and vitality. I can understand how anyone might speculate about the painting's relation to the art of Velázquez. Nevertheless, I do not feel it is by him. It is no closer to his style than the work of any number of painters of the following generation whose styles were profoundly affected by Velázquez's. Although the free brush work in the modeling of the dog's body is reminiscent of Velázquez (that is what these artists were known for), the conception and execution of the landscape are quite different from his ... Your painting does not appear to be a fragment but is instead an intimate portrait of a dog. As such it departs from any painting known to have been painted by Velázquez ... The one artist who is known to have painted such pictures of animals is José Antolínez (1635–1675), one of the extremely talented generation of younger artists who followed Velázquez at the Court and who are regrettably too little known by the general public today.

A beautiful painting, in fine condition, painted by whom? Velázquez or José Antolínez? The difference in value was a million dollars or two.

George Gordon, Senior Director of Old Master Paintings at Sotheby's in London, conducts some of the auctions in New York as well as London, and over the years we have become very good friends. He is always as kind and helpful as he is knowledgeable about old masters, and so I showed him this portrait of a dog and mentioned the varied opinions I had had. He thought that there was a good chance that it could be by Velázquez. The key would be the opinion of the world expert on that artist, Professor Perez-Sanchez in

Madrid. And so, in April 2000, we signed an agreement that Sotheby's would ship the painting to Madrid for Professor Perez-Sanchez's opinion. If he said yes, Sotheby's would offer it as a Velázquez. If not, Sotheby's would try to ascertain the correct name and offer it as such. I suggested that Sotheby's insure it for $1 million, a modest price for a Velázquez in great condition. But George explained that a courier would have to accompany a million dollar painting, at considerable expense. The maximum that Sotheby's would insure it for at their own expense was $150,000, and so, not being a prophet, I agreed.

The specialist of Spanish paintings at Sotheby's, James Macdonald, who was to liaise between the Madrid office and Professor Perez-Sanchez, faxed me on January 12, 2001, "As you are aware the painting is currently safely stored in our office in Madrid. Sadly Professor Perez-Sanchez had to cancel my meeting with him during my last sojourn to Spain, however he has kindly agreed to come into the office on Monday of next week (January 15) to inspect the picture. Although I will not be there in person I will discuss the matter with him over the telephone." "Safely stored" until Professor Perez-Sanchez's visit on January 15. But on Saturday, January 13, Sotheby's office was broken into and our dog and some other works of art were stolen.

The insurance agent, Iain Fairley International, advertised the theft, offering a reward, as did the *International Foundation for Art Research (IFAR) Journal*—all to no avail.

Sotheby's insurance paid us $150,000—with the understanding that if the painting should be recovered within five years, we would have the option to purchase it for $150,000. Were it recovered after five years, we would have the option of acquiring it for $150,000 "in addition to a reasonable sum to reflect interest and expenses relating to recovery." The five years have passed, and we haven't yet had to make the decision whether we want to repurchase it.

The payment of $150,000 gave us a "profit" of close to $70,000, half of this Janet's. But Christophe had turned his interest over to a former business partner, Paolo Affif, resident in Ireland. Affif told me that Janet owed him a considerable sum of money and was hoping that our gem would yield a great deal. So at first, Affif decided not to accept the half "profit" but hope for its recovery and sale. But eventually, in September 2002, he decided that a bird in hand is better than two in the bush and accepted his share of the "profit," $34,646.00.

Will I ever know whether I owned a real Velázquez? Probably not.

### Sargent and Lely

There are times in the lives of most of us when we simply do not know what to decide. The most serious time of indecision in my life was after I received Isabel's letter no. 82 on August 15, 1951, the first letter I had received since September 1950. I didn't know what to do and I made the wrong decision—if I had decided to fly to Canada before she returned to England on August 22, our lives might have been so different!

With paintings there often is indecision. Should I bid, should I take a chance despite all that overpaint? But the greatest indecision in my life regarding a painting was totally different, lasted only half an hour, and solved itself.

In December 2001, Philip Mould of Historical Portraits in London told me of a magnificent portrait (Plate 33) of Arthur James Balfour painted by John Singer Sargent for the Carlton Club in London in 1908. The large canvas, 101 in x 58 in, was exhibited in the Royal Academy that year, and G.K. Chesterton described it in the *Art Journal*:

By far the most important thing in the exhibition, by the perspective of history, is Mr Sargent's portrait of Mr Balfour ... Mr Sargent's most sympathetic portrait is also one of his most sagacious ... It is the portrait of a philosopher and a statesman ... Mr Sargent has left on canvas the record of what was worst at the end of the nineteenth century, after the death of Gladstone and the great crusades: the brazen fashion, the foul finance. Here, perhaps he has left forever the record of what was best in it.

The National Portrait Gallery published an appeal for funds, briefly describing the life of Arthur Balfour. But to me, Balfour had an importance not mentioned in this appeal: he was the father of the Balfour Declaration of November 2, 1917, in which the British government expressed its support for a Jewish homeland in Palestine. The best verbal description of Balfour I had ever seen was a study by Pierre van Paassen written in 1925 when Balfour and Chaim Weizmann, later the first president of Israel, traveled to Palestine for the opening of the Hebrew University. Van Paassen wrote:

Well may one ask, what stirred this strange, often lethargic, more often incomprehensible figure, at one time called "the Eternal Nay" in the Irish Home Rule question, what moved him to champion the cause of the Jewish people at the Versailles conference and become their advocate in the councils of humanity in the days that followed? ... A review of his life would show that only the most profound questions of human activity, only the most momentous events, have ever been able to stir Lord Balfour into anything approaching enthusiasm ... Logic, force, and dignity are his weapons ... There are no sentimental reasons attached to his visit. He is not rejoicing primarily over the happy ending of two thousand years of exile for the Jewish people. He is not inhumane or insensitive, but to him "the existence of man is a mere accident," and the mass of mankind is necessarily doomed to hard and unthankful, unremitting toil, and the struggles of the past must be repeated in ages to come. It is because the People of the Book will again begin an era of conscious, creative, scientific effort, that he is interested.

The best visual description of Balfour was John Singer Sargent's, and I hoped to buy it with Philip Mould.

Arriving at a contract with Arthur Ackerman and Peter Johnson Limited, the company representing the Carlton Club, was not easy, but finally on March 22, 2002, I signed the contract. This called for the painting to be offered to the National Portrait Gallery in London for £900,000, open for acceptance by the NPG until 5 p.m. Friday, July 19, 2002. If not accepted, I would have to pay £900,000 by the next day.

Philip Mould thought it touch and go that the NPG would be able to raise the funds so, on my request, he prepared an invoice in the event that they should not. I wire transferred the £900,000 to Philip's London account so that he could pay the Carlton Club's agents immediately after the painting became mine at 5 p.m. that Friday.

On July 15, the NPG e-mailed this message to its major supporters:

The portrait is contracted to be sold to an American buyer unless we can find £900,000. It would be a marvelous acquisition for the Gallery and we have come a great way to achieving this total. Jacob Simon, our Acting Director, has had some wonderful results including support from the Art Fund, Christopher Ondaatje, Lord Sieff's legacy and funding from the Gallery's own acquisition fund. In total we have raised £551,000 but the Carlton Club has only given the Gallery until July 19 to secure the purchase.

At 3:30 on Friday, July 19, I stopped at Historical Portraits, Philip's gallery on Dover Street just off Piccadilly, and was told that Jacob Simon, the Chief Curator and Acting Director of the NPG, was inviting me to tea at the National Portrait Gallery at 4:30. Philip thought that the gallery had come close to raising the £900,000 and would ask me to extend the deadline to the following week. Would I/should I extend the deadline? As I walked down St. James's Street, past Christie's to Pall Mall and past the National Gallery, I thought of nothing else and also mused that my indecision was so much less important than my indecision in August 1951. I was sorry that Isabel was not with me—she had stayed in Bexhill—I would have loved to follow her advice. Finally, as I entered the National Portrait Gallery, around the corner from the National Gallery, I decided that the way Jacob Simon asked for an extension would decide me. If really friendly, yes; if demanding, no. I need not have worried. Jacob Simon turned out to be very friendly and his first words to me were, "I am very happy to be able to tell you that just this last hour we have succeeded in raising the balance needed."

On July 23, *The Times* wrote, "Portrait is saved. One of the greatest portraits of a Prime Minister has been rescued for the nation at the eleventh hour." I was tempted to write to *The Times* that it was really the twelfth hour less one minute.

On July 26, Jacob Simon sent me a very friendly letter asking me whether I might like to fund a research project on Jewish Iconography through a Bader Fellowship in the History of Portraiture and ended with, "The acquisition of the Balfour portrait has been an extraordinary episode in my career and I am delighted that it has led our paths to cross. I look forward to welcoming you at the National Portrait Gallery on a future occasion."

The National Portrait Gallery is a fine place for the portrait. If Philip Mould and I had acquired it, we would almost certainly have loaned it to the Israel Museum in Jerusalem. I had been in Israel in April and had mentioned to Shlomit Steinberg, the curator of the museum, that the painting of Balfour was for sale and that I hoped to buy it. She later wrote asking if I would lend it, "to display it in our portrait gallery in front of the English dining room. This way there is a possibility that one of our donors will see how wonderfully it fits the collection and will buy it for us … " I replied that "you should never sell the skin until you have the bear."

Is London or Jerusalem the better place for this great portrait? I really do not know, though I think it would be admired more in Jerusalem because Balfour was so pivotal to the history of Israel. I would love to have owned the Sargent of Balfour, but it has gone to a good home, and I share Jacob Simon's delight that our paths have crossed. I shall certainly visit the National Portrait Gallery more often to see the Sargent, and I have gotten to know and like Jacob Simon much better.

Our paths soon crossed, with a totally different painting.

In 2001, Philip Mould and I learned that Christie's London was offering in a private sale one of Sir Peter Lely's finest portraits, that of Barbara Villiers, Duchess of Cleveland, and her son as the Madonna and Child (Plate 34). I purchased this in July 2001 for a bid price of £150,000 which, with premium and VAT, came to £177,187.50, or a little more than $250,000 at that time. The painting was one of the finest portraits in the National Portrait Gallery's Painted Ladies: Women at the Court of Charles II, which was also shown at Yale. Philip and I hoped that one of these museums or one of Philip's other customers would purchase this masterpiece.

After first meeting Jacob Simon at the National Portrait Gallery on that fateful Friday afternoon, I asked him why the gallery was not interested in the Lely and was astounded by his reply: "We could not, and I believe no museum could be interested in its purchase, because Christie's cannot provide satisfactory documentation for 1939–45."

John Stanton, the Director of British Art at Christie's, had written to us, "The research that we have undertaken has not revealed any additional provenance for the picture, neither have we become aware, in the course of that research, of anything which suggests a specific problem in relation to the provenance. We have in addition consulted the Art Loss Register, who has confirmed that they are not aware of any claims in relation to the picture." But this was not enough for the National Portrait Gallery, and Christie's would not supply more information. And so Philip and I decided to offer this portrait for auction at Christie's London on November 24 2004, with a reserve of £150,000, hoping of course that it would bring much more. But it failed to sell, and so I offered it to the National Portrait Gallery at the net price I would have received, had it sold at its reserve. After yet further research into the provenance it accepted my offer, subject to the NPG being able to raise the funds. Its effort was successful, and I was paid £147,000 or a little more than $270,000 in May 2005. The National Portrait Gallery purchased one of Lely's greatest portraits at less than it would have had to pay Christie's. Because of the rising value of the pound, I didn't lose money, and I learned about the importance of provenance research.

How many of the paintings I have bought during the last fifty-five years had been stolen by the Nazis? David de Witt, the Bader Curator at Queen's, looked into this very carefully and at first feared that one of the most beautiful paintings we have given to Queen's, Jan Lievens' *Portrait of an Old Woman*, perhaps Rembrandt's mother, may have been stolen from the estate of a Jewish dealer, J. Goudstikker, and sold in an auction in Berlin in 1940. But then we found, to our great relief, that the provenance of two versions of the painting was mixed up in the catalog of the great Lievens exhibition in Braunschweig in 1979. The other version had belonged to Goudstikker. There was no indication whatever that the Nazis might have stolen the Lely, but even the absence of proof of ownership during the war years discouraged unseen buyers.

## Lot and His Daughters

Gui Rochat, a dealer friend specializing in French paintings and who recognized its quality, drew my attention to an enormous canvas—66 in x 92 in—lot 24, in Sotheby's New York sale on January 22, 2004. The painting of *Lot and His Daughters* (Plate 35), attributed to Hendrick Bloemaert, had been sent to the auction by a club in Des Moines, Iowa, where it had hung in its dining room.

Although Isabel and I often go to New York auctions in January, we go only when there are paintings I feel I have to have, and there were none such that week. But the *Lot* intrigued me. The quality seemed superb; not just the voluptuous daughters but also the wonderful still life with a large pitcher, which reminded me of Adam Van Vianen, and the fruit, which very much resembled that of Jan Davidsz. de Heem. The painting was very dirty and looked Flemish. I thought that it might be an early Johann Liss, an artist I like a lot. Years ago, I had bought one of his greatest works at Christie's in London but then was treated very unfairly by the British Heritage Committee (see Chapter 6) and could not get an export permit. Perhaps this was another opportunity to buy a beautiful Liss.

I knew that George Gordon was going to conduct the sale, and then visit us for a restful weekend in Milwaukee. I called Sotheby's in New York and arranged with Ben Hall that he would call me in Milwaukee the morning of the sale so that I could bid by phone. I had already talked to Otto Naumann and knew that he liked the image, but he had no room in his gallery for such a large painting and did not intend to bid. I had decided that my limit would be $200,000—but I was lucky. The size must have discouraged others, for bidding was slow and I could hear George knocking it down to me for only $75,000, for a total cost of $90,000 after the buyer's premium was added.

I was delighted with my buy, but what was I going to do with it? Certainly not have it sent to my conservators. Charles Munch and Jane Furchgott, who have conserved most of the paintings in my collection, could not take it—their truck and their vacuum table are too small. Fortunately Gui suggested a conservator in lower Manhattan, Michael Heidelberg, who gave me a not-to-exceed price of $40,000 for the conservation. Wow! More than twice what I had ever paid for any conservation—but then, think of the size! Richard Charlton-Jones and George Gordon suggested sending the canvas to London where conservation would cost about half as much. But there was such an advantage to having the work done in New York where Gui could keep a close eye on it and help with any problems as they came along.

The first problem came at once: the truck Gui first considered was too small. I asked Ben Hall how had this ever come from Holland to a club in Des Moines? He promised to try to find out but has not succeeded. Gui finally found a trucker who could help, and the conservator received the painting on a snowy Wednesday, January 28. Carrying such a behemoth up three flights to the conservator was not easy. Carrying a Steinway would have been more difficult, but perhaps not much. Just two days later, on the Friday, Michael called Gui and me in great excitement. Under the later inscription P.P. Rubens, on the lower right, was the genuine two-line inscription A. Bloemaert fe. 1624! And Michael was certain that the painting would clean beautifully.

At almost eighty, I still had a lot to learn. I had thought the painting to be Flemish, perhaps an early Liss; instead, it is the finest, most Rubensian Bloemaert I have ever seen. More good news was on the way. An old friend in Rotterdam, Hubert van Baarle, is most interested in Abraham Bloemaert and was really excited when I told him about this painting. A few days later he wrote that on February 14, 1811, "A. Bloemaert *Lot and His Daughters*, a grand gallery picture [formerly in the collection of Charles II], was sold in London for £39.18, the highest price an Abraham Bloemaert had fetched at the time." "A grand gallery picture" indeed!

Of course, Abraham Bloemaert's work is well known to me—or at least I thought so, just not well enough to recognize the *Lot* as his work. I had bought a fine *St. Jerome Working by Candlelight* many years ago in Holland. And then, in the preview of Christie's sale in South Kensington on December 7, 1995, I had seen a dirty, unframed canvas described as "After Abraham Bloemaert *The Dream of Jacob*" and estimated at £2,000–£3,000. The original was thought to be with a dealer in London where I had already seen it, and I liked this "copy," dirt and all, much better. I was the only bidder in the room, but was bidding against someone on the telephone, who was almost as stubborn as I was—I had to go to a hammer price of £17,000! My friends Jane Furchgott and Charles Munch did a fine job cleaning and relining my painting, and I thought that this was the finest Abraham Bloemaert I could ever own (Plate 36).

Years earlier, in 1976, I had written about *Jacob's Dream* for The Bible Through Dutch Eyes, an exhibition at the Milwaukee Art Center:

The vision of a ladder with angels going up and down on it is unique in Biblical imagery, and so *Jacob's Dream* has aroused artists' imaginations for centuries. The Bible is the book of dreams, par excellence: dreams of individuals, dreams of a people, dreams of all mankind. It is surely no accident that the very first well-known dream in the Bible is not that of a king or of a general but of a man at the lowest point in his life—homeless and hunted, yearning for God's promise that He would return him to his country.

PLATE 19 (top): Rembrandt, *A Scholar by Candlelight.*

PLATE 20 (below): Rembrandt, *Head of an Old Man in a Cap.*

PLATE 21: Rembrandt,
*Head of an Old Man.*

PLATE 22: Rembrandt,
*Head of a Bearded Man:
Study for St. Matthew.*

PLATE 23: Rembrandt, *Small Head of an Old Man in Profile*.

PLATE 24: Artist unknown, *Rembrandt Sketching*.

PLATE 25: David de Witt.

PLATE 26 (above): Eeckhout, *Tobit and his Wife*.

PLATE 27: (opposite top) Caravaggio, the Hermitage *Lute Player*.

PLATE 28: (opposite below) Caravaggio, our *Lute Player*.

PLATE 29 (left): Caravaggio, our *Lute Player*, detail of the vase with flowers.

PLATE 30 (opposite top): Attributed to Caravaggio, the *Lute Player* on loan to the Metropolitan Museum.

PLATE 31 (opposite below): Attributed to Caravaggio, the *Lute Player* in the Salini collection.

PLATE 32 (above): 1985 catalog.

PLATE 33 (opposite): Sargent, *Portrait of Balfour.*

PLATE 34 (above): Lely, *Portrait of Barbara Villiers, Duchess of Cleveland, with her son.*

PLATE 35 (opposite top): Abraham Bloemaert, *Lot and His Daughters.*

PLATE 36 (opposite below): Abraham Bloemaert, *Jacob's Dream.*

PLATE 37 (left): My *Old Woman with a Candle*.

PLATE 38 (below): Rubens, the superior *Old Woman with a Candle*.

PLATE 39: Menzel, *An Afternoon in the Tuileries Gardens.*

PLATE 40: Liss, *The Repentant Magdalene.*

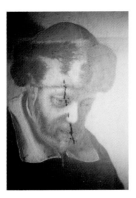

PLATE 41 (left): detail of my Verhout under UV light, showing the deep scratch to the face of the subject.

PLATE 42 (below): Verhout, *Portrait of Cornelius Abrahamsz Graswinckel* restored and cleaned.

How often had I thought of *Jacob's Dream* while in the prisoner of war camp in Canada? That dream is especially meaningful to me.

The great expert on Bloemaert is Professor Marcel Roethlisberger at the University of Geneva, who has published the two-volume *catalogue raisonné* on the artist. He is a most helpful scholar and so, naturally, I sent him photographs of my new acquisition. He replied,

> I am much interested to see how *Jacob's* Ladder has come out. I saw the painting at the sale viewing in London. As you know it was quite dirty, fine in some areas and abraded in others; I felt it was difficult to know what was underneath, but it looked interesting and seemed worth a try. I mentioned it to nobody, nor did anybody ask me, to my surprise. I could not stay for the sale but it was indeed I who bid on the phone, not suspecting that it was against you, otherwise I would have abstained.

In an article titled "Abraham Bloemaert: Recent Additions to His Paintings," Professor Roethlisberger published my *Jacob's Dream*.

The *Lot and His Daughters* is, I believe, in a class by itself—certainly the best of Bloemaert's works that I have ever seen. When Professor Roethlisberger saw it in New York in 2006, he called it a magnificent painting. He was particularly impressed by the beautiful still life, exceptional for the artist.

## Rubens

The first painting I ever bought at auction was an oil on canvas (Plate 37) depicting an old woman with a basket, shielding a candle with her hand, purchased for £28 at Sotheby's in

London during my honeymoon, on July 23, 1952. This lot 153 was just called Jordaens, not Jacob Jordaens, not even J. Jordaens, indicating that Sotheby's did not think it really was by Jordaens. The seller, Lord Mackintosh of Halifax, wrote to me,

> I bought this picture in London nearly thirty years ago and always thought it was by Wright of Derby, but of course you know he specialized in candlelight pictures. I sent it with another Wright of Derby to the Bi-centenary exhibition in his native town of Derby. The authorities there said it was a Jacob Jordaens and showed it as such in the Exhibition and it has always been accepted as such ever since.

But it wasn't by Wright of Derby or by Jacob Jordaens; nor was it by Rubens, as Professor Erik Larsen stated in an expertise he wrote in 1956. It was an old copy after a painting on panel by Rubens that was on loan to the Museum of Fine Arts in Boston between 1948 and 1965. Still, I enjoyed looking at my painting, but did eventually give it to a school in Milwaukee, which sent it to a local auction in November 1965 where it sold for $7,000. The school was happy and so was I. In 1952, I could have bought a better painting, an original, for £28, but we all make mistakes, and hopefully we learn as we live.

Fifty-one years later, when I went to London to view the old master sales at Sotheby's in December 2003, George Gordon showed me the Rubens original that he hoped would come up for sale in July. What a difference between this original and my copy! The original (Plate 38) includes a boy lighting a candle from that of the old woman and shows a clear pentiment of the old woman's left hand, which had originally been painted in a higher position. Rubens produced this night piece around 1616 and etched the subject around 1621. The counterproof of the first state is inscribed in his hand, in Latin, and translates to "Light can be taken a thousand times from another light without diminishing it." The work is on five pieces of wood, a clear indication that Rubens painted this not for sale but for his own enjoyment, and it is included, as no. 125, in the posthumous inventory of pictures found in his house in 1640.

I told George Gordon how much I liked this original and recounted the story of the old woman with a candle, the first painting I had ever bought at auction. In March 2004, he confirmed that the Rubens would be included in Sotheby's London sale on the evening of July 7, 2004, and would be exhibited before then in New York, where Otto Naumann was able to examine it carefully.

Sotheby's catalog described the painting, lot 30, in six carefully written pages with three photographs. Among the many copies, mine in Milwaukee was included. I simply could not understand the estimate, only £2–£3 million. Two years earlier, on July 10, 2002, Rubens' *Massacre of the Innocents*, wonderfully well painted but a ghastly subject, had sold for a hammer price of £45 million. I would much rather look at this wonderful night scene—one of Rubens' few night scenes—and, like the *Massacre*, painted entirely by Rubens, without workshop involvement but for his own enjoyment. Otto thought that he could sell it profitably if we could buy it for £4 million, but I doubted that it would sell that inexpensively.

As at the sale of *The Massacre of the Innocents* in 2002, Henry Wyndham was the auctioneer. Once again the room was packed, not in anticipation of the Rubens this time, but of lot 8, a small painting described as the last Vermeer not in a museum. I did not like the painting and was rather surprised when Rob Noortman told me on the day of the sale that he wanted to buy it. He was indeed the underbidder to the purchaser, Stephen Wynn, who bid by phone. The hammer price was £16.2 million.

Tension in the salesroom eased after this and bidding was rather slow. A number of the paintings in the sale were bought back, but that wasn't going to happen to lot 30, the Rubens. However, there was only one other bidder, on the telephone, and Henry Wyndham knocked the Rubens down to me at £2.2 million, much to my happy surprise. Briefly I wondered whether I should keep this beautiful candlelight painting I had bought so inexpensively, but Otto, of course, was eager to sell and wanted it to go to the Mauritshuis in The Hague. There it was described as a "Topstuk van Rubens," an exceptional painting by Rubens, which of course it is.

In the same sale was another painting that I found very beautiful, the head of an old man by Jan Lievens, from the collection of the late D.G. van Beuningen in Rotterdam. It was estimated at £200,000–£300,000, but there were many bidders, two of them particularly determined. It finally went to Johnny van Haeften (bidding with Richard Green) for £1,650,000, a record price for a Jan Lievens. With commission the price was well over $3 million. I can't buy them all.

For years, I have been writing and lecturing about Jan Lievens, called "*Ein Maler im Schatten Rembrandts*," a painter in the shadow of Rembrandt. Well, I believe the shadow is in our minds. Lievens was a great painter and not just while working close to Rembrandt in Leiden. Over the last forty years, I have bought ten paintings by Lievens, most for just a few thousand dollars, and four of these ten I have given to Queen's. Some of them, one of Rembrandt's mother, for instance, and another of St. Paul, I like even better than the painting of the old man that brought a record price. My favorite is a late work, painted in the 1650s, a portrait of Jacob Junius. I am so happy to see Lievens coming out of Rembrandt's shadow, and I look forward to a Lievens exhibition that will go from the National Gallery in Washington to the Milwaukee Art Museum and then to the Rembrandthuis.

## Menzel

For some years, I have been working with an able gallery in Munich, the Galerie Arnoldi-Livie, owned by Angelika and Bruce Livie, she a charming Bavarian, he an American of Scottish descent. Both are great fun to be with. I have thoroughly enjoyed working with them and greatly appreciate their wonderful hospitality every time we visit Munich. Isabel and I visit them each year, and we were all pleased when they sold two of ABFA's works to German museums.

I was very interested when Angelika told me about a most beautiful painting by Adolph von Menzel that was in a museum, the Staatliche Kunstsammlungen Dresden, but that might possibly be returned to the heirs of the previous owner, Estella Meyer, neé Goldschmidt. In 1935, Mrs Meyer was forced to sell the painting to the museum in Dresden at a price well under its actual value. She was later deported to Auschwitz where she died in 1942. Menzel painted *An Afternoon in the Tuileries Gardens* (Plate 39) in 1867, after he had visited Paris for the world exhibition. He may well have been inspired by Manet's *Music in the Tuileries Gardens*, painted in 1860 and now in the National Gallery in London.

The Livies had been following the discussions about the return of the painting and thought that if Dresden did return it, the heirs might decide to sell. When they showed me the major books on the artist and I realized what a beautiful work it was, I agreed that I would be willing to consider purchasing it and would then entrust its sale to the Livies. Early in March 2005, Angelika and Bruce told me that the museum in Dresden had decided to agree to the restitution in order to avoid a lengthy lawsuit with the eight heirs, who were being helped greatly by the Jewish Claims Conference. However, it was important to the museum that the painting continue to be exhibited in Dresden until it was sold and that the eventual buyer, probably a museum, should consider returning it on loan from time to time in exchange for one of Dresden's great paintings. What museum, be it the Metropolitan in New York or the National Gallery in London, would not be glad to show one of Dresden's wonderful Bellottos or some other of Dresden's great paintings?

Wishful thinking? Perhaps. But my hope was that this beautiful Menzel might go to London. I could just imagine how stunning Menzel's *Tuileries Gardens* would look next to the National Gallery's Manet of the same subject!

Hoping to avoid losing the Menzel, Dresden had made a tentative offer of €1 million. I heard that Christie's in London was reported to have offered the heirs a €3 million guarantee. The question was how quickly would they be paid and would the museum in Dresden be helped with a possible exchange? And with whom? We decided to make an offer, and while we were in Vienna the first week of June, Angelika called me and put me in touch with Dr. Markus Stötzel, the heirs' lawyer near Marburg. In a very pleasant negotiation by telephone, we agreed on a price and then met Dr. Stötzel in the Arnoldi-Livie gallery in Munich on June 15, signed the contract, and arranged for the prompt wire transfer of the funds.

There followed a great deal of publicity, all of it correct and to me very surprising. The *Morgenpost* in Dresden even showed photographs of the Livies, of me as a thirteen-year-old, and with Isabel standing before Herstmonceux Castle—and even of a Bellotto in the museum in Dresden. The publicity was not limited to Dresden or to Saxony; even Germany's greatest newspaper, the *Frankfurter Allgemeine*, published an article on June 17! The gist of all the stories was that an eighty-one-year-old Jew, a dealer and collector, driven from Vienna in 1938, had helped the heirs, the museum in Dresden, and hopefully the museum that would acquire the painting.

*Ende gut, Alles gut*—after the Livies had found the right buyer. Or so I thought, though it did not turn out quite like that. The Livies found the ideal buyer—just as we had hoped—the National Gallery in London. Dr. Christopher Riopelle, the curator of the gallery's nineteenth-century paintings, and two other curators flew to Dresden in October 2005, were welcomed at the museum, and shown the painting. They then asked that it be shipped to London where on November 3 the Acquisition Committee of the National Gallery voted 11:1 to acquire the Menzel at the price asked by the Livies. Dr. Riopelle agreed to return the painting to Dresden for a Menzel exhibition opening at the end of November and thereafter to consider exchanging the Menzel from time to time with one of Dresden's masterpieces. The Livies and I had kept our promise.

Professor Dr. Martin Roth, the *Generaldirektor* of the Staatliche Kunstsammlungen Dresden, had spoken highly of our plans. In an article in the *Sächsische Zeitung* in June, he was quoted, "When you consider Alfred Bader's tragic fate as a Nazi victim, then his actions are a great gesture of humanity, clearly symbolic to everyone. Alfred Bader is helping us to ensure that this world-class painting can be shown from time to time in our *Galerie Neue Meister*. We are deeply grateful to him for this." In July he invited me to come to Dresden to lecture and to express his thanks by showing me the Old Master Gallery personally.

I had already agreed to give two lectures in Vienna and to be at the second presentation of the Lieben Award (see Chapter 16) on November 4. The next week was free, and so I suggested that I come to Dresden to give four lectures. I would give "The Rembrandt Research Project and the Collector" and "The Bible Through Dutch Eyes" on November 9; the latter, I believed, would be particularly fitting on the anniversary of *Kristallnacht*. The following day, I planned to give two lectures in the university's Chemistry Department. All was set: the museum booked a room in a pleasant hotel, and when Angelika Livie called me in Vienna on November 4 to tell me of the

National Gallery's decision, I thought that my two lectures at the Dresden museum would also be a celebration of our dreams come true.

The next day I was staggered to receive a fax from Professor Roth telling me that I was no longer welcome to be the museum's guest. He had learned that we had sold the Menzel to the National Gallery in London without a legal contract for an exchange with Dresden. Naturally I responded immediately that Dr. Riopelle had assured us that the National Gallery was happy to send the Menzel to Dresden at the end of the month, and to consider exchanges thereafter. No mention of a legal contract had ever been made. Professor Roth never replied to me.

The largest headline in the Dresden *Morgenpost* of November 8 was "*Riesenkrach um Millionen Menzel*" (Great Fuss Over Menzel Worth Millions). In a full-page article, Professor Roth accused the Livies and me of having mistreated the museum in Dresden and even the eight heirs because we sold the painting at a profit. I had paid the heirs the sum they requested, about three times the €1 million offered by the museum in Dresden. I wish I knew exactly what motivated Professor Roth to act so irrationally. Other German newspapers, the *Sächsische Zeitung*, the *Süddeutsche Zeitung*, and the *Frankfurter Allgemeine* all wrote about this affair without explanation for Professor Roth's actions.

We did not cancel our flight to Dresden because we had the two lectures at the university, and despite all the brouhaha, spent a very pleasant day there. An old friend, Dr. Tomas Kucera, had come from Berlin to listen to the lectures I couldn't give. We had not known he intended to come but were very glad to see him, since it was a long time since we had last met. His appearance was a really bright spark since we had been "uninvited." However, I did meet Dr. Harald Marx, the director of the Old Master Gallery, and we talked a good deal about the wonderful works of Rembrandt and his students in the gallery. Of course, Dr. Marx could not discuss the reasoning behind the *Generaldirektor*'s actions, although clearly he was as puzzled as we were. In the afternoon, we visited the newly built synagogue, and in the evening we were treated to a most sumptuous dinner arranged by Paul Gerhard Babick and his wife, Dr. Ute Babick Krüger, the historian working with the Jewish Claims Conference to recover paintings stolen by the Nazis.

The next day I gave the two talks in the Chemistry Department of the university. The audience was very small indeed because the museum had told the university that the lectures had been cancelled. However, two journalists, Christiane Kohl of the *Süddeutsche Zeitung*, and Birgit Grimm of the *Sächsische Zeitung*, came and then joined us for lunch after the lectures. They were very interested to hear the real story and wrote fair reports for their papers. We left Dresden for England early on Friday morning, still greatly puzzled by Professor Roth's actions.

Dr. Christopher Riopelle of the National Gallery in London had invited me for lunch with Dr. David Jaffé, the Senior Curator. When I went up to London the following week, they showed me the Menzel, my first look at this magnificent painting. They were delighted with it and perfectly agreeable to return it to Dresden for the Menzel exhibition opening later in the month and then to consider future exchanges. In fact, Dr. Charles Saumarez Smith, the director of the National Gallery, flew to Dresden for discussions and a press conference on November 25 and was asked repeatedly whether he was satisfied with the purchase. Of course he was, yet Professor Roth reiterated that I had lied to him by promising a permanent loan to Dresden. Luckily, Christiane Kohl of the *Süddeutsche Zeitung* had a copy of his July 4 letter to me in which he clearly approved of my intention to sell the Menzel. When she confronted him with this, he turned to his assistant and asked, "Did I really write this?"

I honestly wish I knew what made Professor Roth so angry. In an interview with the *Leipziger Volkszeitung*, he expressed his doubts that an exchange with the National Gallery would take place and ended with, "If Bader loved art, he would give part of his profit to the museum." No museum director has ever treated me so badly and yet he suggested that I help his museum financially. I wonder whether the word "chutzpah" is known in Dresden.

A few days later I met Dr. Saumarez Smith for the first time. He is a charming man who knew a good deal about me because his curator of old masters, Dr. Axel Rüger, studied at Queen's and was one of two editors of the *Festschrift* given to me for my eightieth birthday. Dr. Saumarez Smith assured me once again that the National Gallery was interested in exchanging the Menzel from time to time and that it would be shipped to Dresden on November 30. His parting words to me were, "Please find other wonderful paintings like the Menzel for us." The Livies and I will certainly try.

A delightful postscript to this saga was written by Dr. Christopher Riopelle as part of a going away presentation to Dr. Charles Saumarez Smith when he left the directorship of the National Gallery in July 2007:

> Menzel had long figured on the gallery's informal desiderata list as the most important German painter of the later nineteenth century. His paintings are almost entirely unrepresented in collections outside the German-speaking world. That, as the result of restitution by a major German museum, a Menzel of this ambition and complexity should have come on the market was remarkable. That it should relate to, indeed enter into dialogue with, one of the gallery's most famous modern paintings, is serendipity. Menzel painted the picture after seeing Edouard Manet's *Music in the Tuileries Gardens* of 1862 (NG3260) when he visited Paris five years later. He acknowledges Manet by quoting the top-hatted

figure near the centre of the canvas from that work but then goes on to show how he thinks the painting of modern life should proceed, in a more highly realistic, richly detailed, and anecdotal manner. As soon as the picture was offered to us, Charles recognized the necessity of acquiring it and of doing so quickly. He also had to contend, gracefully, with a German director colleague who was understandably dismayed at losing a great painting and startled to see how fast and effectively the gallery could act when it needed to.

What a contrast between the great director of the National Gallery and the *Generaldirektor* in Dresden!

# 6

## *A Liss Lost*

I am often reminded of my late friend, the great art historian and teacher Wolfgang Stechow. In 1994, a whole flood of memories came back to me when I looked into the Christie's London catalog of its sale in December. There was an illustration of a painting by Johann Liss described as a *Repentant Sinner Turning away from Temptation and Offered a Palm of Salvation by Angels* (Plate 40) consigned by the Cartwright family in Edgcote, Northhamptonshire. It was a most beautiful painting, estimated at only £400,000–£600,000, and I was sure it was the original of a copy I had first seen at the Cleveland Museum early in 1976 when I was visiting a most interesting exhibition in honor of Wolfgang Stechow.

The forty-one paintings were said to be the works of Johann Liss, a brilliant German-born, Dutch-Flemish-and-Italian-educated artist, who died of the plague in Venice around 1630, in his early thirties. Wolf had often spoken to me very highly of Liss, comparing him with Adam Elsheimer and pointing out the great beauty of *Amor Vincit*, the Liss owned by the Cleveland Museum. I spent several hours in the exhibition, thinking of Wolf and wondering whether he would have agreed that all the paintings really were by Liss. I did not and annotated my catalog with comments like "Beautiful" for the A-29 *Amor Vincit*, "okay" for many others and "copy" for some. One of these was A-17, called *The Repentant Magdalene*, from Dresden. Dr. Rüdiger Klessmann, the well-respected German art historian who had written that entry in the Cleveland catalog, believed the Dresden painting was the original. He knew of the painting that now, twenty years later, was for sale at Christie's, but he referred to it as a copy. Clearly he had never seen the Northhamptonshire painting itself, now being offered unframed in London. It was smaller (98.8 cm x 125.8 cm, excluding 2 cm of canvas folded over at the top, bottom, and left edges) than the canvas in Dresden (114 cm x 131.5 cm). The edges of the canvas had been turned over to make it fit on the overmantel of the billiard room of the Cartwright family. So what?! It was a magnificent work, one of the best by Liss that I had ever seen. Otto Naumann, my New York art dealer friend, agreed, and I bought it at a hammer price of £900,000. Rob Noortman was the underbidder; he knew a good painting when he saw one.

In January 1995, I was informed that export from Britain would be stopped. This had happened once before when I bought a German altarpiece of ca. 1510 in December 1993. On that occasion, I had been treated entirely fairly. In fact, I had rather enjoyed my meeting with the Reviewing Committee to put my case for permission to export. Unfortunately, this encounter was to prove totally different. Export of artwork from Britain can be stopped based on one or more of three criteria, called the Waverly criteria: if the work is closely connected with British history, if it is of outstanding aesthetic importance, or if it is of great significance for study.

Julia Willmore, the Reviewing Committee's secretary, informed me that it would meet in its office on 2–4 Cockspur Street at 11:15 a.m. on February 1. I faxed her on January 20 that I would fly to London to be at that meeting and included an outline of my arguments for export:

I believe that this painting does not fall under any of the three Waverly criteria. It does not come under (1) because it is totally unrelated to British history and national life.

It hung unrecognized and unframed in a billiard room with the canvas folded over the top to fit available space!

No one can argue that the Liss is an unimportant picture in today's market. However, there is no question that while it remained in a British collection, it was neglected and abused. Apparently while in the collection of the Cartwright family in Edgcote, the picture was cut down, losing over half a foot on the bottom edge; moreover, the canvas was folded over a reduced stretcher before framing, thereby damaging the original paint at the top edge.

The reduced composition is further evidenced by the existence of another version of the picture in the Dresden museum showing the original, uncut format.

Nonetheless, the painting is a great work by Johann Liss, but Liss is hardly a household name, and chances are that not one in a thousand Britons has ever heard of him.

The National Gallery in London owns a comparably great work by Liss, as does Sir Denis Mahon, whose collection is widely believed to be destined for the National Gallery. Both works are fine examples of the artist's work and are works that have not been cut down. Hence, I do not believe that Waverly criteria 2 or 3 apply.

My most helpful contact at Christie's in London was Nicholas Lambourn, who faxed me on January 19 confirming that the meeting would take place at the Export Licensing Unit at 2–4 Cockspur Street. I phoned him the next day to say that I did not know where Cockspur Street was, and he replied by fax that the nearest tube station was Charing Cross and sent a map showing how to get to Cockspur Street. Immediately after arriving in London on January 31, I called to assure him that I would be at Cockspur Street timely the next morning. He wished me luck.

When I arrived at 11:10 a.m. on February 1, I was told that the venue had been changed—no one had mentioned this to either Nicholas Lambourn or me, though they knew that I was the buyer. When I reached the new meeting place at 11:30, Jonathan Scott, the Committee Chairman, said that they had already decided unanimously to deny export. Before my arrival, a Mr Ron Tabor of Vulcan International Services, a shipping organization employed by Christie's, had presented a report alleging that "the painting was not of outstanding aesthetic importance due to alterations and damage." This was so clearly incorrect that his argument was easily refuted by Neil MacGregor, Director of the National Gallery, acting as expert advisor to the Department of National Heritage. He stated:

The painting under discussion had not been properly studied before the recent Christie's sale and had been dismissed as a copy of the painting of the same composition in the Dresden Gemäldegalerie. The picture has now been universally accepted as an autograph work, and the Liss specialist Rüdiger Klessmann has reversed his view about the relative status of the two works. This is indeed a work of the very highest quality, superbly illustrating Liss's fluid brushwork, his inventive approach to composition and iconography, and his skillful treatment of facial expression. The subject, which is almost certainly the Magdalene turning away from worldly temptation (represented by the sinister figure who offers precious objects on a dish and whose face is cast in shadow) to the angel who extends the palm of heavenly glory, is rare in art, although, significantly, there is a painting with a similar treatment of the subject by Jordaens (private collection, Chicago). The present work is a great deal more sensuous and visually exciting. Liss' chromatic juxtaposition of the golden orange of the central figure's drape with the flashes of blue lining recalls similar passages in the later works of Veronese, and adds weight to the assumption that this painting was made in Venice.

When I demurred, explaining the reason for my late arrival, Mr Scott allowed me to state my case "but be quick about it." And, of course, I understood that I had to be quick about it, because the committee had already decided, and the next painting was already on view. Was this British justice? Ever since the meeting dealing with the German altarpiece, I had been so elated by the fair treatment I had received that I almost looked forward to another export denial. Clearly, I am no prophet, for worse was to come. Despite what I believed were my very good arguments, export was still denied. Diana Forbes-McNeil of the Reviewing Committee on the Export of Works of Art wrote to me on March 24, "I can assure you that as soon as the initial two month deferral period on your painting by Liss has ended, i.e. April 8, 1995, we shall let you know as to whether or not any museum has expressed an interest in acquiring it." Nicholas Lambourn faxed me on April 11 that the Department of National Heritage had just assured Christie's that "we would be notified of the outcome this week, and that if there was no definite interest the export would be approved and the license granted immediately after Easter." Neither promise was kept. We heard nothing.

Otto Naumann, with whom I was working on the Liss, was then approached by a London dealer, Alan Hobart of Pyms Gallery in Mayfair. He alleged that he knew of a UK museum that intended to apply to Christie's for the Liss and thus stop its export, but he also said he had a private collector, Sir Graham Kirkham, in Britain, who wanted to buy it. We did not know of Hobart's reputation and were in a quandary: should we accept his offer of £1,270,000 or take the risk of losing the painting to the museum interested? If we sold in Britain, we would not need an export permit. Unfortunately, we believed Hobart when he told us his "inside information," that a museum was seriously interested. Had we heard from the Reviewing Committee on April 8 that no museum was interested, we would not have accepted the offer, made on behalf of Sir Graham Kirkham.

In July, the Reviewing Committee sent me a draft for their 1994–5 Report alleging that "the representative for the applicant contended that the painting was not of outstanding aesthetic importance due to alterations and damage." Of course, I objected immediately, because Tabor was not my representative. I would not have made that silly statement and, had I not been misled to Cockspur Street, would have made a more cogent argument. My objection was brushed aside. Simon Mitchell, the Committee's Secretary, ended his summary dismissal of August 3 with, "I can assure you that the Reviewing Committee makes every effort to deal fairly as between all parties, and we will endeavour to ensure that if any of your paintings are referred to the Committee in the future, the cases proceed smoothly."

Commercially Otto and I did well: a quick but relatively modest profit. But had the Reviewing Committee kept its promise, this painting would now be in one of the world's great museums. Of course, it has been accepted as one of Liss' greatest masterpieces and is on the cover of Rüdiger Klessmann's *catalogue raisonné* published in 1999. What I have learned is that one cannot rely on the fairness of the Reviewing Committee, or the words of a stranger, and I no longer look forward to meeting with them. Every time I think of it, I feel pained by the Reviewing Committee's ill treatment. Wolf Stechow would have followed the saga with great interest and understanding.

# 7

# *A Horror Story, Plain and Simple*

## (but with a happy ending)

Collectors, art dealers, galleries and museums frequently
lend their paintings for special exhibitions being held
at other galleries or museums, and paintings from my
collection are on exhibit in different parts of the world several
times a year. Exhibitions give art students an opportunity to
study paintings otherwise unavailable to them and give the
public a chance, albeit short, to enjoy them. This is a horror
story about one museum exhibition in 1988.

The Emily Lowe Gallery of Hofstra University in Hemp-
stead, New York, borrowed seven of the very best paintings in
my collection for their exhibit People at Work: Seventeenth
Century Dutch Art, scheduled from April 17 to June 15, 1988.
On May 26, I received a cordial letter from the director of the
Hofstra Museum, Dr. Gail Gelburd, informing me that the
exhibition was going so well that all previous attendance
records were broken. She also informed me of minor damage
to one of my paintings on exhibit—a separation of the varnish
in the top right corner of *The Alchemist*, painted by Cornelis
Bega. She reassured me that the damage was truly insignificant
and could be taken care of easily by the museum's conservator.
On June 2 Dr. Gelburd telephoned and spoke with my secretary, Marilyn Hassmann (I was in England at the time) to
request written authorization to proceed with the repair of
the Bega. Then she mentioned additional damages: "a slight
scratch, only to the varnish of the Verhout" and damage to
one of the frames, that of the Vrel.

My secretary phoned me in England to tell me of the additional problems: the scratch to the varnish of the Constantijn Verhout painting, *Portrait of Cornelis Abrahamz Graswinckel*, and the damage to the Vrel frame (the painting was *Interior with a Woman Darning*), all described as minor by Dr. Gelburd. We faxed Dr. Gelburd written authorization to proceed that same day. Unfortunately, since I was led to believe that the damage was so slight as to be immaterial, I foolishly did not think to ask for photographs before giving permission for the restoration of the painting.

When the paintings were returned, the frame of the Jacobus Vrel (1634–1662) painting was so badly banged up that we threw it out, but I was relieved to see both paintings looking in fine condition. I was particularly pleased that the Verhout showed no signs of damage. Anthony Clark, then director of the Minneapolis Institute of Arts, had said of the portrait when it was exhibited in 1967 at the Kalamazoo Institute of Arts that it "... is as beautiful a piece of still life painting, and as original, daring, and elegant a work of art as anything I know ... It is utterly clean and fresh." The Verhout painting does indeed exemplify the perfection that has endured the span of hundreds of years. It is a treasure, my treasure. Constantijn Verhout is an exceedingly rare artist, and I believe there are only three or four known works by him. His two best works are illustrated in Walther Bernt's well-known three-volume compendium *The Netherlandish Painters of the Seventeenth Century*. One is of a sleeping student, the other is my portrait.

In October 1997, almost ten years after the loan to Hofstra, my very able conservator, Charles Munch, visited us one evening, and naturally our conversation was of paintings and their conservation. I mentioned the Verhout and quite happily took it down, just to show him a pristine seventeenth-century Dutch painting devoid of any restoration and requiring none. Charles, however, always preferred to decide a painting's condition for himself and so proceeded to examine the Verhout under ultraviolet light. My beautiful Verhout, the portrait of a brewer, now had a sharp two-inch-long scratch (Plate 41) across the face of the old man—very clear under UV, but not in ordinary light. I was so shocked I could not speak! And so the horror story that began in 1988 continued.

This painting had been at home in our collection since it was returned by the museum, which had reported and repaired "a slight scratch to the varnish." Clearly the damage had been much more severe. We had been completely uninformed about any restoration to the paint itself, believing that the painting had received just a fresh coat of varnish from the museum's conservator.

As I have mentioned, many of the paintings in our collection have been made available for exhibitions for the past fifty years. Only once before was a painting damaged, and that incident was handled quite differently. I was informed that a painting by Peter Lastman, the teacher of Rembrandt, had split in two. The museum in Jerusalem told me immediately, sent me detailed photographs, and returned the painting in two pieces, as I requested. Charles Munch glued the two panels together, there was no paint loss, and the total cost of the damage, covered by the museum's insurance, was about $300. As the painting had originally been on two panels glued together, there was no lasting damage and no claim for loss of value.

One painting damaged in fifty years of exhibitions and then two paintings and one frame damaged at a two-month exhibition at Hofstra.

Charles asked me to request the condition report from Hofstra Museum's conservator, giving details of the work performed with a photograph taken before the restoration was done. I requested this information on November 3, 1997 in a letter to Dr. Gail Gelburd, the director of the Hofstra Museum. Mary Wakeford, her assistant, sent Mervin Honig's museum conservator's undated report and recommendation. A copy of

107

his invoice dated June 24, 1988 leads me to believe that his recommendations for the treatment of my two paintings were made available to the museum early that same month, but were never provided to me verbally or otherwise. The conservator's recommendation "... The deeper part of the scratch as needed should be inpainted and varnished locally and where it might be necessary, filled with gesso putty ... " If only this had been sent to me in 1988, I would have known immediately that the scratch was not only to the varnish, but was indeed more serious damage. I would then have requested that my own conservator repair this damage and that the museum's insurance company compensate me for the repair and for the obvious loss in value. If only things had been handled differently ... but where should we go nearly a decade later?

On January 14 I sent Ms. Wakeford a certified letter informing her that I intended to have the restoration removed and the filling and inpainting improved by my conservator at a cost estimated to be less than $500, at Hofstra's expense. I also intended to seek compensation for the painting's loss of value from Hofstra's insurance company. If the insurance company would not honor a claim made nine years after damage occurred, I fully expected Hofstra to do the right thing. I requested authorization to proceed with the restoration.

A month later, I still hadn't had the courtesy of a reply. My attorney followed up with a letter on February 24. His letter did elicit a response. On March 3 I received a letter from David C. Christman, Dr. Gelburd's successor as director of the Hofstra Museum, who informed me that the statute of limitations on my claim had expired, and added, "We find no merit in your claim."

I was already feeling hurt that I had not been informed of the damage to my Verhout; Christman's reply really galled me. On March 30 I sent copies of all correspondence to James Shuart, president of Hofstra University. I also wrote to Christman, challenging his statement about the statute of limitations having expired and informing him (as my attorney advised me) that it could be raised or waived. My attorney and I felt that in this case—involving nondisclosure of the damage at the time it occurred—the statute would be extended. As to my claim having no merit, I asked Christman once again to review the facts and respond properly. If this response was not forthcoming, in addition to any other action I might decide on, I would take it upon myself to inform the art community of my experience with the Hofstra Museum so that other collectors and lenders would not risk the danger of receiving the same treatment. I received no reply from either the president of the university or the director of the museum.

In May, I wrote a short essay about the damages to my painting titled, "How Not To Handle an Accident In a Museum." I had one hundred photographs made showing the gouge to my Verhout painting under UV. My secretary and I sent packets containing the Hofstra correspondence, the essay, and the photograph to museums, curators, collectors, galleries, and dealers, a few each day for close to six weeks. I sent a packet to David Christman on August 10 and asked him to advise me if it contained any mistakes.

One of these information packets was sent to Professor Donna Barnes at Hofstra University, who had been the guest curator of the exhibition in 1988. Until she received the information from me, she had been completely unaware of the damage to my paintings while at Hofstra. In an effort to resolve this situation, she met several times with Christman.

I also sent an information packet to Dr. Ira Kukin, my friend from Harvard chemistry days, who knew many people at Hofstra. He pursued the matter with a Hofstra board member, Frank Zarb, who took up the matter with David Christman. The comment was made that Al Bader was riled up (if only they knew how much) and it would be best to settle the dispute. On June 16, 1998, David Christman offered me $300. Charles Munch was charging me $1,150 to conserve the painting properly. The $300 offer was a slap in the face. We had another one hundred photographs made to send along with the horror story.

Many of the art historians I contacted sent replies to me, some to Hofstra. The strongest and most helpful came from a very good friend, Dr. William Robinson at Harvard, who replied to Professor Barnes' request for loans of paintings on July 20, 1999 as follows:

> This is no reflection on your work, but I have to tell you that I cannot recommend to Mr and Mrs Abrams that they grant loans to the Hofstra Museum in light of the museum's unprofessional handling of the damage to Dr. Bader's Verhout in the People at Work show. I have seen the correspondence on this matter, which records the museum's succession of mistakes, cover-ups, and evasion of responsibility from the time of the exhibition in 1988 until last year. It would be convenient if we could blame the old régime, but one of the worst documents in this exchange is a 1998 letter to Dr. Bader from David Christman. I feel sorry for you, because it was not in any way your responsibility, but the record of this incident is so appalling that I would not send Fogg drawings to Hofstra, nor could I recommend that the Abrams' drawings be exhibited there.

It was Professor Barnes who kept working with David Christman, Hofstra University, and me, trying to find an acceptable solution. She surprised me by telling me that David Christman was actually a good human being. She told me that his response to my claim was at the direction of the university's lawyer, Emil Cianciulli, who said my claim had no merit. I accused David Christman of hiding behind Professor Barnes' skirts, for he never gave me the courtesy of a personal letter or a phone call or even a "We're sorry." I told Professor Barnes that after much thought, I had decided not to sue Hofstra for damages. Charles Munch had completed the restoration to my satisfaction and at my expense. While I enjoy a good fight, especially when I am unequivocally right, I preferred to keep sending the information packets cautioning art collectors rather than initiating a lengthy lawsuit.

On October 6, 1998 I sent one of my information packets to Dr. Gail Gelburd, the former director of the Hofstra Museum, now the executive director for the Council for Creative Projects in Lee, Massachusetts. She wrote on November 13, accusing me of professional libel and urging me to immediately cease general dissemination of my complaints containing her name. She, as director of the Hofstra Museum at the time of the damages, was only an employee of Hofstra University, and my misfortunes were clearly a university matter, to be addressed and resolved by them. This was certainly not her problem, she believed.

It seemed as though I might soon be on the brink of a lawsuit, but I was confident that all of my statements pertaining to the former director were truthful, and stated only the facts. I wrote Dr. Gelburd of my decision not to take Hofstra University to court, but if she or any other party chose otherwise, I would proceed with a full claim for damages.

Professor Barnes ultimately prevailed upon David Christman and me to find a happier solution. Christman wrote me on December 9, explaining his response as directed by the university attorney. He apologized for the damage to my Verhout and offered full reimbursement of the conservation fees I had paid Charles Munch, agreeing that it was the museum's obligation to conserve the work in an agreeable manner. It seems that Professor Barnes was right about David Christman being a good human being after all. His extremely cordial letter unruffled my tail feathers—it was time for both of us to end this nonsense.

Actually, there was a real silver lining to this affair. Charles Munch found that Mervin Honig, Hofstra's conservator, had

111

used too much gesso and overpaint, which was so visible under UV. Now, properly restored, the scratch is no longer visible under UV. And with the entire painting cleaned, it looks far better than it did before (Plate 42). Charles pointed out that his charge of $1,150 was not only for the repair of the scratch, but also included cleaning the entire painting. And so I returned $500 to Hofstra University on April 9, 1999.

Naturally I informed the art historians to whom I had written about this happy ending.

Professor Barnes later asked me to loan two of my paintings, a Pieter Claesz still life of 1646 and the now beautifully cleaned Verhout to an exhibition titled A Matter of Taste at the Albany Institute of History & Art in 2002. Donna had visited us in Milwaukee in October 1999. We had become friends, and of course I consented to the loan and told her that I would even loan my fine Jacob van Ruisdael winter landscape to a Hofstra University Dutch winter landscape exhibition if she were responsible for that exhibition.

The Verhout looked beautiful in Albany though not in the really well-written catalog because many of the color reproductions were off color—the Verhout looked a sickly green. The catalog was manufactured in China, and it is almost impossible to get good color reproductions when the printer cannot see the actual painting. Museums can be pennywise and pound foolish—and museums are not alone.

# 8

# A Double Theft

Isabel and I arrived at Amsterdam's Central Station on Saturday afternoon, November 12, 1994, and while waiting for the tram to take us to our hotel, I went to the tourist office to pick up a map of the city, leaving Isabel with our luggage—two suitcases and my briefcase. When I returned minutes later, the briefcase was gone. A swarthy, bearded man had distracted her attention by asking a question about trams while a woman grabbed the case.

It contained many photographs and papers, American and English money, traveler's checks, checkbooks, two pieces of jewelry, and three small paintings that I had planned to discuss with Dutch art historians.

We rushed to the police station in the Voorburgwal near by where Martin Te Pas, a very pleasant officer, took the details. He told us that the money was certainly lost, but the paintings might be recovered.

From the hotel, we called two old friends, one, in London, to ask for help with alerting the London bank about the blank checks; the other, a friend and art dealer in The Hague, Saskia Jungeling, to ask for advice about the paintings.

All three paintings were seventeenth century. I had purchased the smallest at Sotheby's in London the previous July. A sketch of a man, I believe by Gonzales Coques, the Antwerp portraitist (ca. 1635), might seem the most valuable to the thieves because it was in an elaborate carved gilt frame with an eighteenth-century label on the back stating that it was by Anthony van

Dyck. Thieves may not know of the unreliability of eighteenth-century attributions.

The other two paintings, both on panels, I had purchased from London dealers just days before. One depicted Rembrandt's mother (Plate 44) in the manner of Dou, and was probably by a Rembrandt student of around 1630. It was in a padded envelope, unframed. The other, also unframed, was just in a plastic folder, between my papers. The seller had suggested that this study of a man might be by Willem Drost, a well-known Rembrandt student, an attribution I found difficult to believe, but as it was certainly mid-seventeenth century and of fine quality, I liked it immensely and thought it the best of the three lost paintings (Plate 46).

We were exhausted after our phone calls from the hotel, took sleeping pills, and both had nightmares about robberies and paintings. But at least we were physically unharmed, and one couldn't but admire the teamwork of the thieves!

Miracles still happen. At 8:00 the next morning, Saskia called us to tell us of a phone call she had received at midnight from a man in Amsterdam, a Bert Vos (Plate 45), who had found many of the photographs and papers and one painting. At first we thought he might be one of the thieves trying to exchange paintings for more money. That this was ludicrous soon became clear when we met Bert Vos later that morning. He had been returning to his home along tramline 17, several miles from the station, at 11:15 the night before, when he noticed a pile of papers and 8 in x 10 in photographs lying in the gutter between two dustbins. Closer inspection convinced him that this was not rubbish, so he scooped up the pile and took it to his simple, third-story apartment, spread out the papers and photographs to dry, read some of the documents, and discovered the non-Drost painting of a man and my telephone list.

He then called my son in Milwaukee but reached the answering machine; he then phoned the police and the Rijksmuseum because he had seen a letter from Dr. Filedt-Kok to me, but of course at midnight, he was only able to talk to a guard. Then he noticed one Dutch phone number, that of Saskia, who knew of our loss and cautioned him not to dry the painting on panel on a radiator.

The miracle is not that we got our papers and the painting back, but that anyone would do what Bert Vos did. Just think of it: a man living alone, going to the enormous trouble—at midnight—to examine the papers, make those phone calls around the world, and try to dry out the damp material. At first he refused compensation. Only when I insisted did he agree to use it for his Boy Scout troop. Of course we invited him to be our guest in Milwaukee. When I fell asleep the night of our misfortune, I thought I never wanted to be in Amsterdam again. Now I knew that I wanted to go back, if only to get to know this man better. We enjoyed his visit to Milwaukee and have been back to Amsterdam several times.

The thieves had taken the study of Rembrandt's mother out of its envelope, which they threw away with all the other papers, but they overlooked the study of a man, and the panel had not suffered. We took it to the Rijksbureau voor Kunsthistorische Dokumentatie (RKD), the Netherlands Institute for Art History, in The Hague and discovered that the painting came from the Hermitage in St. Petersburg and had been sold in Berlin in 1935. Abraham Bredius, the greatest Rembrandt expert of his day, had considered it to be a genuine Rembrandt and given it No. 226 in his catalog of the master's work. When I first saw it in London, I remembered seeing another, certainly inferior, version in the Johnson Collection in the museum in Philadelphia. Today these sketches are no longer thought to be by Rembrandt, but ours is certainly by one of his ablest students, painted in the 1640s.

At the Mauritshuis in The Hague, Frits Duparc, its director, compared it with a portrait of a man in a helmet by Carel Fabritius, then on loan from the museum in Groningen. There certainly is similar handling of paint, yet I do not believe that Bredius 226 is by Carel Fabritius.

When I showed my panel to Dr. Filedt-Kok, he said, "How nice—the poor man's Rembrandt." When I showed it to Professor Josua Bruyn, the retired head of the Rembrandt Research Project, he agreed with my dating, but thought we might never be able to ascertain the name of the very able student. Whoever painted it, I think of it as my Bert Vos panel.

Naturally we reported the theft to Christie's and Sotheby's in Amsterdam, to the RKD, and to the International Foundation for Art Research (IFAR), which published the theft, illustrating both paintings in the *IFARreports* and the Art Loss Register. Then we waited and hoped.

The break came four years later, on December 23, 1998, when Dr. Rudi Ekkart, the director of the RKD, faxed me that a collector in Utrecht, Dr. Matthias M.B. Schilder, an Utrecht zoologist, had bought my *Rembrandt's Mother* at a small auction in Amsterdam and had then brought the panel to the RKD for identification. Dr. Jan Kosten, the Rembrandt School specialist at the RKD, had shown it to be the stolen painting.

"Unfortunately for you," wrote Dr. Ekkart, "according to the Dutch civil code a work of art that had been bought in good confidence (and in this case even in a public auction) longer than three years after the theft is the legal possession of the buyer." Dr. Ekkart added, however, that "the present owner, who is a very reliable and rational man ... is willing to sell it to you for a reasonable price according to the market value."

Just what was the market value?

Two days before the theft in 1994, I had bought the painting from a gallery in London, Whitfield Fine Arts, for £3,200. Dr. Schilder had bought it, lot 1420 in the De Eland auction on June 25, 1998, for a hammer price of Hfl 600, paying a total of Hfl 762.

Professor Werner Sumowski had written to Dr. Schilder that he considered the painting to be one of the best copies of a lost original by Rembrandt. Another copy is in the Mauritshuis (RRP C-41).

A dealer in Amsterdam had offered Dr. Schilder Hfl 20,000, and now he concluded that "Hfl 35,000 is a correct price ... its value would go up easily to Hfl 50,000 in just a few years as was suggested by an art dealer, who advised me not to sell the painting now."

Naturally I asked Dr. Ekkart whether he still considered Dr. Schilder a very reliable and rational man, and I remonstrated with Dr. Schilder:

You would like thirty-five thousand guilders for a painting which I had purchased in November 1994 from a London gallery (known for its expertise but not its low prices), Whitfield Fine Arts, for £3,200, less than a third of the price you are asking. The second point, selling my painting, you have considered, but that may not be as easy as you think. Knowing the facts, a truly good person will not buy it, and a really knowledgeable person will not either, because he can never get completely clear title. The silver lining is that I now know where the painting is. My worry is not that you will not return it. I can live without it, as I own many better Rembrandt School paintings. Rather, my worry is that you will not return it, but that neither you nor anyone else will really enjoy looking at it for a very long time. That would be a pity. Also, it would be a loss of a very interesting study piece to my university's museum, to which my wife and I are leaving our collection. What do I suggest? Certainly not that you just return my painting without compensation. Then you would be the second victim of the thief, and of the almost unbelievable police carelessness. Think about it, and let me know your reaction entirely at your convenience.

My friend, Dr. Otto Naumann, had suggested that I consult an Amsterdam lawyer, Dr. Willem Russell, himself an astute collector. Dr. Russell discovered that both stolen paintings had been offered for sale at the auction house De Eland in February 1995, but the consignor had demanded so high a reserve that they did not sell and were returned to him. Shortly thereafter, they were seized by the police from a Moroccan drug dealer and kept by the police in their lost-and-found storeroom for the next three years, without anyone checking their own police reports or with IFAR. And then the *police* sent both paintings to De Eland again, where they were sold without reserve on June 25, 1998!

Dr. Russell tried very hard to persuade the Amsterdam police to compensate me, to no avail. They did not even offer to give me the money they had received from the auction house. The lawyer advised me that suing the Amsterdam police would be far more costly than the value of the paintings.

At the time, Dr. Cynthia Schneider was the American ambassador to Holland, and I related these facts to her. She responded most kindly on April 1, 1999:

> Your letter of March 24th regarding the theft of several of your paintings in Amsterdam distressed me more than you might have imagined. As a scholar of Dutch art, recently named American Ambassador to the Netherlands, your name is extremely well known to me. Before assuming my post I was an Associate Professor of Art History at Georgetown University; I received my doctorate at Harvard under Seymour Slive. We have many friends in common, from Bill Robinson to Walter Liedtke to Seymour himself. In any case your story is indeed a distressing one. I will do everything I can to investigate the situation, and I will get back to you with information as soon as possible.

But even the American ambassador could not persuade A. A. Smit, the commissioner of the Amsterdam police, to be fair. I had myself written to the police by registered mail on

February 22, 1999 but received no reply. Dr. Schneider wrote to Mr. Smit shortly after that and he finally wrote to me on May 24, 2001 (two years later!), "Although late, I'll try to answer the questions you asked. But let me start by saying that your version of what happened with your paintings is the correct one ... " Yet he made no offer of compensation.

I replied, "That being so, why does the Amsterdam police not reimburse me for the two paintings it recovered and sold through auction?" There was never any response—an example of stonewalling from the police of the city I had thought to be one of the fairest in Europe.

In December 1994, a Dutch paper, *Het Parool*, had written a delightful article about Bert Vos finding the best of these paintings. On April 10, 1999, the same paper published another article about an Utrecht zoologist asking Hfl 35,000 for the *Rembrandt's Mother* that the police had sent to auction. Another Dutch paper, *De Volkskrant*, published a similar article with a photo of *Rembrandt's Mother* on April 24.

Perhaps these articles and my writing to Dr. Schilder changed his mind. I told him that I had read some of his papers, particularly about ill-treated dogs, and realized that he was an able zoologist, and that I hoped that he would sell me *Rembrandt's Mother* reasonably. What was reasonable? I had bought the painting from Clovis Whitfield for roughly the equivalent of Hfl 10,000, and Schilder finally asked if I was willing to pay that. Of course I was, and Dr. Ekkart at the RKD exchanged my banker's draft for my painting, which now hangs in our home.

We even visited Dr. Schilder in his home, happily smiling about the past and admiring his nineteenth-century paintings. He gave us the De Eland catalog of June 25, 1998, listing the two paintings sent in by the police. What a pity that P.J.C. Trommelen, the director of the auction house, could not tell us who had bought the Gonzales Coques, and that he appears not to have checked whether the paintings were stolen. Had he done so in 1995, they would have been returned to me.

The Historians of Netherlandish Art published a full page advertisement (Plate 43) in their April 2000 issue and, if I live long enough, I may find out about the third and least important painting.

In the meantime, the Rijksmuseum has asked me to lend a Sweerts self-portrait, and the Rembrandthuis asked for two early Rembrandts. I hesitated, thinking of A.A. Smit, the Amsterdam police commissioner, but should I cut off my nose to spite my face? I enjoyed seeing all three of these paintings in the exhibitions, and all have left Amsterdam safely.

Publication of my story of the double theft in the *Queen's Alumni Review* in the summer of 2003 interested Peter R. de Vries, who produces a television program featuring crime in The Netherlands. Mr. Evert Nijkamp of that program came to Herstmonceux Castle in November 2004 to interview Isabel and me and produced a film shown on the television station SBS in April 2005.

We had no response from the Dutch police but received an astounding letter, together with €50, from a Mr. Karl Hammer in Breda:

I saw on Dutch television what has happened to you and found it an utter disgrace. I understand your remark that there is no justice in Holland and must admit it does seem like that.

I have not the means to solve your problem, but I can at least do one thing, to show you that the injustice is (mostly) at the "higher" level.

I am sending you €50, which by your standards is perhaps worth less than a second in your life. But if I tell you that I live on welfare, and that this sum is to me worth a week's food, then maybe you can appreciate it better and will realize that at least there is a desire to give you justice in the heart of the "little" man. I hope this will light up *your* heart a bit, so you will continue your good work in the world. For me, I find my satisfaction in Proverb 21:3.

Best wishes to you and your sweet wife Isabel.

Karl

What a man! He told me that he was forty-five, born in Amsterdam to an Austrian mother and a Dutch father. Entirely self-educated, he taught himself video editing and became editor for current affairs programs and a drama writer/editor. Now he lives very quietly and modestly working on a book, *Satan's Song*, which deals with the theft in 1934 of a panel from Van Eyck's Ghent altarpiece *Adoration of the Lamb*. Some people, including Heinrich Himmler, believed that this work holds the key to unlocking the burial place of the *Arma Christi*, the nails and the crown of thorns of Jesus' crucifixion.

David de Witt (the Bader Curator at Queen's University), has read the Dutch manuscript and told me:

Karl Hammer received his story by way of a set of notes and conversations over several months with the dying former agent who left them to him, with the wish that it all be made open. An adept and passionate journalist, Hammer pieced the material together, and fleshed it out with commentary on historical, theological, and art-historical context. The thrilling description of the agent's extensive investigation is a pleasure to read, but it is also vital, as it introduces important corrections to the story of the theft of the Van Eyck panel. The mystery is not solved, but shocking revelations concerning the role of highly placed persons in various countries in protecting and repatriating Nazi officials are made instead. Naturally the book incorporates a stinging moral message concerning the pursuit of spiritual aims coupled to dubious political motivations.

My respect for Karl increased further when he corrected an

entry for a painting of Moses by Gabriel de Sabato shown on our website, www.alfredbader.com (Plate 47). I had thought that the painting depicted Moses descending from Mount Sinai, but Karl Hammer's explanation, shown on our corrected website, is beautifully simple and clear.

I did not want to keep the €50 he sent me, so sent him €100 saying how amazed and moved I was by his action. He replied that to accept the repayment would nullify his gesture, and so he sent €50 to the World Society for the Welfare of Animals and €50 to the Jewish Historical Museum in Amsterdam.

Now I hope that Karl's book, both in Dutch and English, will sell really well. I can dream: David told me that it is better written and clearer than *The Da Vinci Code*.

# 9

# *Prussian Blue*

The following text is reprinted with the publishers' kind permission from *Chemistry in Britain*, Vol. 33, No. 11, November 1997 and Vol. 37, No. 7, July 2001.

## Part 1: Out of the Blue

A teacher and his student, a famous experiment, and an ambiguous monogram are all that Alfred Bader has to go on in his quest to track down the unknown artist of his oil painting. Read on: there's a handsome reward for the person to point him in the right direction ...

The Museum of the History of Science at the University of Oxford owns a painting, *A Chemist's Laboratory* (Plate 48), with a caption that raises more questions than it answers:

An oil painting of a chemist said to be Sir Humphrey [*sic*] Davy (1778–1829), with an assistant in his laboratory. The painting is signed and dated "LR 1827" (Plate 49), and it is probably a derivative. The interest in this painting lies in the glass chemical apparatus depicted, much of it similar to apparatus from the Daubeny Laboratory now in the museum.

But the teacher does not really look like Sir Humphry Davy, and what is he doing? And who is the student? The date, 1827, is clear, but is the monogram (Plate 49) really LR? It could be an elaborate R, a double R, or perhaps an LR or LSR.

The Oxford museum suggests the painting is a "derivative,"

meaning that it may not be original but based on an earlier painting. We can view it on three levels: first, by looking at the contemporary laboratory equipment referred to in the museum's description (the Nooth's apparatus, much like a Kipp's gas generator); second, at the two men; and lastly, at the setting, surely inspired by some of the Dutch and Flemish seventeenth-century alchemical paintings that were found among English collections in 1827. The painting's juxta-position of modern laboratory equipment with a seventeenth-century interior is also quite odd, a sort of *"homage à David Teniers"* an artist might attempt. The R is similar to the R in the signatures of Ramsay Richard Reinagle (1775–1862) who may have painted the Oxford painting or the work from which it is derived.

Though the identity of the painter remains uncertain, some of the mystery surrounding the Oxford painting has recently been resolved by a chance connection with a second painting that I was offered by an antique dealer in North Carolina in 1989. This larger painting, which I later bought, depicts an almost identical scene (Plate 50). Not only does it answer the question of what the teacher is doing, but it also suggests the identity of the sitters, and provides a possible source for the derivative painting in Oxford.

When I first looked closely at my own painting, I thought, "Why, I have done this reaction myself: two yellow liquids are poured together and a blue pigment precipitates. It is the production of Prussian blue." My observation was quickly confirmed by consulting Floyd Green and his *Sigma-Aldrich Handbook of Stains, Dyes, and Indicators*.[1] Prussian blue is made by adding a ferric salt solution to an alkaline ferrocyanide solution and filtering and washing the precipitate to yield the deep blue inorganic pigment.

But what did British chemists know about Prussian blue in 1827? The most important textbook at that time was William Thomas Brande's *Manual of Chemistry*. First published in

London in 1819, the manual went through six editions and was translated into several languages. His student Michael Faraday had a copy[2] in which he made copious additions and handwritten notes, including notes on Prussian blue. And despite his discovery of electromagnetic induction in August 1831, it appears that Faraday was still following the literature on Prussian blue a year later—his notes go to 1832.

Could the teacher in the two paintings be Brande, with his student, Faraday? Arnold Thackray at the Chemical Heritage Foundation in Philadelphia was the first to suggest that the teacher was W.T. Brande (1788–1866), a self-taught chemist who began lecturing at the Royal Institution in 1812 and became Sir Humphry Davy's successor as professor of chemistry there in 1813. Brande's lectures, described by F. James, the editor of Faraday's correspondence, in an as-yet-unpublished manuscript, " ... were intended for all denominations of students, and were given thrice weekly, from October to May. They were the first lectures in London in which so extended a view of chemistry, and of its applications, including technical, mineralogical, geological, and medical chemistry, was attempted." Initially Brande delivered these courses alone with the help of Michael Faraday, who as the assistant chemist at the Royal Institution was responsible, until 1825, for preparing and executing lecture demonstrations for Brande. In 1824, Faraday gave some of the lectures, and from the following year on, the course was given jointly.

Therefore Faraday, who had been Davy's assistant, became Brande's too. He soon surpassed his teacher, although they remained close friends, as evidenced by a photograph taken in the 1860s. Brande no doubt thought of Faraday as his most illustrious student, and in 1854, Brande and J. Scoffern published a *Course of Ten Lectures in Organic Chemistry* dedicated to Michael Faraday. Three pages of Lecture I deal extensively with Prussian blue.[3]

For years, Prussian blue synthesis was a star attraction of

Brande's and Faraday's lecture demonstrations at the Royal Institution and elsewhere. Faraday's handwritten notes for "A Course of Lectures on the Philosophy and Practice of Chemical Manipulation," given at the London Institution in 1827, refers to Prussian blue as example of precipitation. The notes for his lectures at the Royal Institution also refer in detail to Prussian blue[4]. In 1827, the date of the Oxford painting, Faraday published a laboratory manual[5] that included a description of the preparation of Prussian blue. Similarly, Brande included a long entry on Prussian blue—"this beautiful dark blue pigment ..."—in his *Dictionary of Science, Literature & Art*[6], using the references gathered by Faraday.

What if Brande had commissioned an artist to depict him with his most illustrious student and good friend, Michael Faraday? Might he not have picked the very experiment, the precipitation of Prussian blue, that both had demonstrated so often? However, Brande was anything but bashful. Is it conceivable that he or Faraday would have commissioned this large work without anybody writing about it?

The previous owner of my painting, Michele Johnston, had acquired it unsigned, nameless, and without provenance. She wrote to several art historians at the Metropolitan Museum, Yale University, the National Gallery in Washington, and the National Portrait Gallery in London, the Wellcome Institute for the History of Medicine and the Science Museum in London, querying whether the painting might be by John Singleton Copley. Each told her that it could not possibly be by Copley; some strongly suggested Thomas Sully, others some able English artist influenced by Thomas Lawrence. Thomas Sully did paint in England in the 1830s, but he monogrammed almost all his works and kept a careful record—in which this painting is not included.

The connection between the Oxford painting and my larger version was first made by Wendy Sheridan, curator at the Science Museum. In her letter to William Schupbach, curator at the Wellcome Institute, dated June 18, 1990, she wrote:

> The painting shows considerable individual character and a
> strong rapport between the sitters, at a moment of scientific
> "discovery." The work may be contemporary to its content,
> or possibly executed a little later, in the mid-nineteenth
> century when a genre of nostalgic portraiture was in vogue.

She went on to conclude:

> ... in the chemistry showcases at the Museum of History of
> Science, Oxford is a small oil by "L.R.," 1827, which puts
> this exact subject into a context similar to the Oxford
> Daubeny Laboratory of 1823 and suggests Davy as a sitter.
> It is not known which version precedes which, or if in fact
> both are derivative. The larger is a quality of work, of a kind
> probably executed by a professional painter of the status of,
> for example, Sir Thomas Lawrence and his circle ... By
> comparison, the Oxford version is clearly by a lesser
> although competent hand.

It is often difficult to be certain of the identity of sitters in
an historical painting. The younger man looks like Michael
Faraday, while the older man looks more like Brande than Sir
Humphry Davy. Faraday worked with Brande far longer than
he did with Davy, and it was Brande and Faraday who shared
the interest in Prussian blue.

But when was the larger painting painted? Michele Johnston
had the painting wax-lined, obscuring all canvas marks. When
I had the lining removed, the tax stamp and canvas mark of
Thomas Brown, from 163 High Holborn in London, were
found. Painters' canvases were subject to an excise duty from
1803 to1831, and the stamp was applied to the canvas when
the duty was paid. Cathy Proudlove at the Castle Museum in
Norwich has made a study of such marks and identified this

127

as one used on canvas between 1816 and 1830.

So what are the possibilities? Perhaps an able British artist painted the large work before 1827, and the monogrammist R incorporated the image of teacher and student into the Oxford painting. Or maybe R's painting came first, based on an as-yet-unknown earlier work depicting the student and his teacher. In my opinion, the Oxford painting of 1827 is a pastiche after the larger work. Yet several art historians have suggested that the larger work dates from much later—1840 to 1860—when there was nostalgia for genre paintings depicting important earlier events. This supposes that a canvas produced before 1831 was kept for a long time. That, according to Cathy Proudlove, would be highly unusual. Whichever theory is correct, the large canvas must have been the work of an able artist, and there is likely to be a record somewhere—a mezzotint or at least a printed description. I am offering a reward of £1,000 to the first person pointing to that reference.

Christopher With, at the National Gallery in Washington, wrote in a letter to Michele Johnston on March 22, 1989:

Since trying to identify the artist is like looking for a needle in a haystack, I would suggest a different tack. Namely, if one could identify what scientific experiment is depicted, then one might uncover who the two men are in the painting. Knowing that, it would be easier to track down artists who did portraits of those individuals.

This was excellent advice. I have identified the experiment; it is certainly the formation of Prussian blue. The identity of the two men is also reasonably certain: the student was Michael Faraday and the teacher Sir Humphry Davy or, more likely, W.T. Brande. I am more interested in knowing the reason for this portrayal of such wonderful rapport between Faraday and his teacher. When we learn that, we will probably know the identity of the artist.

*Acknowledgements*: Thanks to the many people who helped me in my as-yet-uncompleted quest, including: Clare Ford-Wille, Peter Funnel, Floyd J. Green, Willem Hackmann, Lee Howard, Frank James, Anne-Marie Logan, Keith Moore, Charles Munch, Cathy Proudlove, William Schupbach, Wendy Sheridan, Arnold Thackray, and Malcolm Warner.

Dr. Alfred Bader is offering a reward of £1,000 for information leading to the name of the artist who painted Plate 50. Anyone who may be able to help should write to him at 924 East Juneau Avenue, Suite 622, Milwaukee, Wisconsin 53202, US.

## Part 2: End of the Mystery

In an article "Out of the Blue" (*Chemistry in Britain*, November 1997, p. 24), I described two paintings, one on panel, dated 1827, in the Science Museum in Oxford, and a larger one in my collection, on canvas that bears a tax stamp used between 1816 and 1830. Each depicts a teacher and a student—I believe William Thomas Brande and Michael Faraday—making Prussian blue. Since I knew neither the identity of the artist nor, with certainty, that of the sitters, I offered £1,000 to anyone who could trace the history of my painting.

The identity of the artist of the Oxford painting came first. I found that the monogram is that of Charles Robert Leslie, who worked in London in 1827. He so admired the works of David Teniers that he made several copies of works by that artist and hung them in his painting room. Leslie must have seen my earlier version and copied that in an "*homage à David Teniers*'.

Several connoisseurs suggested that my work might be by an able portraitist, Thomas Phillips, RA (1770–1845). Phillips painted a number of scientists: William Pearson giving astronomical instruction to his family (1808); Joseph Banks, the

129

great explorer, botanist, and president of the Royal Society (painted several times around 1810), Humphry Davy (1821); and Michael Faraday (1842). Phillips' interest in science earned him a Fellowship of the Royal Society (FRS) in 1819.

Looking at many paintings by Phillips, I could indeed see the similarities in paint handling with mine, but could find no reference to my painting in a thesis[7] on Phillips or in any other articles in the art historical libraries that I consulted.

The teacher in my painting, William Thomas Brande (1788–1866), succeeded Humphry Davy as professor of chemistry at the Royal Institution in 1813, and then divided his time between his duties there and the Worshipful Society of Apothecaries, where he had been appointed professor of chemistry and *materia medica* in 1812.

When I learned of Brande's involvement with the Society of Apothecaries, I turned to Dee Cook, the Society's archivist, who made a great effort to trace the history of my painting. She established that Brande's scientific mentor was Charles Hatchett, FRS, the discoverer of niobium in 1801, and one of the early managers of the Royal Institution; that Hatchett had proposed Brande for an FRS in 1809, when Brande was only twenty-one; and that Hatchett had become his father-in-law in 1818. She was also able to provide biographical details of Brande's family: his father had been a royal apothecary and his brother, Everard Augustus, to whom he had been apprenticed, had also been a royal apothecary as well as a member of the court of assistants of the Society of Apothecaries.

Following extensive research, Cook finally narrowed the field of prominent portrait painters of the early decades of the nineteenth century to Thomas Phillips. Cook then discovered the existence of Phillips' sitters book[8] in which there was an entry for February 1816, noting that he had painted a kit cat [a 28 in x 36 in, three-quarter length portrait] of C. Hatchett, Esq (no. 425) and a three-quarter length picture of T. Brand [*sic*] Esq (no. 426). She also found that both paintings were exhibited at the Royal Academy that year. There the latter was described as one of W. Brand. Brande's initials were W.T. and his name was sometimes misspelled. Phillips' next painting, no. 427, described in his sitters book as an "historical from Milton," was of C. Lyell, probably Charles Lyell senior (1767–1849), a man of many parts—botanist, lecturer at the Royal Institution, and translator of Dante's works. Phillips was more than just a portraitist: he liked to depict his sitters in storytelling settings. What a pity that no. 426 is not described in more detail!

Cook surmises that Charles Hatchett very likely commissioned both paintings, nos. 425 and 426. Brande had been Hatchett's protégé since 1802 and was soon to become his son-in-law. Brande wanted himself portrayed with his clever young assistant, Michael Faraday, in this most colorful experiment, the making of Prussian blue.

Faraday began as Davy's assistant at the Royal Institution in March 1813. From October of that year, Faraday traveled with Davy, nominally as his secretary and scientific assistant, visiting France, Italy, and Switzerland. Returning to London, Faraday resumed work at the Royal Institution in May 1815. But by February 1816, he had worked at the Royal Institution for a little more than a year, and so was virtually unknown in the chemical world and was not even mentioned either in Phillips' sitters book or in the brief notation in the Royal Academy catalog.

All of this evidence, that my painting is of the as-yet-unknown twenty-four-year-old Faraday with the twenty-eight-year-old W.T. Brande painted by Thomas Phillips, is circumstantial, yet is so persuasive that I am convinced, and have given Dee Cook the reward.

There are, of course, many loose ends. Least important: how did Leslie have the opportunity to copy Phillips' painting in 1827? Who first owned my painting: Hatchett, or W.T. Brande, or his brother? And what became of it? It is not mentioned in

Brande's will of 1866, or in Faraday's. Brande and his wife, Anna Frederica, were happily married and were survived by four of their five children. Did one of their descendants sell the painting, which then passed from owner to owner and finally reached a chemist who recognized the experiment and is proud to own the earliest portrait of that truly great and good scientist, Michael Faraday?

The search goes on ...

REFERENCES:
1. F.J. Green, The *Sigma-Aldrich Handbook of Stains, Dyes, and Indicators*, p.590. Milwaukee, WI, US: Aldrich Chemical Co., 1990.
2. The Wellcome Institute Library, no. 2332–2334. Brande's work has been cut up and rebound into three interleaved volumes; Faraday's notes are written on the inter-leaves.
3. The subject matter of a course of ten lectures on some of the arts connected with organic chemistry, delivered before the members of the Royal Institution in the spring of 1852 by W.T. Brande, arranged by J. Scoffern. London: Longman, 1854.
4. Royal Institution notes, "Chemical lectures: Faraday." RI library MS F4K, p.255.
5. M. Faraday, *Chemical Manipulation*, p.231 London: W. Phillips, 1827.
6. W.T. Brande, *A Dictionary of Science, Literature & Art*, 2nd edn. London: Longman, 1852.
7. Charlotte Miller, MA thesis, Courtauld Institute, May 1977, "Thomas Phillips RA, FRS, FSA, with 76 illustrations." Many of Phillips' paintings are untraced.
8. A neatly handwritten copy of T. Phillips' sitters book is at the Heinz Archive and Library of the National Portrait Gallery.

# 10

# Sumowski

One of the most helpful and knowledgeable art historians I have ever known is Professor Werner Sumowski (Plate 54) in Stuttgart. He is also the subject of a most unfortunate episode in my life.

In the first volume of my autobiography, I wrote:

I have heard that students, and even some mature adults, are afraid of Werner Sumowski, professor of art history in Stuttgart; they would not be if they knew him well. He looks so impressive, with his shock of white hair, and he speaks and writes very incisively. He has written two encyclopedic works on Rembrandt students, one on their drawings—ten volumes so far—and the other on their paintings, in six volumes. His work on the paintings alone, a Herculean undertaking, contains an enormous amount of information and over 2,000 illustrations, many in full color. I have spent many an evening studying these volumes.

Werner does not travel much, preferring to work almost entirely from photographs, and, of course, as with almost every art historian who makes attributions, some of them have been questioned. Job's saying is applicable here: "Shall we take the good from God and not the bad?" Werner has helped thousands like myself to understand Rembrandt students better.

Over the last twenty-five years, we had become good friends.

I enjoyed sending him detailed information about Rembrandt School paintings in upcoming sales. We exchanged our thoughts about their quality; he gave his opinions about my acquisitions and suggested paintings that he had been shown that I might be interested to buy. We both enjoyed this give and take over many years, and the formal *"Herr Dr. Bader ... Sie"* of our correspondence moved to a friendly *"Lieber Alfred ... Du"* basis, unusual with German academics.

Every June, Isabel and I and two Stuttgart friends, Doris and Helge Herd, visited Werner for an afternoon, spent two hours discussing paintings, and then enjoyed a simple supper. For me, these hours were a high point of our European trip, as often the high point of my week's reading was to study his by-now-well-worn six volumes of Rembrandt School paintings, which illustrate over sixty of our paintings.

After his retirement as professor at the University of Stuttgart and the death of his beloved mother-by-adoption with whom he lived, it was clear that he was lonelier and quieter, and at our last parting in June 2003, he seemed so stressed that he mentioned wondering whether we would see each other again.

I began calling him a little more frequently, particularly during the hot summer of 2003, and often thought of one really moving sentence he had written: *"Dass Du den alten müden Esel auf Trapp zu bringen versuchst, finde ich rührend. Leider ist die Aussicht auf Erfolg gering."* ("I find it really touching that you are trying to move the old, tired donkey. But the chances of success are slight.")

At an auction in London in July 2003, I had met a German dealer, Hans Ellermann, who offered me a painting once attributed to Rembrandt. There are several versions of this study of a bearded man, Bredius 264, and I thought Ellermann's might well be the best version. He had already been given this opinion by Werner and Professor Ernst van de Wetering of the Rembrandt Research Project. Despite this, I did not think it good enough for my own collection and told Ellermann that I felt I could not resell it profitably.

During our discussion, he seemed to believe that the Rembrandt Research Project could never make a mistake. He spoke so highly of the RRP that I felt it appropriate to point out that in fact they had made some mistakes. I mentioned that in 1981, I had written a very strong letter to Ernst van de Wetering about a painting I owned that the RRP had numbered C-22, not by Rembrandt. I had sent Werner a copy of my letter at the time and he had replied, "Your letter to Mr. van de Wetering deserves complete approval." He was harshly critical of their methods in dismissing paintings from Rembrandt's oeuvre. When he had attended a Lievens symposium in Braunschweig, and had been very disappointed in van de Wetering and Bruyn, he felt completely alienated as a scholar, even referring to himself as a "fossil". All this he expressed in his typically pungent style, not in the least suggesting that this was confidential.

So I sent Ellermann a copy of Werner's 1981 letter, hoping to make him reconsider, because over the years I often thought of Werner's letter and found it correct and historically important. Since then, my opinion of Ernst van de Wetering has gradually changed, and we have become good friends; Werner's opinion of the RRP has changed radically also.

Sometime later, Werner wrote that he had heard that I had sent one of his letters—he did not know which—to Ellermann, and I replied that I had sent his letter of 1981, which I considered so historically important. His reply showed how I may have erred:

Your letter of September 3 upset me even more. It is true that you regret that what you have done has hurt me, but you do not admit in the slightest that it just is not right to send strangers private and confidential letters where the sender is counting on your discretion.

I just chanced to hear about Ellermann. How do I know that you have not been writing for years to every Tom, Dick, and Harry?

I simply do not understand why you sent this copy to Ellermann. If Ernst van de Wetering praises the painting and if Ellermann thinks the RRP important, there was not reason to send this.

It is absolutely *scandalous* that in 2003 you sent a statement of *April 1981* to someone where you don't know what he will do with it.

I know: he will peddle it around, and what I said about the Amsterdam Project twenty-two years ago—before the appearance of the first volume, because of negative impressions at the Lievens Symposium, will be circulated as my judgment *today* about the *Corpus*. Today, knowing the publication and being in touch with van de Wetering, I think totally differently. I can make enemies all by myself; I do not need your indiscretion and your thoughtlessness.

You have deeply disappointed me. I have no confidence in you and really cannot work with you as before. Our association has ended irrevocably.

Best wishes for the future.

Had I known or had any reason to believe that Werner would react in such a manner, I would never have disclosed the contents of his letter.

I have been truly saddened and wrote several times trying to explain and apologize. But each letter was returned unopened. In my last note, I wrote, of course in German, "Both of us are close to the end of life and so I am particularly sorry about my stupidity. What can I say other than '*mea culpa*' and my life is poorer without our friendship. Fond regards, your old and stupid friend." I truly regret that an innocent action on my part has so deeply stressed the man whom I so respect and consider my friend.

Sadly, I cannot live my life over again.

# 11

# Lost Masterpieces and Happy Endings

In my family's apartment in Vienna there were many paintings, only one of which I liked, a small seventeenth-century Dutch landscape. I know exactly where it was hanging in the salon, and when Mother began selling her belongings during the Depression, it was among the first to go. I missed it. I was already collecting stamps, but had no money, so I often spent my time peering through the windows of the city's art and antique dealers, where there were many interesting canvases. It was the seventeenth-century Dutch paintings that I saw in these shops—and during one or two visits to the Kunsthistorisches Museum and the Akademie—that I admired most. After my escape from Vienna in 1938, however, all connection to this world of painting ended for nearly a decade.

When I went to Harvard in 1947, I had the good fortune to attend a number of lectures by Jakob Rosenberg on Rembrandt and his circle. That was it. I was hooked, and since my first purchase of an old master from Dr. Paul Drey in New York, my love of paintings has brought me into contact with art historians, museum directors, and curators around the world.

These gifted and zealous experts have added great richness to my life. One such individual was Edward Dwight. In 1956, as director of the Milwaukee Art Institute, he mounted the beautiful exhibition Still Life Painting Since 1470. This was the first such exhibition that I saw in Milwaukee; I loved it and introduced myself to Dwight. As a result of the friendship that developed between us and the help and encouragement he gave me, I made my first gifts of art to the institute. Over the years, I have donated about forty paintings to its collection. Some of these are masterpieces; some are not so good. It took me years to be able to tell the difference, but exploring this world with so many insightful people has been a wonderful journey. It is this interaction of collectors with directors and curators that has resulted in so many gifts to American museums.

Until May 29, 2001, none of my gifts had been deaccessioned, but on April 30 of that year Russell Bowman, then the director of the Milwaukee Art Museum, sent me a letter with a list of ten that were soon to be auctioned. I replied on May 4:

... I can understand the need for deaccessioning, but would it not make sense to discuss with living donors what their thoughts are before the decision is made? There is one decision that I really question and that is the one regarding the Berchem (Plate 51). Winters [Laurie Winters, a curator at the Milwaukee Art Museum] questioned whether this painting is really by Berchem, but I have no doubt what-soever, as explained in entry 4 of *The Detective's Eye: Investigating the Old Masters*, a catalog for the exhibition that Isabel and I guest curated for the Milwaukee Art Museum in 1989. I don't know of any art historian anywhere who knows as much about just such paintings as Professor Wolfgang Stechow at Oberlin knew. And he didn't just decide on the basis of a photograph, but had the original painting there for study. If you have sent that painting for auction, then at least I hope that the auction house will have the good sense of referring to *The Detective's Eye* entry and Professor Stechow's clear opinion. The Art Museum has no work by Berchem, so the first question in my mind was: Why do you deaccession it?

140

Sadly, Mr. Bowman did not write in reply, and on May 29 Christie's East offered the Berchem as lot 108, by "C. Iwry," an unrecorded artist. There was no reference to *The Detective's Eye*, where there is a detailed, two-page description of the painting, with signature and date, 1650. A perceptive buyer paid $3,760. Unfortunately, I was leaving for England on the day of the sale and didn't have the good sense to leave a bid for this or any of the other paintings.

Laurie Winters, the MAM's Curator of Earlier European Art, has argued that while examining the work she discovered the signature "Iwry"—a "well-known copyist and imitator of Berchem who supplied the English market in the eighteenth century..." She says the piece would have been offered for sale as a "possible Berchem" if she and her associates had not been thoroughly convinced that it was the work of another artist. She makes the case that once the signature was discovered the museum was morally and legally bound to sell it as an Iwry, that anything else would have been fraud. Finally, she suggests that she and Russell Bowman decided not to mention *The Detective's Eye* in the sale catalog so that I would be spared "embarrassment" over my "misattribution."

I would not have been embarrassed at all, because the firm attribution to Berchem came from Wolf Stechow, and the signature is Berchem's (Plate 52). Iwry, the "well-known copyist and imitator of Berchem" Winters refers to, is totally unknown, and the name probably resulted from a misreading of Berchem's signature.

Christie's entry of lot 108 alleged that the painting is indistinctly signed CIWRY and referred to a July 1959 sale at Christie's London, that sold this as "C.IVRY signed with monogram." The 1959 sale preceded Stechow's identification of the signature as Berchem's. The two references to an IWRY or IVRY in the Christie's entries are the only ones I have ever seen.

Another work that was deaccessioned was lot 114, a fine

portrait of a Flemish officer, ca. 1635, so thickly painted that I thought it might have been done for a blind person. It was in fine condition, and I wondered if it was being removed from the museum's collection simply because there was, as yet, no attribution. I learned that a knowledgeable young collector, Avram Saban of Florida, bought it for $4,113. At least this seemed to me a happy ending, since Mr. Saban was very pleased with his acquisition.

Another happy ending came to lot 119, by Jan van de Venne, also known as the Pseudo van de Venne. Although it too was described in *The Detective's Eye*, Christie's stated that the artist was Dutch rather than Flemish. The H. F. Johnson Museum of Art at Cornell University bought it for $4,700. The museum's director, Frank Robinson, was an old friend, and he wrote to me in July 2001: "Just a note to say that this museum just bought your beautiful Jan van de Venne, *A Family Making Music*. We are delighted with it; it is full of the tenderness and realism of this exceptional artist." (Perhaps we should have given the painting to Cornell in the first place.)

In addition to these ten paintings that I had given to the Milwaukee Art Museum, several others were deaccessioned. But all of these, I believe, were unimportant compared to a painting that was deaccessioned in October 2001. This was *The Battle of Gibraltar* for which the artist, Joseph Wright of Derby, was paid £420, the largest sum he ever received for any of his paintings. The purchaser in 1786 was John Milnes of Wakefield who had already amassed one of the largest Wright of Derby collections over a period of some twenty years.

With this painting, as with so many of my art purchases, luck had played a great part. In 1967, Milwaukee dealer Tom Lenz and I purchased some eighty paintings from the Laura Davidson Sears Academy of Fine Arts in Elgin, Illinois. Among these was an enormous *Battle of Gibraltar*, attributed to John Singleton Copley. The pupils at the school had not treated it kindly; all sorts of things, from balls to arrows, had been thrown at it. It had probably been badly restored even before Judge Nathaniel C. Sears bought it in 1923 from the well-known Ehrich Gallery in New York, which had it relined with sailcloth at a cost of $71.

Tom Lenz and I agreed that he would prepare a handsome catalog of the Elgin Academy paintings, which he offered in the Lenz Art Gallery between 1968 and 1970. Many of them were photographed, but the oil on canvas *Battle of Gibraltar*, at 61 in x 93.5 in, was too big to be photographed and did not sell, perhaps because of its size. After two years with the Lenz Art Gallery, the few unsold paintings came to me, the Copley *Gibraltar* among them. I was not much interested in battle scenes, and there was certainly no room for the painting on the walls of our home. It went into the basement.

Luck, however, stepped in once again. I had become good friends with Benedict Nicolson, the great art historian and editor of the *Burlington Magazine*, considered the most important art historical magazine in Britain. He was interested in art in all its forms, and had written the definitive books on Terbrugghen, Georges de La Tour, and the followers of Caravaggio. He had recently completed a two-volume work on Wright of Derby, and although I was not particularly interested in this artist, I wanted to read Ben's book. In Chapter 8, I came upon a lengthy description of a *Battle of Gibraltar*, whose location was unknown. As I read his discussion of this missing painting, I became more and more excited. I wondered: could it possibly be the "Copley" in my basement? Ben had written:

On September 13, 1782 the British garrison at Gibraltar decisively defeated the Spanish floating batteries, thereby restoring some of that British prestige which had been shaken by the loss of the American colonies ... The subject was an obvious one for any history painter following in the footsteps of Benjamin West, and most of all for Wright whose specialty was fire, and who could visualize the contribution he alone could make to the events of that memorable day: the firing of red-hot missiles at the Spanish ships; the ensuing conflagration in the harbor; the dramatic feature of the Mole; the proud garrison standing back to survey the blaze ... He worked hard on the picture during 1784, as far as failing health and torpor would permit, finishing it on February 17 the following year ... He also thought of raffling the picture, but was relieved of this necessity by the appearance of Maecenas in the guise of John Milnes who carted the vast canvas off to Yorkshire, paying him a more handsome sum for it than he had received for any other work.

I now had a great incentive to find out more about this large canvas and decided to send it, without the frame, to Mary D. Randall, a conservator in London. I asked her to reline it, to remove the large amounts of overpaint, and then to ask Benedict to look at it. She put a great deal of work into this project over many months. When finally Ben saw the canvas stripped, he could see that it was in very poor condition but came to the conclusion that it was in fact the missing Wright of Derby. He and I talked at length about this discovery—my first foray into the work of this major British artist—and when it was returned to Milwaukee, I offered it to the Milwaukee Art Center (as our museum was then known). In January 1973, they bought it with funds given in memory of Paula Uihlein by the Charleston Foundation, which she had created.

Once *The Battle of Gibraltar* was on view at the Art Center, Professor Damie Stillman, the chairman of the Art History Department of the University of Wisconsin-Milwaukee, became very interested in it and directed one of his students, Biruta Erdmann, to mount an exhibition and to submit a paper to the *Burlington Magazine*. Benedict Nicolson accepted the piece, and it was published in May 1974 (volume 116, pp. 270–272). Ms. Erdmann began her paper,

This painting (lent by the Milwaukee Art Center) and Wright's two drawings, the *Sea Battle* and *British Gunboat in Action* (lent by the Derby Museum and Art Gallery), were exhibited at the University of Wisconsin-Milwaukee, Art History Gallery, from February 27 through March 27, 1973. This exhibition was designed to clarify the authorship of the painting, which was previously listed as attributed to Copley.

This paper cleared up everything—or so I thought, until I looked at the Christie's East catalog of October 2001. There, as lot 46 from the Milwaukee Art Museum, was *The Siege of Gibraltar* listed as a work by a follower of Joseph Wright of Derby, with an estimate of $8,000–$12,000. There was no provenance of any kind, not even a mention of its being a gift from the Charleston Foundation in memory of Paula Uihlein, nothing about Benedict Nicolson's opinion, and no reference to the seminal paper in the *Burlington Magazine*.

*Should I try to buy it back?* Years earlier, I had helped Queen's University to purchase a collection of seven small landscapes by Wright of Derby. Now I suddenly had the opportunity to add Wright's most ambitious work to the Queen's collection. But would either the Getty or the Yale Center for British Art see this Christie's entry and connect it with the *Burlington Magazine* paper of 1974? To the Yale Center, it would of course have been clear that the painting was historically very important, even in its poor condition. If either institution bid, I believed I would have no chance. Hope springs eternal, however, and I asked my old friend, Otto Naumann, to send his secretary to bid for Queen's up to $100,000. As it turned out, there was only one other bidder, and the painting was sold to Queen's for $10,000.

The MAM had shipped the painting without its frame in order to save money; I was delighted to be able to buy it from the museum and reunite painting and frame, which I believe may be the original, chosen by Wright himself. I was very

145

pleased that the museum also gave me its files on the *Gibraltar*, which included some interesting, and to me unknown, correspondence from a very able art historian and collector in London, Dr. Gert-Rudolf Flick. Dr. Flick had first written to the Milwaukee Art Museum in 1998 requesting a photograph and any assistance they could give regarding the *Battle of Gibraltar* listed in the *Burlington Magazine* of May 1974 as attributed to Wright of Derby. He knew that Judy Egerton of the Tate Gallery believed it was not by Wright, but he hoped he could trace the painting to a sale in 1921. As a result of the documentation he received from Milwaukee, he became convinced that the painting was indeed by Wright of Derby. When I received the file on the painting and read these letters, I contacted Dr. Flick and learned that he was working on a book, *Missing Masterpieces, Lost Works of Art 1450–1900*, and had planned to include *The Battle of Gibraltar*, but would not now do so.

In the introduction to his fascinating book, published in 2002, Dr. Flick wrote,

> As I began to research the subject, it soon became clear that many works of art which were listed as missing had either been destroyed or were in fact extant. For example, a painting of *The Siege of Gibraltar* in the Milwaukee Art Museum (U.S.A.) was sold recently as by a "Follower of Joseph Wright of Derby," but has now been firmly identified as the original by Wright of Derby—the very painting that was always thought to be missing. In this case the difficulty in making the correct identification arose from the ruinous state of preservation of the painting, which made a comparison with preparatory drawings hazardous, although not impossible.

Why were these paintings deaccessioned without literature references? Was it the confluence of a director who was just not knowledgeable about the paintings, a hard-working curator,

Laurie Winters, who was not experienced in deaccessioning, and Christie's careless omissions?

The Milwaukee Art Museum and especially its curator Laurie Winters have enjoyed great successes in recent years, giving them reason for confidence. She has succeeded brilliantly in bringing a wonderful collection of art, including a Leonardo, from Poland. Moreover, the new Calatrava wing (a 2002 addition to the Milwaukee Art Museum designed by Spanish architect Santiago Calatrava) really put Milwaukee on the art world map.

When I asked her why she did not send literature references with the Berchem and the Wright of Derby to Christie's, she told me that such references might have undermined her research. This surprised me, because the inclusion in the catalog of provenance and literature references would surely have increased interest and the prices realized. Laurie had indeed studied the problem of the *Gibraltar*. She had received a letter from Judy Egerton, at the Tate Gallery in London, who had looked at the painting very carefully in 1986, and had written to the museum,

... I cannot believe that it is by Joseph Wright of Derby, even though Benedict Nicolson came to think so. There is a lumpishness about the figures, and a failure to extract maximum light and shade effects from the burning ships, that would never have suggested Wright's name to me, though I agree that now we have to find the missing Wright.

In her 1990 catalog for a Wright of Derby exhibition, she wrote that it "is now widely thought not to be by Wright." Other art historians concurred, some suggesting Loutherbourg as the artist. One of the guiding spirits of our museum is Dr. Myron (Ronnie) Laskin, who has great knowledge, particularly about Italian art, and possesses a wonderful visual memory. He told me that he did not believe Benedict Nicolson

147

could possibly have accepted the *Gibraltar* —but in fact he did, both verbally and in writing, and he was the editor of the *Burlington Magazine* when Biruta Erdmann's article was published in 1974. Nicolson's opinion is also included in "Wright of Derby: Addenda and Corrigenda," published post-humously in the *Burlington Magazine* in 1998. As I have said many times, it is possible to be convinced *and* mistaken. Yet even if Ben and I had been mistaken about the attribution of the *Gibraltar* to Wright of Derby, surely giving the literature references and Nicolson's opinion would have aroused more interest in this work. Surprisingly, Christie's did have the reference to the *Burlington Magazine* article, but Sarah Lidsey, the Vice President of Old Master Paintings, was so certain that the painting could not be by Wright of Derby that Christie's decided not to include this important reference.

It is certainly true that the painting was in very poor condition, but as soon as Queen's University's Agnes Etherington Art Centre received the canvas, the decision was made to search further for information. A provenance researcher in London, James Mulraine, found that *The Battle of Gibraltar*, last recorded as a Wright of Derby in the Overstone Park Collection catalog of 1877, was sold in a sale of *that* collection in 1921. However, at that time, the painting had no attribution and was sold nameless by the minor auction gallery Curtis & Henson, which simply described lot 982 as hanging in a hall corridor, "A large gallery painting, *Naval Battle Scene at Night*." The Ehrich Gallery in New York, which acquired it, labeled it "Copley" and offered it as such to Judge Sears in Elgin, Illinois, in 1923.

Recently Queen's sent the *Gibraltar* to a Canadian government laboratory in Ottawa for extensive tests, and then employed a conservator, Barbara Klempan, to continue the process of conserving the painting properly. This painstaking work is now completed. There can no longer be any doubt that this is Wright of Derby's *The Battle of Gibraltar* (Plate 53).

As Dr. David de Witt, the curator at Queen's, has written,

Even before the cleaning, this canvas reflected Joseph Wright of Derby's sense of atmosphere and monumentality, in the large proportion of the composition given over to the sky, filled with billowing clouds and dramatized with contrasts of light and color. But the cleaning went on to reveal daring, lively brushwork, with direct strokes and even his characteristic scratches with the butt end of the brush. Most importantly, however, was the revelation of several scenarios of firelight reflected off fabric, wood, figures, and faces, in the burning ship at the left edge, the exploding barges at the centre, and especially in the dynamic figures in the boats to the lower right. These remarkable passages showcase the particular achievement of which Wright of Derby was himself proud: the rendering of artificial light in night scenes.

The importance of this painting was stressed in a letter I received from Dr. John Bonehill at the University of Leicester in June 2005. He told me that he and Dr. Matthew Craske in Oxford were collaborating in a study of Wright's one-man exhibition of 1785 in which *The Battle of Gibraltar* was the centerpiece. Dr. Bonehill had learned from Christie's in New York that I had bought their view of *Gibraltar* by a "follower" of Wright of Derby, and he was interested in this copy. When I sent him our provenance he was very excited to learn that the "copy" is in fact the original, and he now looks forward to seeing the conserved painting.

There is no question that museums have received many gifts—and have even made purchases—that prove less than important (and sometimes embarrassing). These take up space, and money from their sale can certainly be put to good use, but any deaccession should be undertaken with great care. The director, curators, and board of trustees should work together—to share their knowledge, expertise, and their hunches. Members of an institution's brain trust may have decades of experience under their belts, but there is always something to be said for thorough consideration, attention to detail, and open-mindedness. Needless to say, every effort should be made to obtain the highest possible price for items sold. Finally, if donors are alive, I believe they should be contacted to discuss deaccession and to provide their own insights.

The Milwaukee Art Museum has a very fine collection, which today is housed in a spectacular new building. It has taken many daring steps to become one of the world's great art institutions. But along the way it has allowed some of its intriguing treasures to slip away. One of these now resides at Queen's University's Agnes Etherington Art Centre, to the delight of staff and visitors. And so, at least, we can reflect on yet another painting's long journey, and eventual happy ending.

# Stolen from Alfred Bader
# in Amsterdam on November 12, 1994

### Gonzales Coques (1614-84)
### *Portrait of a Man*
### Oil on panel, 10.2 cm. x 8.3 cm.
### Provenance: Sotheby's, London, July 6, 1994, Lot #186

Theft reported to the Amsterdam police and to IFAR (illustrated in IFAReports, 16, 4, No. 236).

Three paintings were stolen. Of these, the best (previously attributed to Rembrandt, *Bredius* 226) was discarded by the thieves and found that evening. The two others, a period portrait of Rembrandt's mother and the Coques *Portrait* were sent to the auction house De Eland in Amsterdam, were offered for sale in 1995, but returned as reserves were not reached. Shortly thereafter, the Amsterdam police recovered the paintings, checked neither their own police report nor IFAR, kept both paintings in their Lost and Found for three years and then sent them to auction (again to De Eland) where they were offered and sold on June 25, 1998, as lots 1420 and 1421.

*Rembrandt's Mother* was bought by an Utrecht collector, Dr. M.B.H. Schilder, who took it to the RKD where it was identified as one of the paintings stolen from Bader. Dutch law gives buyers at auction legal possession of their purchase if acquired three years after the theft. Hence, Bader negotiated a repurchase of *Rembrandt's Mother* from Dr. Schilder and would like to negotiate a similar repurchase with the buyer of the Coques.

**Please contact Dr. Alfred Bader, 924 E. Juneau Avenue, Suite 622, Milwaukee, WI 53202 USA. Phone (414) 277-0730. Fax: (414) 277-0709. E-mail: baderfa@execpc.com**

PLATE 43: The Historians of Netherlandish Art advertisement.

PLATE 44: The painting of Rembrandt's mother that was among the stolen items.

PLATE 45: Bert Vos with my painting.

PLATE 46: The Rembrandt School painting that Bert Vos found among my stolen papers.

**ABFA #2163** *SOLD*

**Artist:** Gabriel De Sabato

**Price Range:** *Less Than: $20000.00*

**Title:** *Moses*

**Dimensions:** 40 by 29 Inches

**Description:** Oil on canvas. Signed on the paper marking the book Gabriel de Sabato. We believed that this painting depicts Moses descending from Mount Sinai the second time, but why a book rather than tablets? We thought that we would never know, but then Karl Hammer in Breda, Holland sent us a beautifully intriguing explanation: "Moses is holding the Book of Deuteronomy, largely a record of speeches that Moses delivered to the people. While the other books of the Torah are a direct transmission of God's word (finger pointing upwards), Moses said Deuteronomy was "mipi atzmo" or "on his own" (explaining the gesture to himself)." We will be happy to send a copy of Mr. Hammer's essay to anyone interested.

Contact Us About This Painting

PLATE 47: The ABFA website showing Karl's explanation.

PLATE 48 (above): *A Chemist's Laboratory* at the
Museum of the History of Science, Oxford.

PLATE 49 (below): The artist's monogram—a clue to
the origin of the Oxford painting.

PLATE 50: My own painting of teacher and student
making Prussian blue.

PLATE 54: Werner Sumowski.

# 12

# The International Study Centre

Isabel and I have watched the development of the International Study Centre (ISC) at Herstmonceux Castle (Plate 55) with care and concern. Only now, years after the purchase contract was signed in August 1993, does it seem to be on a stable course.

Principal David Smith's choice of Jane Whistler as the first coordinator was most fortuitous. Jane was a friend of David's wife, Mary, with whom she had taken courses at Queen's in Kingston some years earlier. Jane had also lived near Herstmonceux for many years; she was just the right person for this new venture. As I wrote in my first *Adventures* (p.280):

> She already knew many people in the area and was familiar with the intricacies of obtaining planning permissions, which would have to be secured before Queen's could consider acquiring the property. Jane was so tireless in her negotiations with government bodies, heritage committees, and planning authorities, as well as the local people, that she made me think of a "Swiss army knife." She could tackle anything, yet is full of charm.

The ISC's first executive director, appointed in 1993, was British-born Dr. Maurice Yeates. Although the dean of graduate studies at Queen's, he was at the time on leave of absence at the Ontario Council of Graduate Studies in Toronto and was not able take up this new position until spring 1994. Once

151

he was appointed, however, Jane was no longer able to liaise directly with Kingston, and communications through Maurice were so slow that relations became strained to the point where Jane felt she could not make any progress, and she decided to leave at the end of the year. This was a real loss for the ISC, as the direct contact between Queen's and the local authorities and builders in England was broken. During the next few months, Maurice made several trips from Canada to learn about the project in order to keep things moving. Jane remained in place for a time to ease the transition, and Gillie Arnell, who had taken the position of secretary, held things together until the arrival in March of the newly appointed operations manager, Sandy Montgomery (Plate 56).

The original hope was to begin the first courses in the summer of 1994, and in an attempt to expedite work, Principal Smith decided in February to ask Don MacNamara, professor of international business at Queen's, whether he might be able to become the ISC's executive director. Don had to decline for a number of reasons, but did accept the position of associate director to run the Kingston-based ISC office and be responsible for curriculum development, staffing, and marketing. He assumed that role in May 1994 and worked tirelessly to promote the castle and its programs both in and outside Canada.

Maurice eventually took up residence at the ISC, and in September 1994, he welcomed the first group of fifty third-year students who moved in just as the builders began to move out. We were as thrilled as Principal Smith to know that at last our dream of having teachers and students at Herstmonceux was a reality. The castle had come alive, but there were a great many difficulties still to surmount. David Smith retired as principal in 1995 and Maurice resigned as director in April of that year, so the new venture had to be handed on to Bob Crawford, who came out to work with Sandy Montgomery, who luckily had remained to tackle whatever problems arose.

Bill Leggett, who succeeded David Smith as principal of Queen's, turned to Don MacNamara, whom he asked to step up as executive director to run the ISC from Kingston with an academic director who would be appointed for two years in England. As well as working with the academic directors to build the curriculum, Don was instrumental in proposing and designing the "field study" models for the academic European trips that every student takes. Don's enthusiasm in Kingston and Sandy's dedication at the castle were the two factors that held the ISC together in the first years. However, the division of executive management in Canada and limited two-year academic direction in England, a situation that continued until the end of 2003, never allowed the ISC to develop to its full potential. It was very difficult to take a long-term overall view for development when control was in Kingston and the directors in England changed so often. The one firm constant was Sandy. He was the backbone of the ISC and richly deserved the recognition he received in May 2004, the Queen's Distinguished Service Award (Plate 57), which tells this clearly.

Financial problems had existed through the 1990s, when the Canadian government grants to universities were cut drastically. The loss of millions of dollars in funding affected every aspect of the university's organization. When Queen's bought the castle in 1993, Isabel and I did not realize that quite a few Queen's academics would strongly object to the ISC. Tighter financial stringencies in Kingston simply increased their opposition. "Why spend money in England when it is needed so badly in Canada?" was their complaint. Some even referred to the castle as a "boondoggle," a "sinkhole," and when a program for first-year students was added to increase enrollment, detractors referred to it as "the International Summer Camp."

There were times when the Board of Trustees came close to giving up. A real-estate firm was consulted and reported that the market for castles in England was so poor that Queen's might receive only $10 million from a sale. The Board met to consider selling. It was Don MacNamara's appeal that persuaded the Board not to close the ISC. Don remembers our telephone conversation in which he related the decision and my reply: "Praise God. He has sent you to save the castle." Principal Leggett flew to Milwaukee to ask us for an additional $1 million, which we gave. Funding has remained a constant problem as costs and the number of students has fluctuated over the years. In 2002, we offered to pay all ISC deficits for a period of five years and are very pleased that the financial situation has improved so that further help should not be necessary.

The problem of the short-term appointments of directors had still to be addressed. The last two-year academic director (2001–2002), Patrick O"Neil, struggled valiantly to persuade Queen's to alter and strengthen the leadership by appointing an executive director in England for a term of five years. Dr. David Bevan (Plate 58), not already a Queen's academic but with wide international experience, accepted this appointment in January 2003. The ISC has benefited greatly from the new management structure. Straightforward and hardworking, David has worked splendidly with Sandy Montgomery, who is happy not to have to shoulder so much responsibility.

Efforts to encourage students from a variety of universities in different countries have had varied success. Even the number attending from Queen's and other Canadian universities has at times been disappointing. Reports of possible closure, anxiety caused by terrorist activity, and the difficulties some students experienced of fitting into the home university after the time abroad have all played a part in less-than-optimal enrollment. Fortunately, numbers have increased steadily nevertheless. The maximum of 180 students in a term was first reached in 2004. As a result, the 2003 deficit of CAN$914,000 declined to CAN$348,000 in 2004, to CAN$187,000 in 2005, and was fully eliminated in 2006.

Largely unaware of all this, the students have from the

beginning really enjoyed themselves and learned a great deal. For many of them, this is the first time they have been abroad. If they are first-year students, they and their parents have the assurance that they will be in a safe environment. They also benefit from the fact that, as Andrew Loman, who taught at the ISC for three years, has written in a history of the castle: "The small classes, the committed students, the field study program, and above all the opportunities for daily intellectual exchange with academics from different fields make the ISC overwhelmingly a pleasure." For many of these students, it is a life-changing experience.

British immigration policy makes it almost impossible to hire Canadians on any long-term contract. There is no problem with British and European staff who come from countries in the European Union, but Canadian academics must be hired on a limited-term work permit and thus are not on a tenure track.

In 1997, however, the ISC had the opportunity to welcome two brilliant Canadian musicians, Dr. Shelley Katz and Diana Gilchrist Katz (Plate 59), he an outstanding pianist, she a world-class singer. Had they "only" been musicians, they would have been classed as entertainers and would not have been given permanent residence. Luckily, Shelley is also a composer whose work was published in Germany, and so he was allowed permanent residence as an artist! Their activities with the students, local residents, and visiting professionals have truly enriched the cultural life of the whole community. The castle concerts they presented several times a year have always been highlights. In the years since the family has moved to Cambridge, Shelley and Diana have come down during the week to continue their work with the students, many of whom bring their instruments from home to play with some of the local musicians in a small orchestra or chamber group under Shelley's direction. The choirs get better and better, and everyone looks forward to the concert at the end of the semester.

One of the hopes we had from the very beginning was that the students would have an opportunity to get some flavor of English life. Their time is short, the courses are intense, and many weekends are taken up with field trips, to London, Stratford, and Brussels. We are very grateful that a number of the local residents have invited students to their homes to tea and meals, have taken them on favorite walks on the downs, and have given them a peek into life in rural England.

Many of these local people were among those who, in 1988, formed the "Friends of Herstmonceux Castle," hoping to prevent the estate's falling into the hands of developers. After they actively opposed a number of proposals, they were relieved to hear that a university, Queen's, was hoping to buy the property, and were particularly pleased to learn that Queen's was a Canadian university. A great many Canadian soldiers had been stationed in this part of Sussex during World War II. This seemed to be an acceptable new owner for "their" castle. From the earliest days and for the next ten years, the ISC was blessed to have one of these "friends", Mrs. Gillie Arnell, as the wonderfully capable secretary who worked first with Sandy Montgomery. She was truly helpful not only to students but also to each successive academic director.

It was Celia Scott, another of the committed Friends of Herstmonceux Castle, who proposed me for a CBE, Commander of the British Empire, an honor given by the British government. Many of our family traveled to Washington to be with us when the British ambassador presented me with the medal, which I was very proud to receive (Plate 50). It is a "thank you" for our efforts, not only to provide an international study center for students from many countries, but also to help the economy of the region of Sussex where Isabel lived and worked for thirty-two years. And we were especially glad to celebrate this honor again, some months later, with a large group at the ISC, where we enjoyed a reception in the courtyard followed by a short musical interlude provided by the Katz family. We have had so many happy times with these friends we have made in Sussex.

Isabel and I are always thinking of areas where we feel we can make a difference, and the ISC clearly offers many opportunities. The estate was the home of the Royal Greenwich Observatory from 1952, when the telescopes were built, until 1988, when operations were moved to Cambridge and La Palma, in the Canary Islands. Of the seven telescopes, only the largest, the Isaac Newton, was moved to La Palma; the other six remained in place, largely in working order. For many years after the Observatory closed, a group of scientists, including Patrick Moore, Richard Gregory, and Stephen Pizzey, hoped they might someday be able to set up a science centre on the site.

When it became clear that the ISC would not be likely to make use of the telescope complex, they asked for and were granted a short-term lease to set up temporary exhibits until they could make the building usable. Working tirelessly, with volunteer help, Stephen Pizzey built a very successful centre, and in 1995, the Observatory Science Centre signed a fifty-year lease with the ISC that enabled it to apply for and eventually win a heritage grant to make necessary improvements to the property. The centre has become a major venue for youngsters to be involved in hands-on physics, and thousands of them visit each year. Nor is it only for youngsters. There are evening courses for adults in astronomy and the exploration of space, and the ISC now offers a course in astronomy, with telescopes better than the one I knew in Kingston during my student days.

Set in woodland, apart from the main group of domes, the Isaac Newton Observatory building, visible for miles around, has remained vacant. This seemed a waste of a grand space. In 1999, Isabel and I funded a study by an architect and supported the formation of an Isaac Newton Arts Trust. The building had been condemned as unfit for use, but the

157

architect's report found the structure sound and estimated that it would cost £3 million to convert the building into an art center to include a concert hall, restaurant, and space for art exhibitions. We offered £1 million to the Arts Trust, headed by Stephen Phillips, who had considerable experience in the arts world. He hoped they would be able to raise an additional £2 million from Arts Councils and the National Lottery with which to make major alterations to the building. Various efforts so far have failed, but until they find additional funding, the plan is to try to convert the area *peu à peu* with help from the European Union.

Some progress has been made. A large amphitheatre-shaped area on one side of the building has been cleared of scrub and protected by the planting of hundreds of trees. A number of outdoor events have taken place in the castle grounds and in the amphitheatre. The Isaac Newton Arts Trust has recently signed a fifty-year lease with the ISC, and our hope is that some day both it and the Observatory Science Centre may combine and work together as an Arts and Science Centre.

At the end of July 2005, the ISC held a Tenth Reunion for ISC alumni. It was also the twelfth anniversary of the ceremony held in July 1993 when Principal David and Mary Smith, Chancellor Agnes Benidickson, Isabel, and I rode into the grounds of Herstmonceux Castle for the "Cutting of the Ribbon" ceremony. What an exciting gala day Jane Whistler had arranged for us and for the hundreds who came to visit the grounds, open to the public for the first time after so many years. On Thursday evening, July 28, 2005, the new Queen's principal, Dr. Karen Hitchcock, with a number of members of her family, was making her first visit to the ISC to welcome thirty-two ISC alumni who had returned from many parts of the world for this reunion. It was also a time for many Friends of Herstmonceux Castle to meet the new principal and the students who had returned.

We were a very happy group: new people to meet and so

158

much to learn about what had been happening since the students had graduated. But reunions would wait, at least until the buffet supper, after the concert specially arranged for me by the Musicians in Residence. "A Musical Tribute: Themes of a Life" was beautifully presented by Shelley and Diana Katz, joined by three guest musicians and their sons, David and Nathan Katz. I had a hard time holding back tears of grief at the *Ani Mamin*, in memoriam of the *Shoah*, and of joy at the end, "Once you have found her, never let her go." Whenever I have heard this, I have thought of Isabel, and here she was sitting right beside me with four members of her family who had come from Canada to be with us. My happiness could not have been greater!

On Friday, Isabel and the family, Jane Whistler, and Mary Smith went to Glyndebourne to see Smetana's *The Bartered Bride*, while I stayed at home in Bexhill to discuss the manuscript of a long history of the castle written by Andrew Loman. Andrew had come over for the reunion and on Saturday afternoon was to give a lecture about the history of the castle, which would be followed by my talk: "Why I Love Queen's." Diana and Shelley had prepared a CD, "Love Live Forever," that had been planned as an accompaniment to Andrew's book. In the meantime, everyone who came to the reunion received a copy of the CD, which we can now play if we need a reminder of the castle.

During our discussion, Andrew mentioned another reason, apart from the legal problems Canadians have in receiving permission to work in England, why coming to teach at the ISC is difficult. There are just two cottages and two very recent small apartments, very little accommodation for families, and since most of the staff come from afar and for a relatively short period, it has been necessary to house them in a section of Bader Hall, where the students live. This is a situation that has long needed attention. When we discussed this with Sandy Montgomery, he suggested that it would be possible to rebuild on foundations of existing buildings and to alter part of Bader Hall to make more adequate provision for academics. This seems to us a very important step to take, and we have given Queen's the funds. Since we would not have given the castle to Queen's without the vision and our wonderful rapport with Principal David Smith, we suggested that we call this residence, completed in 2007, the David Smith Hall.

## 13

# A Canadian in Love

One of our gifts that made Isabel and me so happy, without any of the problems that often accompany major gifts, was the Isabel Bader Theatre at Victoria University in Toronto.

The idea of building arose because of Isabel's Canadian/ English connections. During her years in England, Isabel had seen many fine plays performed at the Old Vic, one of the oldest theatres in London and famous throughout the English-speaking world. All theatre lovers were very sad when it fell on hard times in the early 1990s. The appearance of the well-known Mirvish family of Toronto as the saviors of the theatre was a matter of great pride to Isabel. Despite major investment in renovations and reorganization, however, and with difficulties in their theatres in Toronto as well, they decided to concentrate their efforts in Canada. Early in 1999, we learned that they wanted to sell the Old Vic. I immediately called Principal Leggett at Queen's to inquire whether Queen's might like the theatre, and his answer was "No thanks, we have enough problems with Herstmonceux Castle!"

My next call was to Roseann Runte (Plate 61), the president of Victoria University in Toronto. As intelligent as she is gracious, Roseann had become our good friend, and so we asked her whether Vic might be interested in owning the Old Vic. Her reply was encouraging: "No, we don't want the Old Vic, but if you are interested in a theatre for us, why not build a new Vic? For close to a hundred years we have had the land right

161

here on Charles Street. It is just being used as a tennis court, because we have never had the money. Even though Victoria has the oldest dramatic review in North America, an annual comedy show called 'The Bob' and many graduates have become distinguished directors and actors, we have never had a theatre." This idea had a definite appeal. And how much would it cost? I have never had an answer from Roseann that wasn't clear and simple: CAN$6 million.

We had previously been involved in only one major building project, the expansion of the Agnes Etherington Art Centre at Queen's University. This had necessitated an architectural competition, at considerable cost, and a great deal of bureaucratic hassle and disappointment. There were no such complications at Vic. Roseann wanted a Toronto architect, Peter Smith, who had designed many other theatres. Smith described the project as "an 'intimate' two-level theatre; it will have basic staging and audio-visual equipment in the first year, with room to grow." The faculty wanted another floor for lecture rooms, and so the university raised an additional CAN$2 million. There were no cost overruns.

On June 4, 1999 Isabel, Roseann, and I turned the first sod for the theatre during Isabel's fiftieth reunion. There were some delays completing the building because of strikes of workers supplying concrete, but finally, on March 3, 2001, there was a wonderfully happy celebration for the opening with our families sharing our joy. Roseann said about this largest gift that Victoria University had ever received, "When Alfred gave us the money for the theatre, it was because he wanted to make a gift to Isabel. It's a kind of a double generosity, and a true love story." If only other major gifts led so simply to truly happy endings.

While getting to know, like, and admire Roseann, it occurred to me that she might be just the right person to edit and publish the eighty-two letters Isabel had written to me between July 21, 1949 and August 11, 1951. I had kept all of her letters, and on each November 1, her birthday, had read some of them. Isabel now often faults me for looking back too much, but how could I not, having met a woman of such inner and outer beauty. It took considerable persuasion to get Isabel's reluctant agreement to let us go ahead. But Roseann did a fine job as editor of *A Canadian in Love*, published in 2000 as a limited edition of 1,000 copies by the University of Toronto Press. The eighty-two letters appear unchanged, as do two of Isabel's mother's letters, written in 1951. The book ends with Isabel's brief letter, no. 83, written in March 1975, and my long reply written after our meeting in April.

Roseann's Introduction, describing our lives and love, is a gem. Some evenings when I am too weary to sleep, I read some of the Introduction with a few of Isabel's letters and then fall asleep happily. Isabel thought that she had destroyed all my letters to her—they were too painful to look at. But after *A Canadian in Love* appeared, she did find a few that we then showed to Roseann, who commented that they contained no surprises. Of course, we have also kept the hundreds of letters we wrote to each other before our marriage in 1982.

As a wonderful postscript, Roseann sent Isabel:

### Words of Love, for Isabel

*some would maintain that chance runs rife*
*that a force beyond set the date*
*when twice we met, tourists in life*
*in love, a twist of fate*

*yet if only I could utter*
*the words I know you wish to hear*
*if only I could defer*
*if only you were here*

*words rise in my heart, flow steadfast*
*course down my veins, oh, my prince of men*
*only to be betrayed at last*
*by this, my very pen*

*I carried your sad smile with me*
*in my mind's eye for many years*
*not to be forgotten you see*
*or dulled by time and tears*

*in my solitude by the sea*
*of you I think and often pray*
*can you feel my sighs for thee*
*mingling in the salt spray?*

*silence dwells in my heart you know*
*where once I heard the chords of love*
*trembling in the air so sweet and low*
*whisp'ring on the wings of doves*

*it is said, hearts that meet at sea*
*must wait out storms, sail mists and more*
*yet true soul mates will finally*
*return to home's harbour*

*pride stayed my voice, and yet you knew*
*of my love, though I spoke it not*
*my hand you won with a small blue*
*true blue forget-me-not*

*and now where once sadness did reign*
*at last two hands in one enfold*
*at last, dear heart, I can speak plain*
*my love, I do behold*

*thoughts borne upon the wind*
*barely uttered may yet be heard*
*true love in truth need not be penned*
*nor speak a single word.*

*A Canadian in Love* led to a delightful film of the same name, produced by Golden Reed Productions. Sue Read and Jim Golding had made two films we admired. One was *The Children Who Cheated the Nazis*, about the almost ten thousand children who came on the *Kindertransporte* to England in 1938–9. I had left for England on the first of these from Vienna in 1938. The second film, titled *Rescued—A 60-Year Journey*, described the lives of a few children who were hidden from the Nazis—often under dreadful conditions. Among these was the Nobel Laureate in chemistry Roald Hoffmann, who asked the haunting question, "How many more contributions to world chemistry would there have been had not 95 percent of the Jewish children in Poland died in the Holocaust?"

The film *A Canadian in Love* depicts our lives, from our meeting in July 1949. It was first publicly shown at the Jewish Film Festival in Toronto in May 2007.

In 2005, we learned that the Music Department at Queen's hoped to build a recital hall and wondered whether we might help. But Queen's had no real campus theatre either. The beauty and simplicity of building the Isabel Bader Theatre in Toronto made us wonder whether we might not fund a Performing Arts Centre at Queen's. This could offer greater facilities for the arts. Building at Toronto had been simple because Victoria University had the land in the middle of the campus, and Roseann chose just the right architect. This was not the case at Queen's. There was very little land available on its campus. Karen Hitchcock (Plate 62), who became principal of Queen's in 2004, agreed that a center to house music and drama would be great. The City of Kingston owned a beautiful 3.3-acre parcel near the campus and right on Lake Ontario, which Queen's was able to acquire for CAN$1.7 million, the first part of our gift. Now we hope that we will be able to attend a celebration of the opening, as we did in Toronto in March 2001.

If universities knew who is really responsible for our actions as a couple, Isabel, rather than I, would have received more of the honorary doctorates. She has received two, one from Emmanuel College of the University of Toronto in 1995, Doctor of Sacred Letters, the highest distinction a lay person can receive from the college, and one from Queen's University, an Honorary Doctor of Law degree (Plate 63) in June 2007.

We have taken part in so many really enjoyable events. The latest of these was the celebration for Isabel on her eightieth birthday on November 1, 2006 at Herstmonceux. Orchestrated by David Bevan, Sandy Montgomery, and Diana and Shelley Katz, the festivities were spread over two days. Afternoon tea with a few close friends gave us all time to catch up on the latest news at the ISC. Then we met Principal Karen Hitchcock and various friends who had just come over from Kingston to be present at the wonderful concert in the evening. Specially arranged by Diana and Shelley, it began with my favorite "Some Enchanted Evening" from *South Pacific*, arranged by Shelley for Diana and tenor Andrew Forbes-Lane. Andrew then sang his own version of "'Twas on a Monday Morning for Isabel" with apologies to Flanders and Swann. Recognizing Isabel's interest in the theatre, he sang Noel Coward's "Mrs Worthington" with great feeling, and followed that with two much more romantic Coward favorites.

Most remarkable to us were three moving Hebrew pieces sung by the sixteen members of the ISC Women's Chamber Choir, who had had just a few weeks to learn the texts perfectly. The concert ended with "Libiamo" from *La Traviata* presented by all three musicians and the full ISC choir of sixty-five students, the largest choir ever at the castle. The music was so touching, but so was the students' enthusiasm to honor Isabel.

After a light meal and many congratulations, we fell into bed at 11 p.m., happy and dead tired, sent off to sleep by a final goodnight birthday call from our family back in the US. What a gala eightieth birthday party!

Fortunately, the birthday dinner was scheduled for Thursday evening, a dinner for twenty-four, carefully prepared by Sandy Montgomery. After drinks in the Elizabethan Room, we went upstairs to a five-course dinner that included some of our favorites: lamb, apple tart, and custard. The seating for the three tables of eight had been chosen very thoughtfully—to Isabel's left, the principal talking about the future; to my right, Jane Whistler, who had been so instrumental at the beginning of the ISC, talking to me about the past. Isabel was given some lovely gifts, and there were brief speeches, including one by me, referring to another Thursday, November 2, the one in 1941 when I was released from the camp on the Ile aux Noix and two weeks later was on the way to Queen's.

Before we cut the birthday cake, we had a good laugh at a funny cartoon from the *New Yorker* with which it was decorated. It showed one young girl saying to another, "I never thought turning eighty would be so much fun." Nor did Isabel and I. The evening ended with Diana Katz singing some Lieder and ending with "Summertime" from *Porgy and Bess*, one of Isabel's favorites, because it reminds her of another wonderful soprano who sang it at the first concert she went to in Toronto in 1945.

How wonderful to have shared Isabel's eightieth birthday with truly good friends.

# 14

# My Eightieth Birthday

## Home

The date April 28, 2004 was a special day, my eightieth birthday, and as busy as could be. I knew that my son David would be coming in from Pennsylvania and Charles Munch from his home near Madison, so I wanted to get as much work done as possible before they arrived.

Despite many phone calls and e-mails that required my attention, I couldn't help thinking of April 28 in years past. I have often wondered what my parents' lives were like before I was born. Were they overjoyed at the prospect of a second child? Was my father concerned at this addition to his family? He was not a reliable provider, addicted to gambling; was he aware that his financial position was very precarious? Did Mama, my biological mother, have any inkling of this? Were they delighted to have a son? Within two weeks, my father was dead, the cause of death unclear, suicide or murder. I shall always wonder about this.

On what was to be my last birthday in Vienna, in 1938, Muttili, my mother by adoption, gave me a slip of paper, a promissory note for a trip up the Danube. I knew at the time that the intent was good, but it would be impossible because we had no money, and life was so precarious because the Nazis had marched in the month before. I couldn't know that within seven months, I would be leaving Vienna on the first *Kindertransport*.

By my sixteenth birthday, a Sunday in 1940, the war had begun. No one in Hove, England, where I was living remembered that it was my birthday. It was a sad day, but on Monday, a letter came from Muttili wishing me a very happy birthday, always concerned for me, always worrying about my health. I was so pleased to have her letter. Within days, Holland and Belgium fell, Britain expected an invasion; within two weeks, I was arrested as an enemy alien, interned, then shipped to Canada as a prisoner of war. My next birthday was spent in the internment camp on an island in Quebec, Canada. How long would I be kept there? That was the question we all asked ourselves, but at least we were safe from the Nazis, and by April 1941, conditions were very much easier than on our arrival.

Certainly my seventeenth birthday was a happier day than the lonely Sunday in England. I kept a diary in German of our lives in the prisoner-of-war camp and made the following notation for April 28:

28.4.41. Seventeen. When I compare my last birthday with this and consider what happened in this last year, I ask myself "was the last year a lost year or not?" Materially, certainly, mentally, certainly not. In free life I could never have had these experiences, and what is much more important, is not a true friend, a friend you can really trust, worth much more than material gain? And now, should I pass the matriculation exam in June, I will certainly not look back to my sixteenth year as a wasted year.

It is customary on one's birthday to make resolutions, and some years I set goals which seemed hopeless from the start; this time, however, I know that I will reach my goal: I will try to bring myself mentally, morally, and physically to the level of Pong [my best friend in camp].

My birthday passed well. The weather was and still is beautiful, and many of my friends have given me small presents. Bobby, Max, Arno, Heinz, Walter, and Bruno [the Canadian sergeant] were among the first—my box is full of oranges, apples, coconuts, chocolates, and cookies! Rudi gave me an Agatha Christie, chocolates, and cookies. My greatest pleasure came from Muttili's and Pong's letters received yesterday and Pong's book. The day is coming to an end, may my seventeenth year see the world at peace, and me in freedom, united with Muttili and Pong.

Heinrich (Pong) Wohlaŭer, my best friend in camp who had returned to England, had written in English: " ... and I shall think of the lone island in a river in Canada, where my friends are, and just are celebrating the birthday of one of them, the one whom I liked most of them. Alfred, become a good and honest man! There are so few about now and the world is in need of them!"

My hopes for freedom came true six months and four days later, so that on my eighteenth birthday, I was a free man, although I had to report each week to the Royal Canadian Mounted Police. I had been taken into the heart of the wonderful family of Martin Wolff in Montreal, and I was enrolled in Queen's University, where I had been welcomed and helped in every way. I was working hard and knew that my life lay before me.

So for the next many years, birthdays are a blur until my seventieth and seventy-fifth, when we had wonderfully happy celebrations with family and friends, some of the best of whom are no longer with us. Marvin Klitsner has died since, as has Bill Schield, the best stockbroker I have ever known. He and his wife died in a tragic car accident while vacationing in Spain.

I am blessed to have reached my eightieth birthday and to have so many friends who have sent greetings from around the world. Among the most memorable was an e-mail from Yechiel Bar-Chaim, which read in part:

Your generosity has changed the way I work and liberated certain instincts from within that perhaps were there before well hidden and perhaps not. I can say that as a result in communities like Belgrade, Zagreb, and Sarajevo there are now Jewish activists involved in helping others—inside and outside the community—in ways we wouldn't have imagined just a few short years ago.

At least as important to me, however, have been the new friends and contacts to whom you have introduced me in London, Prague, and Brno. Looking forward to our dinners in Prague scheduled in June with some of the best of them.

When I got home from the gallery, there was a beautiful orchid from Margarete, the wife of David Harvey, then CEO of Sigma-Aldrich, and a card that read:

Dear Alfred,
Congratulations on this very special day! I wish you—and Isabel of course—good health and many happy returns of the day.

While I am thinking of all your achievements, I want to thank you for having brought our entire family over the Atlantic to Milwaukee. You may have mixed feelings on that subject, but I for one am very grateful for it.

So thank you again and many successful years of hunting, finding, and selling (and uniting) those extraordinary works of art that we all love.

Fondly, Margarete (and David)

As I walked into the living room, I saw that my good friend Otto Naumann had filled our house with eighty tulips in eight vases, an unforgettable sight! Charles Munch brought me a beautiful sketch painted by his partner, Jane, a sketch that will join the two that Charles and Jane gave me for my seventieth and seventy-fifth birthdays. David and Daniel gave us a beautiful flat-view television set for our living room, which will allow us to see all sorts of programs much more clearly. Ann

Zuehlke, my very helpful gallery manager, gave me a back massager to ease the occasional discomfort I get in my lower back and a large jar full of cookies to add to my weight.

Isabel and I had intended to have a quiet evening at home, but David would not hear of it, so he and Daniel had invited us instead for a quiet dinner in a secluded room at the University Club with Linda and her parents, our dear friend Lucy Cohn, Charles Munch, Ann Zuehlke, and Michael Hatcher, our bookseller friend. It was so good to be with family and friends. By the time we came home shortly before ten o'clock, I was dead tired, happy with my first day as an octogenarian.

The celebrations have continued.

On Monday evening, May 3, there was another birthday dinner at the home of friends Joe and Audrey Bernstein at which Rabbi Israel Shmotkin and his family presented me with an extraordinary map portraying my journeys in life. The Bernsteins and Rabbi Mendel Shmotkin, a charismatic Lubavitch rabbi, have become our close friends in recent years, and Joe and I have been working together both charitably and in business. This was a very different and very special party.

## Queen's

May 12 and May 13, 2004 were among the most memorable days of my life. Principal Leggett, the Art Centre, and the Art History and Chemistry Departments at Queen's had invited Isabel, Daniel, and me to a gala celebration, continuing my eightieth-birthday festivities. Those who know me will understand why.

Sixty-four years earlier, on May 12, 1940, I had been picked up at the religious school of Middle Street Synagogue in Brighton to be interned for the next sixteen months. At the time, I did not realize that my months as a prisoner of war would give me a wonderful education and lead to my being admitted to

Queen's University on November 15, 1941. My connection to Queen's has been close ever since, particularly for the last thirty years.

So it was that on this May 12 Isabel, Charles Munch, and I joined Daniel to fly to Kingston. We were bringing the very fine Michael Sweerts *Self-Portrait* as my annual gift of a painting to Queen's.

Although Charles and his partner Jane Furchgott have conserved the majority of the old master paintings we have given to the Agnes Etherington Art Centre, Charles had never been to Queen's before, but he had not been to Ottawa either, so he drove to the National Gallery there. Isabel went to Summerhill, where we were staying, to unpack, and I spent an hour with David de Witt, the Bader Curator at the Agnes, discussing various paintings.

At noon, we went to the first of the events prepared for the next two days, a luncheon at the new chemistry building where Victor Snieckus, the Bader Chair for Organic Chemistry, presented me with a truly moving compilation of greetings from more than fifty chemist friends around the world. Many of these—in Canada, in the United States, in Britain, France, and Switzerland—I had not heard from in years, and these greetings brought back such happy memories of our visits to them in their laboratories.

Then, between 1:30 and 5:00, there was a chemistry symposium with two lectures, followed by a reception. The first lecture, by our old friend the Nobel Laureate Barry Sharpless, was a lighthearted review of his travels and of his great chemical discoveries. The second, by one of my best chemist friends, Professor Gilbert Stork of Columbia University, dealt with his efforts over the years to look at various synthetic routes to morphine.

We were surprised but delighted to see Eva Kushner, the former president of Victoria University, who had come in from Toronto to bring us greetings from President Paul Gooch of

174

Victoria University. She and Isabel went to the Bader Gallery in the Art Centre and then on to Summerhill to catch up on news, since Eva would be in Europe in June when we planned to be in Toronto for Isabel's fifty-fifth reunion.

After the reception, I went off to our room at Summerhill for a few minutes' rest while Isabel visited the costume store and the conservation department, where Sheilah Mackinnon is working on some of the museum's costume collection. Before long, she was back and waking me to say that some friends were waiting to talk to me before the principal's dinner. To my amazement, there stood Volker Manuth, the previous Bader Chair in Northern Baroque Art, now in Nijmegen, Holland, and two of his former students; Axel Rüger, the curator of the National Gallery in London; David de Witt; and my two sons, to present me with a *Festschrift* titled *Collected Opinions: Essays on Netherlandish Art In Honour of Alfred Bader* (Plate 64). Isabel, David, and Daniel had written the Forewords. I could hardly walk downstairs for the dinner because I was laughing so hard at what they had written about me. "As soon as we could speak intelligently—maybe by age five—our conversations with our father went something like this:

"You want to eat lunch? What for? We have to go look at that painting auction preview."

"Don't take a taxi—take the Tube."

At the moment of presentation, I was too weary to realize fully what a wonderful gift this was. Twenty-one art historians had written important art historical essays, some dealing with paintings in my collection. One historian, Astrid Tümpel, had written two delightfully thought-provoking short stories. Charles Munch had drawn a sketch of me looking at a Rembrandt. The editors, Volker Manuth and Axel Rüger, must have worked incredibly hard to put this together. And four of the writers, Bill Robinson, Arthur Wheelock, David de Witt, and Martha Wolff, had visited us recently without any hint. What a conspiracy! It took me many hours, some while I could not sleep, really to understand what I had been given.

Downstairs there was a fine buffet hosted by Principal and Mrs William Leggett who had invited Rosetta Elkin, Martin Wolff's daughter from Montreal (who had just turned ninety), and some of the many good friends we had made during our years at Queen's. The high point was the presentation of a plaque inscribed as follows:

## BADER LANE

In Victoria's reign she was *Alice Street*, a gently curving passage through residential estates at Kingston's rough-hewn edge. While John Macdonald crafted a country and the town grew, more homes populated Alice's pastoral greens. So would the limestone halls of Queen's University, born years earlier by Royal Charter. Alice, appropriately, assumed the name of her academic neighbour. In time Queen's Crescent would accommodate Gray House, built at the dawn of the new century by a philosophy professor's nephew, and Ban Righ, cornerstone of a future women's residence, erected in 1923.

Seventeen years hence, propelled over an ocean by the winds of a European war, a young *Alfred Bader* found landfall and open arms at Queen's. Mentors and friends there offered a grounding in chemistry, history, and humanity; the student, in turn, excelled. And so it began: a globally renowned career in chemistry, a passion for fine art, and a borderless philanthropic quest to advance chemical knowledge and the preservation of beauty on canvas.

Life is a busy and unpredictable thoroughfare. Mind, toil, and molecules spawn a fortune; art, and Isabel, inspire it. Queen's welcomes a youth; the adult enriches Queen's with old masters and its students with generations of opportunity.

And today, as *Alfred Bader* enters his 80th year, Queen's

honors its most generous benefactor by declaring that of May 8, 2004, Queen's Crescent, the street born as *Alice* shall now be known as **Bader Lane**.

The new Bader Lane (Plate 69) is a street bounded on the south by Ban Righ Hall where, in my student days, girls were carefully protected from men, and on the north by the Agnes Etherington Art Centre.

What a gift!

May 12, 1940 had been one of the unhappiest days of my life. May 12, 2004 was one of the happiest, but there was still more to come.

The next day, the Art Department and the Agnes Etherington Art Centre held a joint celebration. David de Witt, Sebastian Schütze (the Bader Southern Baroque Chair), and Volker Manuth discussed three paintings, two Dutch and one Italian, in the Bader Gallery. At noon, we enjoyed a delicious luncheon hosted by Professor Gary Wagner in Ban Righ Hall with many of the students who had received our scholarships.

My talk at 3:00 about the history of Aldrich and Sigma-Aldrich was well attended and was followed by a public reception from 4:30 to 6:00, complete with another birthday cake and champagne.

Dinner in the evening was hosted by Mrs Merle Koven, a member of the Queen's Board of Trustees and very active in the Kingston Jewish community. It was attended by Harvey Rosen, the Mayor of Kingston, and his wife, and many others who have worked hard to establish the program of Jewish studies at Queen's. A long day of happy celebrations.

The next morning, we met with Bob Silverman, dean of arts & sciences, David Wardle of chemistry, and John Osborne of art history to discuss all sorts of financial matters relating to our gifts to their departments. One discussion centered on the endowment for the two chairs, one in Northern and the other in Southern baroque art; the second was about the Bader

Chair in organic chemistry; the third dealt with the declining deficit of the International Study Centre at Herstmonceux Castle, which we had agreed to cover for five years.

The last item of discussion was the question of whether we might be the lead donors to build a music and drama centre to be named after Isabel. Of course we agreed.

After a brief visit to Rabbi Daniel Elkin, Rosetta's son, we drove to the airport. Unfortunately, the plane developed mechanical problems, the replacement was caught in a thunderstorm, and two other replacements also could not make it until 11 p.m., but fortunately we had no urgent plans back in Milwaukee, so we spent a leisurely afternoon and evening and caught a plane home the next morning.

These full and truly wonderful days, far more moving than we could have imagined, are now memories to be relived and savored at leisure.

Until Monday, March 22, I had not thought much about my birthday. Why should an eightieth birthday be so different from my seventy-ninth or eighty-first? But clearly it was, for on that Monday, Yechiel Bar-Chaim arranged for a fine birthday luncheon in London. We had a quiet family birthday party in Milwaukee on April 28 and another at the home of Attorney Joseph and Audrey Bernstein on May 3. Then followed the two-day celebration in Kingston and more parties in Brno and Prague in June. Again I can say with King David in the 23rd Psalm: "My cup runneth over."

## Brno

Our first birthday event in Europe took place in the Czech Republic. Jiri Damborsky (Plate 65), the Loschmidt professor of chemistry at the Masaryk University in Brno, and Professor Skursky, one of our first contacts there, worked immensely hard to arrange a three-day celebration. Festivities began on

June 14 with a sumptuous lunch at Masaryk University, attended by the university's rector, vice-rectors, dean, several professors, and the governor of Moravia who, after a welcoming speech in Czech, gave me a beautiful book on Moravia. My Czech, however, is nonexistent, and so I had to thank him in English. I enjoyed being able to tell him that my mother's great uncle, Otto Count Serenyi, had also been the governor, *Landeshauptmann*, of Moravia from 1910 until 1917.

Lunch was followed by a symposium in the Museum of Applied Arts. After my lecture on Josef Loschmidt, six Bader Award holders gave presentations of the work they are doing in the Czech Republic. It was a great pleasure to meet these young chemists, many of them for the first time. The break for a cup of tea was very welcome, too much to eat, but a good opportunity to talk to some of the many chemists and friends who had come for this event. When we returned to the hall, we were treated to a video conference with three Bader Fellows and Professor Henry Pinkham, dean of science at Columbia University. This was the first such hookup I had ever seen at a university; it went seamlessly and was a great success with us all.

I was able to speak directly to these three students and remind them that we had not established fellowships for Czech students in order to lure them to the West but in the hope that they would return to the Czech Republic. This exciting episode was followed by brief talks by three other Bader Fellows. Miloslav Nic received his PhD in London and returned to take a position at the Technical University in Prague. Kamil Paruch, working at Schering-Plough, also plans to return, perhaps to the Masaryk University, and Zora Wörgötter, who received a Bader fellowship in art history, became a curator at the Moravian Gallery in Brno. We seldom have a chance to spend time with the young people we try to help, so this was a very welcome opportunity.

We then moved to the International Hotel, where the rector

gave me a most surprising gift, the Imperial Order of the Iron Crown, III Class, the very award that had been given to Josef Loschmidt in Vienna at the time of his retirement. During an elaborate reception afterwards, I had time to talk to many more chemists and also to my distant cousin, Vera Bader Weber, and her husband Peter, who had come from Kyjov, my grandfather's home town. Although we felt we couldn't, and certainly shouldn't, eat a bite, the caterers had outdone themselves. We couldn't resist.

What a day it was! Jiri had worked so hard to make it a success, and he did want us to meet his family. We were glad to spend a couple of hours quietly that evening at home with him, his wife Martina, and their young son David. Martina had prepared a simple soup that reminded me of Isabel's soups at home. It was so good to end the day just chatting quietly with Jiri and his family.

We waited a long time for the Masaryk University to find a suitable chemist for the Loschmidt Chair, but I am so pleased with their appointment of Jiri Damborsky. He is a brilliant, hard-working biochemist and such a fine human being. He has worked very hard to learn as much about Loschmidt as he can, studying material he collected when he spent three days with us in Milwaukee. Much of this he has loaded onto a website (www.loschmidt.cz), which will help make Loschmidt known not only in the Czech Republic but throughout the world.

After an interview with Czech television the next morning, we set out for Prague by way of Nelazehoves Castle, where Prince William Lobkowicz was interested in discussing our suggestion that we fund a very able Czech art historian, Dr. Vladan Antonovic, to work with some important prints in the Lobkowicz collection. Vladan received two Bader fellowships and his PhD from Innsbruck, but despite excellent work, he has found it very difficult to obtain a suitable position in the Czech Republic.

In Prague that evening, Yechiel Bar-Chaim had arranged another birthday celebration with a very interesting group who do all the groundwork for us in our efforts to help Roma and others in need. Then, finally, on our last evening, there was yet another dinner, this time with art historians. For more than ten years, Professor Milena Bartlova has worked diligently to choose Bader fellows to study art outside the Czech Republic, many of whom have done very well. We are well satisfied with this project. It shows us that some of our efforts have been very fruitful indeed, and we really appreciate all the effort that so many good friends made to give us these wonderful three days in the land of my ancestors.

## ACS

The rest of my eightieth year settled down until mid-March 2005, when celebrations took off again for a last big bang, this time in San Diego. Over two astounding days, chemistry students, chemist co-workers, and academic friends took the opportunity at the American Chemical Society (ACS) convention to remind me of some of the happiest times of my life. A symposium titled Current Aspects in Synthetic Organic Chemistry had been organized in my honor by two of the Nobel Laureate Herbert Brown's former students, P.V. (Chandran) Ramachandran, professor at Purdue, and Clint Lane, who had come from Purdue in 1972 to head the new Aldrich Boranes, retiring as the president of Aldrich in 2002.

Clint and Chandran represented my long years of close collaboration with Herb on borane chemistry. We had looked forward to sharing time with Herb and his wife Sarah, for whom the symposium had been specially arranged for Sunday afternoon and Monday morning so that they would not find it too tiring. How sad we were when we learned a few weeks earlier that Herb had died. His contributions to chemistry

181

have been enormous—a whole new field, hydroboration. The hundreds of young students attending the symposium lost the opportunity of seeing this outstanding Nobel Laureate, at ninety-two, still intensely interested in scientific research and students.

I was delighted to see that the symposium was sponsored by major chemical and pharmaceutical companies (Plate 67) including, to my surprise, Sigma-Aldrich. Eight brilliant chemists, longtime friends, gave riveting lectures, often referring briefly to connections Isabel and I had with them over the years. From the first, Ronald Breslow's lecture on biomimetic control in synthesis, to the last, Samuel Danishefsky's discussion of potential new cancer drugs, the audience—at times exceeding a thousand—was listening to the research of truly great chemists. There was sometimes laughter, for instance when Barry Sharpless showed a picture of Isabel and me as an example of "click" chemistry at work (Plate 66) and Victor Snieckus showed a delightfully doctored photo (Plate 68) of a painting in which he had substituted me for Brande teaching Michael Faraday how to make Prussian blue.

On Sunday evening, Isabel and I had the great pleasure of attending a Project SEED (Summer Educational Experience for the Disadvantaged; see Chapter 18 for more on SEED) dinner chaired by James Burke, Chair of the American Chemical Society Board of Directors, and Madelaine Jacobs, CEO of the American Chemical Society. We have long taken part in this outstanding ACS project to help young students pursue "college education in chemistry." A group of bright, happy, enthusiastic Bader scholars discussed the impact of the scholarships on their lives and presented us with a beautiful album with twelve moving letters describing their work. It was heartening to see how they have used chemistry as a stepping-stone to careers not only in chemistry but in dentistry, medicine, pharmacy, biology, and pharmaceutical companies.

The following evening, Stephen Quigley and I received the

PLATE 55: Herstmonceux Castle.

PLATE 56 (left): Sandy Montgomery.

PLATE 57 (below): Sandy's Distinguished Service Award.

Awarded to

# *Alexander Montgomery*

**by Queen's University Council**
**for Distinguished Service to Queen's**

*May 7, 2004*

WILLIAM C. LEGGETT, PRINCIPAL AND VICE-CHANCELLOR

A. CHARLES BAILLIE, CHANCELLOR

Queen's University Council, in its 129th year, presents a distinguished service award to

*Alexander (Sandy) Montgomery*

From Kingston to England and beyond, your amazing administrative feats built the International Study Centre into a magical place, thus extending the University's international reputation. We recognize you today as the cornerstone of the Castle since its inception as the ISC.

Your outstanding character, faithful commitment to the ISC vision, is illuminated by a well-known, uniquely idiosyncratic humour. No less than seven Academic Directors benefited from your association, and have relied on your ingenuous and mischievous ability to make them smile even on the really tough days.

Others celebrate your loyal support of Queen's, to seeing the ISC experience through, as one who worked on the budgets, reworked those budgets and reworked them again. All the while, you have been a constant source of energy, raising spirits, encouraging those at the Centre at times when it stumbled or soared.

We see today the ISC as a product of your loving care as artist and administrator, an achievement of your belief that it could be this strangest of all things: a Canadian study centre in rural UK that was at once a Castle, a true home for students and viable venture.

In grateful appreciation for your service, your selfless dedication and outstanding accomplishments, Queen's is proud and honoured to bestow upon you an award for distinguished service.

PLATE 58 (top): David Bevan.

PLATE 59 (center): Shelley and Diana Katz.

PLATE 60 (below): Receiving my CBE.

Plate 61 (top left): President Roseann Runte.

Plate 62 (top right): Principal Karen Hitchcock.

Plate 63 (above): Isabel receives her doctorate.

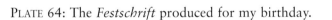

COLLECTED OPINIONS
Essays on Netherlandish Art

In Honour of Alfred Bader

PLATE 64: The *Festschrift* produced for my birthday.

PLATE 65 (top right): Jiri Damborsky.

PLATE 66 (below right): 'Click' chemistry.

PLATE 67 (below): The sponsors of the chemistry symposium, San Diego.

1951–2001: FIFTY YEARS OF CHEMISTS HELPING CHEMISTS

# Aldrichimica ACTA

VOL 34, NO. 2 · 2001

PLATE 68: Me in the Prussian blue painting.

PLATE 69: The new Bader Lane.

Henry Hill Awards given by the ACS for public service, and we then went briefly to a reception hosted by Madelaine Jacobs, and on to one of the most enjoyable dinners sponsored by Sigma-Aldrich that I have ever attended. Hosted by Chandran and Clint, the room was just full of old friends, among them Dr. Jai Nagarkatti, now CEO of Sigma-Aldrich in St. Louis; and Clint, Ike Klundt, and Harvey Hopps, able chemists formerly at Aldrich. I just knew it would bring back some wonderful memories. They told all sorts of funny, often long-forgotten, stories about me accompanied by slides that really almost brought tears to my eyes.

I had not expected to be asked to speak, but was happy to say how good it was to be with so many old friends. Although my expulsion thirteen years earlier had been a very painful experience, I was able to assure them that I had become happier and wealthier because I am able to choose the people with whom I work and because, although my first sale of Sigma-Aldrich call options was the excuse for my dismissal, I have since earned a good deal through further sales.

Our visit to booths in the exhibition the next day was a trip down Memory Lane. So many familiar faces, but so many changes as chemical firms have merged and re-formed over the years. Finally, on our last evening, I was able to present the Alfred Bader Award in Bioinorganic or Bioorganic Chemistry in person to Sir Alan Fersht, an old friend from Cambridge University. And there was Gilbert Stork, receiving the Herbert C. Brown Award for Creative Research in Synthetic Methods. We don't often go to the ACS meetings these days, and I could not fail to be proud that this and three other awards came from Sigma-Aldrich. Who could have dreamed that the merger I worked so hard to achieve in 1975 would have resulted in our giving more ACS awards than any other firm. The Aldrich motto has always been "chemists helping chemists."

George Olah's Priestley Medal address at the end of the evening was a down-to-earth review of his scientific journey from Budapest to Dow, Cleveland, and the University of Southern California. Here was another refugee from Europe, whose work culminated in the Nobel Prize, and on that evening in the Priestley Medal, the highest award given by the American Chemical Society.

So many happy memories of work with chemists for half a century, but art, after all, was my first love, so before we left for the airport, we visited the Timken Museum. When I introduced myself to John Petersen, the director, he apologized that he had little time to talk because he had to rush off to a meeting at his bank to arrange for payment of £1 million for a beautiful painting by van Dyck, a portrait of Mary Villiers, Lady Herbert of Shurland, which had once belonged to Charles I. I had bought this painting with Philip Mould in August of 2001, and he had sold it through Christie's to the Timken Museum. I don't recall anyone ever having to cut our meeting short to attend another for a better reason. As we left San Diego, I thought yet once again of the 23rd Psalm: "My cup runneth over."

# 15

# *Josef Loschmidt*

In Chapter 16 of the *Adventures of a Chemist Collector* I described Professor Christian Noe's and my efforts to follow in Bill Wiswesser's footsteps to bring Josef Loschmidt's chemical work to the attention of the world. In this we have, I think, succeeded and textbooks in chemistry are beginning to describe Loschmidt's work correctly.

I have summarized the literature through 1998, and the editor of the *Bulletin for the History of Chemistry* has permitted me to reprint this paper.

Professor Jiri Damborsky, the Loschmidt professor of chemistry at the Masaryk University in Brno has prepared a widely read website, www.loschmidt.cz.

# THE WISWESSER-LOSCHMIDT CONNECTION *

*Alfred Bader, Milwaukee, WI*

William Joseph Wiswesser (1914-1989) [Fig. 1] graduated from Lehigh University with a B.S. in chemistry in 1936 and received an honorary D.Sc. from that institution in 1974. He was employed by Hercules, the Trojan Powder Company, the Picatinny Arsenal, the Cooper Union, Willson Products, the U.S. Army at Fort Detrick, and finally by the Agricultural Research Service of the U.S.D.A., Being interested throughout his varied career in simplifying chemical structure descriptions, he developed the Wiswesser Line Notation (WLN), which made possible the single-line depiction of every molecule, no matter how complicated. Research organiza-

*Figure 2*. Josef Loschmidt

tions in the 1980's had millions of WLN records in their computers. The Aldrich Chemical Company even offered its catalog in WLN.

Wiswesser learned about the chemical work of Josef Loschmidt (1821-1895) [Fig. 2] from Moritz Kohn's paper in the *Journal of Chemical Education* (1), which is based on Richard Anschütz's paper (2) and reprint (3) of Loschmidt's 1861 volume (4). He felt that he had made a great rediscovery, also believing that this somewhat obscure chemist was the forerunner of the WLN; and he wanted the world to know about it.

*Figure 1*. William J. Wiswesser

186

22                                                            Bull. Hist. Chem. **22** (1998)

He submitted a manuscript to the present author (A.B.) for the *Aldrichimica Acta*, which at the time was being distributed to over 200,000 scientists worldwide. Although the initial response was one of reluctance, I became enthusiastic about the subject after reading Loschmidt's book (3) and some letters, in particular one by Wiswesser to Linus Pauling (see Ref. 16), and collaborated to expand the paper, which appeared in *Aldrichimica Acta* in 1989 (5).

Wiswesser described Loschmidt's chemical firsts:

1. The first correct cyclic structure of benzene and of many aromatic chemicals, 121 in all.
2. The first representation of the allyl moiety.
3. The first representation of the vinyl moiety and of many others.
4. The first representation of cyclopropane, 21 years before it was made by Freund.
5. The first picture book of molecules, containing graphic displays with atomic domains, rather than abstract bond lines.
6. The first double- and triple-bond marks (within the overlaps).
7. The first realistic displays of atomic sizes and bond distances (largest overlap with triple bonds).
8. The first set of diagrams with correct C = 12, N = 14, O = 16 formulas.
9. The first textbook use of atomic-group symbols.
10. The first use of the valence prime marks on these and atomic symbols ("Valenz" was introduced by Wichelhaus in 1868, 7 years later).
11. The first LINE-FORMULA NOTATIONS ("rational formulas").
12. The first revelations of hexavalent and tetravalent sulfur.

The article also outlined Loschmidt's life and work, based largely on the biography Richard Anschütz published with the 1913 reprint. Wiswesser also prepared indices of Loschmidt and Anschütz citations, by author and subject. He translated Loschmidt's chemical names into English and collated structures with page numbers.

On the occasion of our last meeting in Reading, PA, Wiswesser gave me a great deal of his material on Loschmidt, even copies of the original plates, which he had hand-colored Expressing concern about his own failing health, he urged me to continue his work on Loschmidt. I remember his pleasure upon receiving the *Acta* containing his article, just a few days before he died.

Since then, I have been trying to continue his work, by giving many lectures, first at the Boston American Chemical Society meeting in April 1990 (6), to which he had been invited, and then at chemical society meetings and in chemistry departments, and finally by publishing several papers (7). All of these lectures and papers were based on Wiswesser's seminal paper in the *Aldrichimica Acta* (5). I have been greatly helped in these efforts by Professor Christian R. Noe, formerly at Loschmidt's alma mater, the Technical University in Vienna, and now at the J.W. Goethe University in Frankfurt.

Our papers have been attacked quite sharply by two historians of chemistry, Professors A.J. Rocke (8) and G.P. Schiemenz (9). Rocke presents three main arguments:

(1) "Loschmidt clearly believed that the most probable structure for benzene (Schema 182) was a formula constructed from multiple fused cyclopropyl rings, using only single bonds. (8)"

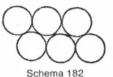

Schema 182

However, all of Loschmidt's more than 100 aromatic compounds are based on Schema 185 as the basic benzene structure.

Schema 185

(2) "... Kekulé himself did not recognize Loschmidt as a predecessor for the benzene structure because he cited Loschmidt's benzene proposal in his first paper on the subject. If Kekulé had consciously taken the idea for benzene from this obscure source, or regarded the Loschmidt structure as similar to his own, the last thing he would have wanted to do was to draw attention to it. (8)"

Kekulé did not "cite" Loschmidt's proposal. All he said in one footnote in French (10) and one in German (11) was, "I prefer my structure to those of Loschmidt and Crum Brown." Aside from these denigrating footnotes - not citations - and one brief abstract (12), there were *no* references to Loschmidt's book in the *entire* 19th century. Rocke points to the *Dictionary of Scientific Biography*, where more space is devoted to Loschmidt than to Kekulé. Loschmidt was indeed well known in the 19th century, but as a physicist, not a chemist. Not until Anschütz's first paper (2) was Loschmidt recognized as a highly competent chemist.

(3) "Even if Loschmidt had suggested a cyclical benzene structure in 1861, I would argue for its insignificance, because no empirical evidence could then be adduced to support the idea. (8)"

This is the kind of argument that can be made against much purely theoretical work.

Schiemenz criticized Wiswesser *inter alia* for claiming that Loschmidt was the first to consider a 6-carbon monocyclic structure for benzene, and also for stating that Loschmidt's book of 1861 was practically unknown and that he was "a shy and self-effacing man."

> "Die Idee einer monocyclischen Anordnung der sechs C-Atome des Benzols kommt nach allem bei Loschmidt auch nicht andeutungsweise vor. (9a, 9c)" *["Nowhere is there in Loschmidt's book even the slightest hint of a monocyclic arrangement of the 6 carbon atoms in benzene."]*

But consider the following structures to represent aromatic compounds aniline, benezenesulfonic acid, benzoic acid, and cinnamic acid.

Aniline                   Benzenesulfonic Acid

Benzoic Acid

Cinnamic Acid

In a letter to *Chemistry and Industry*, Schiemenz wrote (9b):

This misunderstanding that Loschmidt's benzene structures might symbolize a monocyclic formula was already discussed by E. Rey in 1965, who aptly commented that one must interpret the circular symbol as what it really means and not as what it could be, and hence not as a circular array of six carbon atoms. The argument also holds true for all of Loschmidt's formulae (by the way, there were not 386!) which may have some superficial resemblance with modern molecular models. To date molecular modeling back to 1861 is just anachronistic.

Schiemenz's English summary of his longest paper states (9c):

> In 1989, W. J. Wiswesser claimed that the correct, monocyclic structure of benzene was not conceived in 1865 by A. Kekulé, but already in 1861 by J. Loschmidt. It is shown that this view is neither correct nor new. As a symbol for the benzene nucleus $C_6$, Loschmidt used a circle which Wiswesser believed to stand for a cyclic array of the six carbon atoms. In fact, this circle represents, in the two-dimensionality of the printed page, a sphere. Similar, but smaller 'circles' (*i.e.* spheres) represent hydrogen, carbon, nitrogen, oxygen and sulfur atoms. Their sizes are chosen so that the volumes of the corresponding spheres reflect the respective atomic weights (72 for $C_6$). This meaning soon passed into oblivion. As a consequence, gradually a misinterpretation developed which culminated in Wiswesser's view which recently has been popularized by C.R Noe and A. Bader.

The most telling indication that Loschmidt thought of a monocyclic structure is in his Schema 229 for *p*-phenylenediamine (13):

> *Schon der Anblick des Schema zeigt die Möglichkeit von isomeren Modificationen.* ["Just looking at Schema 229 shows the possibility of isomeric modifications."]

Schema 229

Schiemenz counters (9d):

> Auch eine Anmerkung *Loschmidts* zum 'Semibenzidam'='Azophenylamin' (Phenylendiamin), Schema 229, gehört hierher: 'Schon der Anblick des Schema zeigt die Möglichkeit

24 Bull. Hist. Chem. **22** (1998)

von isomeren Modificationen' (*Loschmidt* (1861), 34). Entgegen der Auffassung von *Noe* and *Bader* (*Chemistry in Britain* 29 (1993) 402, Corrigendum: S.573; vlg. dies., in *Wotiz* (1993), 233) einer Interpretation als o-, m-, p- Positionsisomerie noch nicht zugänglich (*Anschütz* (1913), 132), kann diese Bemerkung nur im Sinne einer Konstitutionsisomerie verstanden werden (vgl. *Loschmidt* (1861): *Isomerie*, S.8-11). Mithin muß bereits *Loschmidt*, der anderswo N-N- und auch O-O-Bindungen hat (Schema 176,178), an die Atomverknüpfung des Phenylhydrazins gedacht haben.

Thus, Schiemenz dismisses this argument by claiming that Loschmidt must have been thinking of an isomer like phenylhydrazine (which had not yet been made). However, in his discussion on isomerism, Loschmidt distinguished between isomers "*im engern Sinne,*" like o-, m-, and p-isomers, and isomers "*im weiteren Sinne,*" like phenylenediamine and phenylhydrazine. The former you can predict just by looking at them, but not the latter (14):

... wir **Isomerie im engern Sinne nennen**. Solche Isomerie findet statt zwischen Milchsäure und Paramilchsäure, zwischen **Alphatoluolsäure und Betatoluolsäure**. Die anderen Arten der **Isomerie im weiteren Sinne sind**: erstens jene Fälle, wo zwei Substanzen denselben Kern und dieselben Aufsatz-Atome haben, wo aber die letzteren zu anderen Aufsatzelementen gruppiert sind. **So haben Nitrotoluol und Benzaminsäure** [*i.e.*, aminobenzoic acid] nicht nur dieselbe Zusammenstellung $C_7NH_7O_2$, sondern auch denselben Kern $C_7^{VIII}$ und dieselben Aufsatzatome $NH_7O_2$." [Emphasis added]

Schiemenz points out that Loschmidt did think of six-atom monocycles such as his Schema 237, 1,4-diphenylpiperazine, and claims that this is "unambiguous proof that he did not think of such an array for [the $C_6$ nuclei). (15)" Yet, in fact, Loschmidt came even closer to Kekulé's cyclohexatriene structure in his Schema 239 for the 1,3,5-triazine derived from aniline and 2,4,6-trichloro-1,3,5-triazine.

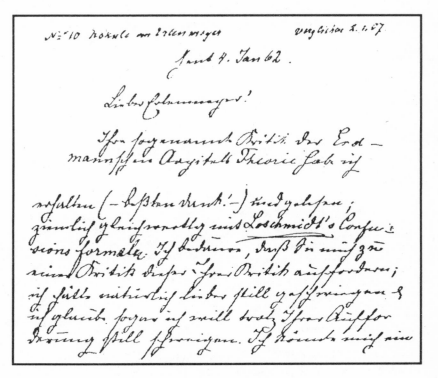

*Figure 3*. Letter from Kekulé to E. Erlenmeyer

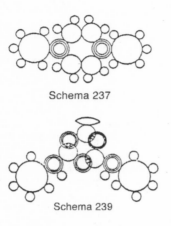

Schema 237

Schema 239

Rather than being unambiguous proof that Loschmidt did not think of benzene as a six-carbon monocycle, it suggests that he must have considered such a structure but did not know how to do this without the inclusion of double bonds, hence, his decision to leave that *"in suspenso.* (16)"

Shortly after Loschmidt's book appeared on January 4, 1862, Kekulé wrote a letter to Emil Erlenmeyer [Fig. 3], in which he alluded to *"Loschmidt's Confusions formeln* (sic)." Why would Kekulé have chosen such a description for Loschmidt's structures? Because in 1861, Kekulé stated that you cannot write formulae of constitution, and so considered Loschmidt's structures *"formulae of confusion* (17):

> Which of the different rational formulae one wants to use for specific cases is essentially a question of appropriateness. Based on the observations already given, there can be no doubt that one may use different rational formulae for the same substance. At the same time, one must also, of course, keep in mind that the rational formulae are only formulae of reactions (*'Umsetzungsformeln'*) and not formulae of constitution (*'Constitutionsformeln'*), and that they do not in any way describe the constitution, i.e., the position of the atoms in the compounds. This should be clearly stressed, because oddly enough some chemists still believe that by the study of chemical reactions, one can derive with certainty the constitution of compounds, and thus depict the positions of the atoms in the chemical formula. That the latter is not possible warrants no special proof ... Yet a basic task of natural science must of necessity be to discover the constitution of matter or in other words, the position of atoms; this, however, can only be at-

tained by the comparative study of physical properties of the existing compound and certainly not by the study of chemical reactions ... But even when we have succeeded in this, different rational formulae (*'Umsetzungsformeln'*) will still be appropriate. [Emphasis added]

As R.B. Woodward stressed in his 1972 Cope lecture (18):

> He [Kekulé] was, in truth, too much under the influence of the theoretical and physical chemists of the time, who were inordinately opposed to the idea of fixed chemical structure—so much so that, until 1886, the infant *Berichte der Deutschen Chemischen Gesellschaft*, born in 1868, would only print structural formulae using dotted-and-dashed lines; the use of solid lines to represent the nearest neighbor relationships would have imputed too much reality to an hypothesis which leading theorists of the day simply would not accept.

Schiemenz (19) has claimed that Loschmidt's 1861 book became well known after its publication. As is clear from Kekulé's letter, he and Erlenmeyer knew of it (20). So did Herman Kopp who reviewed it briefly (12). Before Anschütz's publications of 1912 (2) and 1913 (3), however, there were only three references to it: two brief and disparaging footnotes (10, 11) in Kekulé's papers and Kopp's review (12). If indeed Schiemenz (19) is correct in asserting that Loschmidt's book was widely known, chemists may have 'borrowed' from it without bothering to cite it; but that seems unlikely (21).

Schiemenz faults Wiswesser for describing Loschmidt as "a shy and self-effacing man." How could a man "who was a member of the Imperial Academy of Sciences, founder of the Chemical-Physical Society, institute director and, at one time, dean of the faculty of philosophy of the University of Vienna be 'a shy and self-effacing man'? (22)" Although this may indeed be difficult to understand, many who knew Loschmidt personally wrote about that very quality. Franz Exner, Loschmidt's successor as professor of physics at the University of Vienna, had known Loschmidt well for many years because Loschmidt had been a student and friend of Exner's father at the University of Prague. At the 100th anniversary of Loschmidt's birth, Exner wrote that Loschmidt had "a rare goodness of heart and modesty; totally without jealousy, he could enjoy the scientific successes of others just as much as his own. (23)" Alexander Bauer, the grandfather of the Nobel laureate Erwin Schrödinger, described his unsuccessful attempts to bring the *Chemische Studien* to the attention of scientists during a trip to England (24):

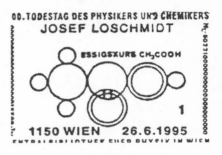

*Figure 4*. Commemorative Stamp

Only one, the mathematician Liouville (25) in Paris showed great interest and gave it a very favorable review. That publication [*Chemische Studien*] was quickly forgotten. It cannot be denied that its author was much to blame for that, because he later did nothing to draw attention to it, even though he had many opportunities.

Loschmidt's best friend, Ludwig Boltzmann, said, "...everywhere Loschmidt's excessive modesty prevented his being appreciated as much as he could and should have been. (26a)... He just could not stand it, when people talked about him and his merits.(26b)"

Richard Anschütz questioned why Loschmidt did not point to his own work of 1861 at the time of the *Benzolfest* in 1890 which celebrated the 25th anniversary of the correct benzene structure. Anschütz believed that Loschmidt's silence was "...because of the undemanding modesty which was an integral part of his character. The discovery of *Chemische Studien* ... his old, unnoticed and forgotten work, he left to chance (27)"— and, luckily, we must add, to Richard Anschütz and William Wiswesser.

A high point in Loschmidt's recognition as a chemist came at a symposium at the University of Vienna in June, 1995, at which many well known chemists paid tribute to Loschmidt, who had died 100 years earlier in July, 1895. Among the lecturers were Max Perutz, Carl Djerassi, and Sir Herbert Bondi, all originally from Vienna, and Ernest Eliel, Albert Eschenmoser, Christian Noe and Günter Schiemenz. The papers, which dealt

with chemistry and physics, have been published in English by Plenum (28). It was Wiswesser's recognition of Loschmidt's remarkable insights into chemical structure which sparked the renewed interest in and a greater understanding and appreciation of the *Chemische Studien*, culminating in the 1995 Symposium.

*Figure 5*. First-day Postmark

The Austrian postal service issued a commemorative stamp [Fig. 4] showing one of Loschmidt's many correct aromatic structures, that of cinnamic acid. The postmark of the first-day cover [Fig. 5] showed the structure of acetic acid, one of Loschmidt's many firsts.

Did Wiswesser make mistakes? Of the twelve "famous firsts," No. 1, "The first correct cyclic structure of benzene and of many aromatic chemicals, 121 in all," is somewhat of an overstatement. Loschmidt was the first to consider a monocyclic six carbon ring, but he did not know what to do with the double bonds. Kekulé's cyclohexatriene of 1865 appeared to be an improvement, but the puzzle about its unsaturation was still to be addressed (29). Wiswesser was correct in describing Loschmidt's other firsts and in ending his paper with, "....that tiny book of 1861 was really the masterpiece of the century in organic chemistry."

## REFERENCES AND NOTES

*This paper was presented with a poster session at the American Chemical Society meeting in San Francisco in April,1997, HIST 005.
1.   M. Kohn, *J. Chem. Educ.*, **1945**, 22, 381.
2.   R. Anschütz, *Ber. Dtsch. Chem. Ges.*, **1912**, 45, 539.
3.   R. Anschütz, Ed., "Konstitutions-Formeln der Organischen Chemie in graphischer Darstellung," Ostwalds Klassiker der exakten Wissenschaften," No. 190, Leipzig, 1913. Reprinted by the Aldrich Chemical Co., Cat. No. Z-18577-9. NOTE: All subsequent references to structures labeled as "Schema" are taken from this booklet.

4.   J. Loschmidt, *Chemische Studien I*, Carl Gerold's Sohn, Vienna, 1861. Reprinted by the Aldrich Chemical Co., Cat. No. Z18576-0.

5.   W. J. Wiswesser, "Johann Josef Loschmidt (1821-1895): a forgotten genius. Benzene rings and much more in 1861," *Aldrichimica Acta*, **1989**, *22* [1], 17.

6.   C. R. Noe, A. Bader, and W. J. Wiswesser, "Loschmidt, not Kekulé, published first benzene ring diagrams" presented at the symposium on the Kekulé's Benzolfest, 100 years later, 199th American Chemical Society National Meeting. Boston, April 22, 1990, HIST 008.

7.   (a) A. Bader, "Josef Loschmidt, the Father of Molecular Modeling," *Royal Institution Proceedings*, **1992**, *64*, 197; (b) C. R. Noe and A. Bader, "Josef Loschmidt," in J. H. Wotiz, Ed., *The Kekulé Riddle*, Cache River Press, Vienna, Illinois, 62595, 1993, Ch. 16; (c) C. R. Noe and A. Bader, "Facts are Better than Dreams," *Chem. Br.*, **1993**, *29*, 126; (d) A. Bader, "Out of the Shadow," *Chem. Ind. (London)*, **1993**, 367; (e) A. Bader, *Adventures of a Chemist Collector*, Weidenfeld & Nicolson, London, 1995, Ch. 16; (f) A. Bader, "A Chemist Turns Detective," *Chem. Br.*, **1996**, *32*, 41; (g) A. Bader, "Loschmidt's Graphic Formulae of 1861: Forerunners of Modern Structural Formulae," in W. Fleischhacker and T. Schönfeld, Ed., *Pioneering Ideas for the Physical and Chemical Sciences*, Plenum, New York, 1997; (h) A. Bader, "Richard Anschütz, Archibald Scott Couper, and Josef Loschmidt", Ref. 7g.

8.   A. J. Rocke, "Waking up to the Facts?" *Chem. Br.*, **1993**, *29*, 401-403.

9.   G. P. Schiemenz, (a) "Good-bye, Kekulé. Joseph Loschmidt und die Monocyclische Struktur des Benzols," *Naturwissenschaftliche Rundschau*, **1993**, *46* [3], 85; (b) "Further out of the Shadow," *Chem. Ind. (London)*, **1993**, 522; (c) "Joseph Loschmidt und die Benzol-Formel. Über die Entstehung einer Legende," *Sudhoffs Archiv*, **1994** [1], 41; (d) Ref. 9c, p. 57, footnote 120; (e) "Spheres from Dalton to Loschmidt. Insights into the Ways of Thinking of a Genius," in W. Fleischhacker and T. Schönfeld, Ed., *Pioneering Ideas for the Physical and Chemical Sciences*, Plenum, New York, 1997.

10.   A. Kekulé, "Sur la constitution des substances aromatiques," *Bull. Soc. Chim. Fr.*, **1865** [2], *3*, 100.

11.   A. Kekulé, "Untersuchungen über aromatische Verbindungen," *Ann. Chem. Pharm.*, **1866**, *137*, [2], 134.

12.   Liebig's *Jahresbericht*, **1861**, *1*, 335. [ See Ref. 3, p. 100.]

13.   Ref. 3, p. 68.

14.   Ref. 3, p. 15.

15.   Ref. 9b; Ref. 9c, p. 47.

16.   I want to thank William F. Reynolds for pointing out that Loschmidt was probably reluctant to accept a benzene structure with double bonds, of which he was well aware, since this seemed inconsistent with the known chemistry of benzene. As Wiswesser pointed out in a letter to Linus Pauling (August 2, 1987, copy in author's personal collection). Loschmidt provided "amazingly perceptive graphical visualizations" in 1861 of increasingly tighter, overlapping bonding in ethane (Schema 9), ethylene (Schema 56, 57), and acetylene (Schema 59). Photocopies of this letter are available on request from either the author or the editor of the *Bulletin*.

17.   A. Kekulé, *Lehrbuch der organischen Chemie*, F. Enke, Erlangen, 1861, p. 157.

18.   R. B. Woodward, unpublished manuscript, courtesy of R. Hoffmann and the Chemical Heritage Foundation.

19.   Ref. 9c, pp. 42-43.

20.   "Knowing" and "understanding" are not always the same. In the heat of discussion during the Boston American Chemical Society meeting (6), I suggested that Kekulé may have plagiarized Loschmidt. I no longer think so. Kekulé 'knew' Loschmidt's book but did not 'understand' it as Anschütz and Wiswesser did. Loschmidt's Schema 185 for benzene may have led to Kekulé's snake dream, but we can never know for certain whether he even had that dream. The first six-carbon monocyclic benzene structure was Loschmidt's; the first cyclohexatriene Kekulé's. Most recently E. Heilbronner and K. Hafner have reviewed this controversy ("Bemerkungen zu Loschmidts Benzolformel," *Chemie Unserer Zeit*, **1998**, *32*, 34). The authors approve particularly of Schiemenz' (Ref. 9c) "ausgezeichneten und akribisch recherchierten Richtigstellung" [Schiemenz' excellent and meticulously researched correction] and of Hafner's "August Kekulé, dem Baumeister der Chemie zum 150 Geburtstag," Justus von Liebig Verlag, Darmstadt, 1980. There (p. 76) Hafner wrote, "...again Kekulé succeeded brilliantly. His irresistible desire for clarity and his unusual power of imagination again helped. Basically the benzene formula is a logical conclusion from structural history. Today it seems obvious, but over a hundred years ago it was an extraordinary mental leap, comparable to the intellectual effort once necessary before man could exchange sled runners for the wheel. *The idea that a hydrocarbon might have a circular structure was totally foreign to chemists of that time. The circle was the symbol for the indivisible, the atom.*" [emphasis added]. But 13 years earlier Ferdinand Kirchhof ("Joseph Loschmidt und die Benzolformel," *Chem. Appar.*, **1967**, *91*(2), 48) had written, "*The idea that a compound might have a circular structure was totally foreign to chemists of that time. The circle was the symbol for the indivisible, the atom, and the merit of having depicted the $C_6$ nucleus as a circle belongs unquestionably to Loschmidt.*" [emphasis added].

21.   Recently, F. W. Lichtenthaler ("Emil Fischer's Proof of the Configuration of Sugars: A Centennial Tribute," *Angew. Chem. Int. Ed. Engl.*, **1992**, *31*, 1541) has suggested that Adolf Baeyer, Hugo Schiff, and Rudolph Fittig were the first to depict sugars correctly, around 1870. Anschütz pointed out that Loschmidt was the

192

first—nine years earlier—to show the correct structures of mannitol and other sugars (Ref. 3, pp. 119-120, footnotes 63, 66, 69, 70 and 72). But are Baeyer, Schiff, and Fittig likely to have known this?

22. Ref. 9c, p. 57.
23. F. Exner, "Zur Erinnerung an Josef Loschmidt," *Naturwissenschaften*, **1921,** 9, Heft 11, March 18.
24. A. Bauer, *Oesterreichische Chemiker-Zeitung*, **1913,** XVI, No. 18, 241, September 15.
25. Jean Jacques has kindly pointed out that this was Joseph Liouville (1809-1882), but his review of *Chemische Studien* appears not to have been published.
26. L. Boltzmann, "Zur Erinnerung an Josef Loschmidt," a eulogy presented to the Imperial Academy of Sciences in Vienna on October 29, 1895 and published by the executive committee for the erection of the Loschmidt monument, Vienna 1899; (a) p. 14; (b) p. 16.
27. Ref. 3, p. 109.
28. W. Fleischhacker and T. Schönfeld, Ed., *Pioneering Ideas for the Physical and Chemical Sciences*, Plenum Press, New York, 1997; see also Ref. 7g, h, 9e.
29. For a clear discussion of Kekulé's benzene formulae, see G. P. Schiemenz' "Where did Kekulé Find 'his' Benzene Formula?" Ref. 7b, Ch. 9.

## ABOUT THE AUTHOR

Dr. Alfred Bader, 2961 North Shepard Avenue, Milwaukee, WI 53211, earned his Ph.D. under Louis F. Fieser at Harvard University in 1950. He founded the Aldrich Chemical Company in Milwaukee in 1951 and was the co-founder of Sigma-Aldrich in 1975. Dr. Bader, now 74, continues to pursue vigorously his interests in chemistry, art, and the history of art and chemistry.

# 16

## *The Lieben Award*

Isabel and I have been to Vienna many times, usually to visit our chemist friends at Loba Chemie and at the University of Vienna. One of the happiest occasions was the Loschmidt symposium in 1995, when many eminent chemists from around the world honored Josef Loschmidt on the 100th anniversary of his death.

Another important visit was early in June 2003 when Isabel and I attended a very interesting two-day symposium at the university, at which scientists and historians discussed how the Nazis dealt with Jews at Austrian universities and how this affected intellectual life in Austria after the war. Among the speakers were two Nobel Laureates, Eric Kandel and Walter Kohn, and two old friends, Edward Timms and Ruth Sime. Many of the talks showed us how positively Austria has changed in the last fifty years.

That week, two old friends, Dr. Robert Rosner and Professor Christian Noe, told me about a most interesting prize, the Ignaz Lieben Prize, which had been the most important scientific award in the Austro-Hungarian Empire until its collapse, and then just in Austria. Begun thirty-five years before the establishment of the Nobel Prize, it honored fifty-five eminent scientists, including four who later received the Nobel, and Lise Meitner, who was the first female recipient of the Lieben Prize, which has sometimes been called the Austrian Nobel Prize.

Our friend Robert Rosner was the sales manager of Loba

Chemie, Aldrich's valued supplier in Vienna. When he retired, he took a history degree at the University of Vienna, specializing in the history of chemistry in Austria. During his studies, he learned about the Lieben Prize. An Austrian banker, Ignaz Lieben (1805–1862), left 10,000 Gulden in his will "for the general good," and his son, Adolf Lieben, an eminent organic chemist and the first Jew to hold chairs in chemistry in Prague and Vienna, persuaded the family to use 6,000 Gulden to fund the prize, which was administered by the Academy of Sciences and first given in 1865. The family increased the award substantially in 1898 and in 1908. During the terrible inflation of 1923, the capital was lost, but the Lieben family continued to pay 1,000 Austrian Schillinge until 1938, when the Nazis discontinued the prize. The last donor, Heinrich Lieben, Adolf Lieben's son, died in Buchenwald in 1945.

Dr. Rosner had shared the information about this virtually forgotten prize with our mutual friend, Professor Christian Noe, with whom I had collaborated so well on the chemical work of Josef Loschmidt. Rosner and Noe explained that the academy was eager to reinstate the Lieben Award and asked Isabel and me whether we might be interested. What an opportunity: a prize for young scientists that had been started by a Jewish chemist to be reinstated by another Jewish chemist. Of course our answer was yes, provided the Lieben family did not object in any way. That very week, Professor Noe invited Dr. Wolfgang Lieben-Seutter, a grandson of Adolf Lieben, to discuss our plans. Dr. Lieben-Seutter assured us that he had no objections.

We decided quickly that the prize should again be administered by the Austrian Academy of Sciences, that it should be open to young scientists from all countries formerly in the Austro-Hungarian Empire, that it should be $18,000 annually, and that it should be guaranteed by us for thirty years (Plate 70).

I was asked a number of times by the academy to give my

reasons for reinstating the award, and these are given in the Appendix to this chapter. The first Lieben Award was to be given on Tuesday, November 9, 2004, sixty-six years after *Kristallnacht*, and we flew to Vienna on November 7 to enjoy the next four days.

We were welcomed on Monday night beginning with a press conference, where once again the emphasis of the questions was on our reasons for funding this award.

The public festivities began with a welcoming speech by Georg Winkler, the rector of the University of Vienna, followed by a reading of a duolog written by Professor Carl Djerassi, the father of "the pill," entitled "Sex in an Age of Mechanical Reproduction" and read by Carl Djerassi and Maria Hartmann. This heated discussion deals with the possibility and the ethics of the fertilization of a human egg with a single sperm by direct injection under the microscope, followed by reinsertion of the egg into the woman's uterus. An interesting question period was followed by a pleasant, semi-formal dinner.

The following day, we were again interviewed by some journalists and photographers. After this we went to the beautiful Austrian Academy of Sciences for the first presentation of the new Lieben Prize. The ceremony began with greetings from Herbert Mang, the president of the Academy, a lecture by a Hungarian academic, and music by the Mozart Ensemble of the Vienna Volksoper. This was followed by the presentation of the Lieben Award to Dr. Zoltan Nusser, a thirty-six-year-old Hungarian neurophysiologist, who had studied in Oxford, at University College London, and at UCLA before returning to the Hungarian Academy of Sciences in 2000. The Austrian Academy of Sciences award committee had chosen him from more than fifty applicants.

After a further Haydn trio by the Mozart Ensemble, the academy president presented Isabel and me with the "Bene merito" gold medal and certificate. I had been asked to present a few minutes' acceptance speech in German. I stressed the

Liebens' and my Jewish and Austrian backgrounds, and explained that my view of Vienna had changed during the last fifty years (see Appendix on pp.200–201).

More music was followed by another brief talk by the academy president and buffet lunch.

The symposium at the university lasted for a day and a half, the lecturers dealing with the Lieben family, the fifty-five Lieben prize winners, Jewish culture and anti-Semitism, and the migration from Austria after 1938. This was accompanied by two exhibitions at the university, one depicting the lives and works of the fifty-five prizewinners, the other "1924–A Good Year" illustrating the lives of six scientists, myself included, born in Austria in 1924.

We had never been to the Konzerthaus in Vienna, and really enjoyed a fundraising concert there that evening. Two young female musicians, a violinist and a pianist, were playing modern music with a great deal of spirit. I had heard music by Maurice Ravel and Bela Bartok before, but not of the other three composers, Otto Zykan (whose work had its first performance ever), Manuel de Falla, and George Enescu. Nor had I ever watched a young violinist play with such vigor.

Dr. Wolfgang Lieben-Seutter invited us for supper with his family. Isabel had bought a special dress for this occasion and, as usual, was the most beautiful woman around.

Some of the lectures at the university were hard to understand, but several were brilliant and informative. Early on Wednesday afternoon, Yechiel Bar-Chaim of the American Jewish Joint Distribution Committee (the Joint) joined us on his way from Paris to the Balkans. He gave me the "Via Bona" award which he had accepted for me in Prague in September for " ... support of civil and human rights and ... baroque art history and chemistry in the Czech Republic." And of course we discussed our help for the following year, mainly for the neediest in the Balkans.

Wednesday evening we went to the opening of a Lieben

exhibition in the Jewish Museum, which was most interesting, showing the rise and fall of this family, with many documents, photographs, and paintings. What I found most surprising was that the family continued to pay for the Lieben Prize even after the bankruptcy of the Lieben Bank in 1932.

A young historian, Georg Gaugusch, specializing in genealogy, told me that he had found out a good deal about the family of my grandmother, Hermine Freund. He eventually helped me identify the four Freund family portraits we have at home!

Wednesday evening ended with supper in the Augustinerkeller near by—lots of talk with Paul Löw Beer's daughter Kitty, her former husband Professor Arnold Schmidt, and Christian Noe.

Thursday morning began with an hour's breakfast with Dr. Vladan Antonovic, who had come from Innsbruck, a very able young Czech art historian whom I am trying to help—not an easy task. My high school in Vienna had invited me to speak on Monday morning, and to return on Thursday morning, to answer more questions from the students. On Thursday afternoon, we met for tea with an Austrian historian, Professor Gerhard Botz, who would like to publish an abridged German translation of my autobiography. Why not?

Thursday evening was most difficult for Isabel. The Jewish Museum had invited me to present "The Bible Through Dutch Eyes," and I had requested two projectors and two carousels to show two slides side by side. This was impossible in the set-up provided, and Isabel had to rearrange everything and stand on a ladder—for fifty minutes!—to move the slides. Isabel and I have worked together quite often presenting this talk—but never like this. The museum gave me many Austrian stamps commemorating the revival of the Ignaz Lieben Prize; I wished that they had spent that money instead on facilitating showing slides.

After the talk, we invited our old friend Bobby Rosner for

supper. He was really the guiding spirit to the revival of the prize. He was happy about all the happenings and about the publication of his book *Chemistry in Austria 1740–1914*, which had appeared that week.

There was a lot of publicity about the new Lieben Award. *Profil*, an Austrian *Time*-like magazine, had a two-page article with photographs of Isabel, Bobby Rosner, and myself in its October 29, 2004 issue. Most Viennese dailies published reports on November 10, 2004, the most detailed in *Der Kurier*, headlined "Help for the Ablest and the Poorest" and showing a photograph of Isabel and myself with Dr. Nusser and the president of the academy.

We left Vienna for London on Friday morning, happy about the week, but Isabel weary after having to stand on a ladder for so long.

APPENDIX

### The Lieben Prize

Our reasons for funding the Ignaz Lieben Prize are varied and complex.

We first learned of this award in 2003 from two friends in Vienna, Dr. Robert Rosner and Professor Christian Noe. The Lieben Prize was the first privately funded award in the Austro-Hungarian Monarchy. Others, such as the Baumgartner Award, followed.

Established in 1862 by the wealthy Viennese banker Ignaz Lieben, a Jew, the prize was to be given to an able young scientist. Until the Nobel Prize some thirty years later, it was the most prestigious award in the Monarchy. The element Meitnerium was named after the first woman awardee, Lise Meitner, and four other awardees later won Nobel Prizes.

The original sum of 6,000 Gulden given to the Academy was increased by the Lieben family in 1898 by 36,000 Kronen and again in 1908 by an additional 18,000 Kronen. We wonder whether they chose these sums because in Hebrew 18 stands for Chai, life, and 36 twice Chai. This is certainly the reason why we chose $18,000.

The capital for this award and all others administered by the academy was lost in the great inflation of 1923. However, the Lieben family gave 1,000 Austrian Schillinge annually to continue the Lieben Prize until 1938, when it was stopped by the Nazis. Heinrich Lieben, who made the last donation to the Academy, died in Buchenwald in 1945.

We know almost nothing about Ignaz Lieben, but his son Adolf Lieben was a brilliant organic chemist. After studies in Heidelberg and Paris, he was invited by Stanislao Cannizzaro to the chair of chemistry in Palermo, then moved to Turin and eventually was the first Jew to hold chairs in Prague and Vienna.

When I first returned to Vienna occasionally after the war, the idea of establishing an award for Austrians was unthinkable. Whenever I met an Austrian older than myself, born in 1924, I wondered what that person had done in 1938. Yet most old Nazis have died, and I sense that the younger generations are better people.

Now that the Czech Republic, Slovakia, and Hungary are joining the European Union, Vienna will again be the true center of Europe, so an award to a scientist in a country of the old monarchy, again with the 18, Chai connection, seems really fitting.

There are also strong personal reasons for our re-establishing the Lieben Prize. "Muttili," my father's sister, who was my loving mother-by-adoption, often spoke of the "*Guten alten Zeiten,*" before World War I. She was inordinately proud of her father, my grandfather, Moritz Ritter von Bader, who was knighted by Emperor Franz Josef. She was proud to be an Austrian, refused to leave Vienna, and died in Theresienstadt. And my mother, born a Hungarian countess, spoke of our direct ancestor Count Franz Gabriel and his brother Johann Karl Serenyi, one of the defenders of Vienna against the Turks in 1683. He held the imposing title of *Generalfeldwachtmeister und Vize-Oberbefehlshaber der Streitkräfte in Wien.* Mama took me several times to St. Stephen's Cathedral to show me the plaque thanking Count Serenyi for his efforts against the Turks, and to listen to the second mass on Good Friday, praying for the infidel Jews. This always troubled me, brought up a Jew by my caring Muttili.

Under Hitler, many Austrians treated Jews worse than the Germans did and have made restitution more slowly and less generously. There were decent Austrians, some of whom I knew well—just not enough of them. But the past is behind us, my roots are in the Austro-Hungarian Empire, and the Lieben Award will go to able young scientists, the very people we want to help.

## 17

## *Family and Friends*

Life since my expulsion from Sigma-Aldrich in 1992 has been happy and productive; the only serious cloud was when my son David's wife, Michelle, left him in the summer of 2002. David was totally distraught, thinking until then that he was happily married to Michelle, who was carrying his third child, Noa, a daughter born in January 2003.

Since their divorce, David and Michelle have shared custody of the children, and as Michelle does not live far away, Helena, Isaiah, and now Noa spend alternate weeks in their lovely home near the Delaware River. We were all relieved to see that the children seemed to adapt very well to this new lifestyle, and when David eventually met a caring woman, Michelle Berrong, whom the family call Chellie, it was wonderful to see how the children came to love her as much as she loves them.

David and Chellie were married in April 2005 (Plate 71), and the family is overjoyed to have a new baby, Faye Ella, born in December 2006. Isaiah hoped for a girl so he would be the only prince in the family. Upon reflection, which didn't take long, he decided that a boy would have been more fun for him but he would make do with the situation. Noa emptied out her big doll crib for her new younger sister and wanted to do everything for her. They are a very busy household and we love to be with them (Plate 72). We spent a wonderful few days with them in the summer of 2006, together with the Milwaukee Bader family and Isabel's sister, Marion. We were able to celebrate both David's and Linda's birthdays. David's love of dramatics provided us with two hilarious birthday parties. And then at the end of March 2007 all of us flew east again for Faye's naming ceremony, a really fun weekend.

Daniel and Linda and their three children (Plate 73) live just a few blocks from us in Milwaukee, so we see them much more often. Two of their children, Carlos and Jessie Gisela, were adopted in Guatemala. Their son Alex, who has Down's syndrome, has benefited from the great love and care both parents and his siblings give him. He is making great strides with all the help he has received at school and in therapy for some of his difficulties. They are a strong, lively family of whom we are very proud. Daniel does a great deal of traveling, largely in connection with his position as president of the Helen Bader Foundation, which gives ten to twelve million dollars annually to help education in Milwaukee and Israel and on care for Alzheimer patients. Linda holds the family together while he is away, often with the help of members of her family. Together they make a wonderful team.

Daniel's work was recognized with an honorary doctorate from the University of Wisconsin-Milwaukee in May 2006, twenty-six years after I received my first honorary doctorate from that same university. Honorary degrees and awards are fun to receive. In the last ten years, I have received a number, but the one I have enjoyed the most was the Centennial Human Relations Award presented to Daniel and me jointly by the American Jewish Committee on May 30, 2006 (Plate 74).

Daniel gave a moving speech outlining the work of the Helen Bader Foundation, Yechiel Bar-Chaim of the Joint sent a video presentation from Paris (see Appendix on pp.212–213), and I tried to summarize my life's aim:

This is the first time that my son Daniel and I are being honored together and naturally this gives me a great deal of pleasure.

But of course I am mindful of the advice that I gave my

Sunday school students at Temple Emanuel every second year when we were studying the Books of the Prophets. It gave me immense pleasure to shake hands with eighteen of these students this evening! Jeremiah in Chapter 9 put it so clearly, "Let not the wise man glory in his wisdom, neither let the mighty man glory in his might, let not the rich man glory in his riches: But let him that glorieth glory in this, that he understandeth and knoweth me ...

Knowing and understanding means knowing and keeping the commandments.

There are some rabbis who say that each of the 613 commandments is equally important, but I find this hard to believe. To me, among the most important commandments, next to the Ten Commandments, are the commandments Justice, Justice You Shall Seek, and You Shall Not Stand Idly by the Blood of Your Neighbor.

Another of the important commandments is one which I say twice a day: *Veshinantom Levonecho*. You shall teach your children, and I am truly happy to know that I have taught my sons, and they have learned.

Recently, I read a wonderful speech given by Professor Yehudah Bauer, the director of Holocaust Studies at the Yad Vashem in Jerusalem. In that speech, given in January 1998 to the German Parliament, Professor Bauer outlined most cogently how it could happen that in the center of European culture, in Germany, Nazis could grab and retain power for twelve years and plan for the final solution to kill every Jew. Just the day before yesterday the German Pope Benedict XVI visited Auschwitz and, speaking in Italian (so as not to offend the Poles), explained that the Holocaust was the Nazi effort to banish belief in God. The Pope's speech last Sunday was, I think, very much guided by Professor Bauer's speech. Professor Bauer ended his great speech by saying that perhaps we should add to the Ten Commandments three more:

1. That neither you nor your children nor your children's children should ever become perpetrators.

2. That neither you nor your children nor your children's children should ever become victims.

3. That neither you nor your children nor your children's children should ever stand by passively during mass murders.

And yet since the Holocaust we have seen mass murders in Bosnia, in Rwanda, and now in Darfur, and right here in Milwaukee there is such poverty. My sons and I are trying as much as we can never to stand by idly. The keys in Milwaukee are education and employment. The Helen Bader Foundation is trying to help education, Jewish education, and in the inner city. And the first buildings Aldrich bought were at 29th and 30th Streets and Meinecke Avenue, so that we would find it easier to employ African Americans. And it gives Isabel and me a great deal of pleasure to attend the annual Aldrich award dinner and to note that about half the employees attending are people of color.

But is not standing by idly enough?

I am reminded of what Martin Buber in his *Tales of the Hasidim* calls the Query of Queries asked by Rabbi Zusya of Hanipol shortly before his death in 1800. Rabbi Zusya said, "When I come before the Heavenly Judge, He will not ask me, Zusya, why were you not as great as Moses, our teacher. He will only ask me, Zusya, why were you not as great as you, Zusya, could have been?"

When I come before the *Dajan Emes*, I will not be asked, Alfred Bader, why were you not as great a chemist as you could have been? Why were you not as great an art dealer as you could have been? I will be asked, as I ask myself many times, and not only on Yom Kippur, why were you not as good a husband, why were you not as good a father as you could have been?

When my son Daniel comes before the Heavenly Judge, I hope many years from now, he will *not* be asked, why were you not as great a president of the Helen Bader Foundation as you could have been? Why were you not as good a husband, a father, a son, as you could have been? Because I am convinced that my son Daniel is truly as good as he can be.

I cannot conclude without mentioning Marvin Klitsner, the ablest lawyer I ever knew and my best friend. Our success in life would not have been possible without him. When the company was very small, he arranged for each of my sons to own 6.5 percent of Aldrich which, now Sigma-Aldrich, is the world's most profitable chemical company. Marvin helped Helen Bader to write her will, leading to the Helen Bader Foundation. And he helped Isabel and me to write our wills which will lead to a similar foundation to be headed, I hope, by Daniel.

I can say with King David, "The Lord is my Shepherd; *causi revojo*, my cup runneth over."

I believe that as a family, the Baders are all trying to do the best they can. Yet it is hard to see yourself as others see you, and so I was delighted to read a description of Isabel and myself in *A Song of Stone: Herstmonceux Castle*, a book written by Andrew Loman, now teaching English at the University of Newfoundland. Andrew taught at the castle for three summer terms and hopes to teach there again. He wrote:

When I first heard that a septuagenarian millionaire had donated Herstmonceux Castle to Queen's University, I envisioned a wizened Donald Trump, a man conferring magnificent gifts on his *alma mater* in order to construct a vulgar shrine to his own eminence. I imagined silk ties and pinky rings, tailored suits and cigars, wealth and a trophy wife, and more power than principle, a man in the mould of Jeffrey Archer or Conrad Black. It would have been repulsive, and it would have been sordid, and it would, in its way, have been fabulous.

The reality is far different. Bader is a small man who wears a beige overcoat and who shuffles. He's unassuming to the point of invisibility, and he dresses down to an almost alarming degree. (In his rise to riches, a wag might say, he has not forgotten the rags; he wears them still.) Physically—but only physically—he calls to mind Laszlo Carreidas, the millionaire who never laughs in Hergé's *Vol 714 Pour Sydney*, the man to whom Captain Haddock, mistaking him for a pauper, gives money.

And just as Bader spectacularly defies one's expectations, so too does Isabel Bader. Her manner reflects her childhood in rural Canada (she comes from Kirkland Lake in northern Ontario); she is the picture of a pioneer matriarch, a woman who won't brook nonsense, an angel of common sense. Her eyes are steely, her manner sober. Together they are far from what one would imagine a couple to be that can virtually on a whim buy a castle and then give it away. They seem like a couple that, in a frenzy of extravagance, would order a third cookie with their coffee.

Their asceticism is principled, however. Alfred Bader raised the issue of his appearance himself when I interviewed him. It's true, he admitted, that he doesn't dress fashionably. But the less we spend on ourselves, he said, the more we can give away. And perhaps the most astonishing thing about Alfred Bader is that when he says such things, he's in earnest. I try to imagine what I'd do with his resources, and I'm afraid I'd spend my money on silk ties and pinky rings. The Baders no doubt have their indulgences. But they also donate extraordinary sums to charity; the castle is only the most striking example of many. As one learns the scope of their generosity, one can't help but be impressed and humbled. "I am at heart a socialist," Bader told me, and one might plausibly suggest that his charity is a function of his political convictions, born of the tension between his socialist heart and his capitalist success.

We are so thankful that during the last few years we have become really good friends with two Milwaukeeans who have enriched our lives in very different ways. I have known Lucy and Norman Cohn, good friends of Jane and Marvin Klitsner, for many years, but not really well. Only after Norman died in 2000 did Isabel and I really get to know and love Lucy (Plate 75). We have never known a woman in her eighties so active and caring of others. She received a diploma in nursing from the Jewish Hospital in Cincinnati, and after working as a nurse, a head nurse in psychiatry, a time in the army, many volunteer jobs, and bringing up a family, she eventually took a bachelor's degree in nursing from the University of Wisconsin-Milwaukee and, in 1972, a doctorate in psychology, guidance and counseling from Marquette University.

Lucy now spends much of her day counseling patients referred to her by doctors who know of her wonderful ability and kindness. These patients often come early in the morning or after 5 p.m. so as not to interfere with their work. Lucy then spends much of the day in nursing homes. Hardest but most gratifying for her may be the Thursdays spent at the Columbia—St. Mary's Hospital hospice. One day a nurse in the hospice said "Lucy Cohn is as close to a saint as you can find."

Lucy and Isabel really enjoy spending time together going to plays (where I sometimes join them), ballets, and concerts. Early in June 2006, she went with us to Ottawa when I received an honorary doctorate there. She stayed with us with Isabel's sister Marion, and we all appreciated the easy direct flight, courtesy of Daniel's gift of a time-sharing flight. We returned to Milwaukee on Friday, June 9, to leave for England the following Monday. That Saturday, Lucy was taken to Columbia Hospital for a heart valve replacement, followed shortly

thereafter by the insertion of a pacemaker. Always very slim—
she says she had to go on a diet of extra bananas and
milkshakes to put on weight before she could get into the
army—Lucy now weighs less than 80 pounds, and so these
operations must have been very difficult.

They went well, but a nightmare followed when she was
taken for rehabilitation to the Sarah Chudnow Campus, a
facility of the Jewish Home and Care Center. The community
spent millions on impressive bricks and mortar, but the care
experienced by Lucy was abysmal. Lucy's cardiologist impressed on the staff that the pills to be given daily were vital.
They were not given to her there, and when she left they were
not with her other pills. She observed even worse treatment of
other patients, and when she left, she handed the administrator
a detailed report (sadly without keeping a copy). That administrator was just quitting; I wonder whether she gave the report
to her successor. One of the most important commandments
in the Bible is in Leviticus XIX: Do not stand idly by the blood
of your neighbor. I hope that when Lucy is fully recovered, she
will keep that commandment by ensuring that others of the
Jewish community do not encounter what she experienced at
the Sarah Chudnow Campus.

Our second great friend is Joseph Bernstein (Plate 76), one of
Milwaukee's ablest lawyers, of the firm of Godfrey & Kahn,
with a BS in economics from the Wharton School at the
University of Pennsylvania and a juris doctor from the University of Wisconsin Law School. I don't know whether he
spends more time on his legal practice, specializing in financial
planning and various investment ventures, or with *pro bono*
activities. These include the Blood Center of Southeastern
Wisconsin, the Blood Research Institute, the Milwaukee Public
Museum, and many Jewish organizations. Joe and I worked
together first eliminating our local Chabad's substantial debt
and are now building its endowment fund. We have formed
a partnership, Bader-Bernstein, LLC, with investments in

chemical companies. One of these is Materia, utilizing the catalysts invented by the Nobel Laureate Professor Robert H. Grubbs. Joe has joined Materia's Board of Directors, and I would not be surprised if Materia grew to be as important a chemical company as Sigma-Aldrich has become. Incidentally, Sigma-Aldrich is the exclusive seller of research quantities of Materia's catalysts.

Joe often joins me for Friday lunch at the Astor Hotel, and our conversation moves briskly from chemical companies to Jewish charities and on to art. He and Audrey, his wife, love art, though mainly modern art, but have now also acquired some fine old masters from Alfred Bader Fine Arts. Luckily they own two homes, one here and the other in California, so lack of wall space has not yet become a major problem. Unfortunately for me, he and Audrey spend a lot of time in California, but we really enjoy the shared interests we have. I think that Joe and I have a very similar outlook on life, and my friendship with him has helped fill the terrible void left by Marvin Klitsner's death.

As I think back on my life, I realize how lucky I have been. If I had stayed with my biological mother, Mama in Vienna, I probably would not have survived the war. If mother, Muttili, had not applied for me to go on the *Kindertransport* to England in December 1938, I might well have died with her in Theresienstadt. If I had not found such a good summer job with the Murphy Paint Company in 1943, I might not have gone to Harvard, nor come to Milwaukee in 1950. Most importantly, if I had not gone on the *Franconia* to England in July 1949, I would not have met Isabel, and what would my life be like today? If I had not met Danny, would I have two such good sons? If I had not met Marvin Klitsner, where would Sigma-Aldrich be today, and would the Helen Bader Foundation exist? And what if Aldrich in its first twenty years had had serious competition rather than only one major competitor, Eastman

211

Kodak, not really interested in the business, and eventually leaving it altogether?

And on and on. Muttili had a word for it: "*beschert*;" it was meant to be, that I should live to help many, the neediest and the ablest, as Isabel and I are trying to do.

APPENDIX

A Video Presentation about Dr. Alfred Bader
*On the occasion of his receiving the Centennial Humanitarian Award from the American Jewish Committee in Milwaukee, Wisconsin*

**Introduction**
For you to understand the following remarks, I need to introduce myself and describe how I came to know Dr. Alfred Bader.

My name is Yechiel Bar-Chaim, and I represent the American Jewish Joint Distribution Committee in the Czech Republic; the various successor states to the former Yugoslavia, Algeria, and Tunisia.

When Alfred Bader asked to channel through the Joint his annual grants to various programs in the Czech Republic, I became his liaison. Soon, in addition to his gifts for chemistry prizes, traveling fellowships in the history of baroque art, and community development projects for Roma (Gypsies), Alfred began to give substantial donations to the Joint to be used at my discretion to "help the most needy people you come across' in the former Yugoslavia.

In the course of my work I am exposed to a wide range of people:
- Living in seven countries
- Representing all generations
- Active in different fields of interest
- Showing such a variety of character and temperament that sometimes I find it mind-boggling.

Being able to respond to this multiplicity of contact demands:
- Attention
- Concentration
- Patience, and
- A duty to Empathize.

At the same time, by the very nature of things, I am myself indelibly marked by this experience.

I have to learn to recognize complexity and be sensitive to differences and nuances, to respect aspects of life and attitudes that are far from anything I knew before or was ever brought up to appreciate:
- Orthodox Jews and old-time Communists
- Holocaust survivors and rebellious youth

212

■ Introverted, serious-minded Czechs and observant yet playful Jews from the island of Djerba in Tunisia.

And then—without any advance warning—into my very own art gallery of character portraits, carefully collected and sorted and analyzed over many years, walks Dr. Alfred Bader.

■ Viennese and American
■ A chemist and an art collector
■ A Bible expert and a businessman
■ A hard-driving entrepreneur and a self-made man who is also a pretty stubborn old-school moralist
■ This hopelessly romantic husband and yet shrewd judge of men and ideas
■ Someone careful with every penny, who yet can turn around and give away so much with an open hand
■ A philanthropist whose projects must suit his personal convictions, who at the same time will say to me, "Use your own discretion and I hope you"ll come back to me when you need more!"

In all honesty nothing in my—fairly rich—experience ever prepared me to meet up with my good friend Alfred.

Now, when I am still perplexed and in the middle of trying to figure him out, you're already signaling with this great humanitarian award an act of completion. For me we are just in the midst of a process.

What I can share with you on this occasion are the marks Alfred has imprinted on me.

He has freed up and spurred my moral imagination, and after encountering him I suddenly find myself caught up in new and unexpected fields of activity.

What did I have to do until now with Gypsies and their virtually insolvable predicament?

Who knew anything about developing job opportunities for the disabled?

Why should anyone focused on dealing with Jews and others in distress end up negotiating for chemical laboratory space at a major Czech university?

And how did I find myself initiating a post-graduate seminar in baroque art and involved in a few other weird projects that frankly have no link to what I started out to do?

Once I complained to Alfred when the complexities of the Gypsy dilemma became too great for me, "Alfred, you got me into this!" to which he somberly replied, "Yechiel, I'm not the one who said Thou shalt not stand idly by the blood of thy brother."

The confidence he has shown humbles me, while at the same time his expectations stretch my capabilities to the utmost.

Into my world of practical good deeds Alfred has introduced his own far-reaching dimensions. So please count me as one of his many beneficiaries.

Yechiel Bar-Chaim
Paris, May 2006

PLATE 70: A poster advertising the Lieben Prize.

PLATE 71 (left): David and Chellie's wedding.

PLATE 72 (below): David's family.

PLATE 73: Daniel's family.

# CENTENNIAL HUMAN RELATIONS AWARD
## *presented to*
# Dr. Alfred Bader & Daniel Bader
### BONNIE BOCKL AND LEON JOSEPH, CO-CHAIRS

*How do you say thank you to one of the most committed and generous families Milwaukee has ever known? Dr. Alfred and his son Daniel Bader not only do good but they also do it so well, and they leave a better world in their wake.*

*All of us are charitable to the best of our capacities, but the Baders are unique in bettering the human condition, whether by the incredible donation of a castle to the Canadian University that welcomed Dr. Bader, when others had quotas limiting the presence of Jewish students or by the ongoing commitment to special needs early childhood education in Israel, sweaters knitted in Kosovo, soup kitchens in Sarajevo, music for youth in Milwaukee, Jewish education, scholarships and awards for promising chemists, and everything in between; it is almost impossible to count.*

*Through their strong commitment to a diverse range of causes they do not stand idly by the pain and needs of their neighbors, but actively and passionately seek out ways of healing the world.*

*Though it is impossible to adequately thank them, please join us as we try.*

*Sincerely,*

Bonnie Bockl Joseph          Leon Joseph

Milwaukee Chapter
62nd Annual Meeting
Tuesday, May 30, 2006

*The American Jewish Committee* AJC

*honoring*
Dr. Alfred Bader
and Dr. Daniel Bader

AJC
American Jewish Committee
A Century of Leadership

PLATE 74: The American Jewish Committee Award.

PLATE 75 (top): Lucy Cohn.

PLATE 76 (below): Joseph Bernstein.

22.1.42. Food 050
28.1.42. Cinema 030
29.1.42. Haircut 040
31.1.42. Laundry 038
Foto 025
3.1.42 Projection 010
4.1.42. Envelopes 005
Mail 025
R. [Cal. Cert] 020
6.1.42. Surveying 010
Stamps 006
12.1.42. I.S.S. 010
Room & Board 800
15.1.42. Co. gum. 15
Food 05

15.1.42. Laundry 048
Mail 25
Stamps 32
Stamps 130
16.1.42. Book 005
Ch. 010
17.1.42. Stamps 015
22.1.42. Room Bd. 1600
Cinema 20
Stamps 06
Draughting 10
Stamps 10
25.1.42. Rachel 165
Ins. Schauff. 150
Stamps 143

PLATE 77: My expenses.

PLATE 78 (top left): Adina Shapiro.

PLATE 79 (top right): Yechiel Bar-Chaim.

PLATE 80 (left): Rabbi Mendel Shmotkin.

# Alfred Bader: Chemist cares for Karlín

**PRAGUE PROFILE**

BY ALAN LEVY

## Making money work wonders

W hen Alfred Bader was growing up in his native Vienna in the early 1930s, he used to spend summers visiting the family of his Jewish governess, Hilda Kozáková, in the south Moravian village of Miroslav, near the Austrian border. Hilda's brother Robert Herzog was a businessman traveling from village to village visiting butchers to buy the skins of slaughtered animals in order to sell leather to village shoemakers. The boy would tag along to help unload hides, salt them and store them in the family cellar.

Watching Herzog, then a communist, sweet-talk his clients or bargain with a tanner from Mikulov "was the beginning of my business education," says Bader, now a 79-year-old multimillionaire philanthropist who gives away half of each year's income to good causes, many of them in the Czech Republic. He makes annual gifts of at least $5 million (135 million Kč); this year's "will certainly exceed $15 million."

There were weekend journeys to Prague, too, centered around the Old-New Synagogue and the Jewish Cemetery. Near there, a vendor sold drawings for 5 Czechoslovak crowns apiece. "Given the choice of spending 5 crowns on a drawing or on 10 ice-cream cones" Bader recalls, "I usually bought the drawings, many of which I still have."

This was the beginning of Alfred Bader's career as an art collector and dealer, whose milestones include buying a painting for $55,000 in 1979 — a study of Rembrandt's father that was originally disqualified as an authentic Rembrandt by experts in Amsterdam — and then proving it was a real Rembrandt. It was recently appraised at $10 million when he gave it to his Canadian alma mater, Queen's University in Kingston, Ontario. Since he also founded and headed the Sigma-Aldrich global chemical conglomerate from 1955 to 1991, his candid memoir is appropriately titled *Adventures of a Chemist Collector* (see box for details).

Alfred Bader became a Nazi target at 13 when Hitler annexed Austria. But when the British government allocated 10,000 visas for Jewish children between 12 and 16, Bader was placed on the first *Kindertransport* train, which left Vienna Dec. 10, 1938.

Lodged with a Jewish family in Brighton, he enjoyed a good year in school. But when he turned 16 in the spring of 1940, he was interned as an "enemy alien" in a roundup of potential threats between ages 16 and 65. Thrown in with German prisoners-of-war and labeled a POW himself, the teenager was sent to prison camps on the Isle of Man and then in Canada, where a guard named Bruno, father of six, used to wake him every morning by "playing with my penis." Fortunately, the son of his British sponsors resided in Montréal and Bader was released to them after 15 months of internment.

Though he'd passed the matriculation exam for McGill University, he was rejected there and by the University of Toronto because their Jewish quotas were filled. Accepted by the applied-science faculty of Queen's University, the young man with a thick German accent proved a brilliant student who, in three successive years, was awarded bachelor's degrees in engineering chemistry (1945) and history (1946) and a master's in chemistry (1947). He is now Queen's University's most generous benefactor.

Young Bader's appetite for paint and chemicals was whetted by a summer job as a lab technician at a paint company in Montréal. Upon graduation, he went south of the border on a

VLADIMIR WEISS/The Prague Post
**Benefactor Bader** will pull the puppet strings for Patrik Gadžo, 8.

fellowship in organic chemistry to Harvard, where he took another master's in 1949 and a doctorate in 1950. That year, he moved to Milwaukee, Wisconsin, which is still his home city, to work as a research chemist for the Pittsburgh Plate Glass Company.

### A marriage deferred

During his 1949 Harvard summer vacation, Bader sailed from Québec City to Liverpool for his first return visit to Europe. Two days before the ship docked, he met Isabel Overton, the daughter of a Protestant lay preacher from northern Ontario. After a week's courtship in London, he proposed marriage to her. She hesitated — mostly because of their religious differences and his determination to raise any children as Jews, meaning that their mother would have to be Jewish or convert to Judaism.

Their courtship continued by correspondence after he returned to the States and she settled in England as a schoolteacher in Sussex. In her 80th letter to him (he kept them all), she wrote that she didn't think their marriage would work.

On the rebound, he met Helen Ann Daniels, from a South Dakota religious background similar to Isabel's but willing to convert. They were

married in Milwaukee by an orthodox rabbi in 1952 and had two sons.

His heart, however, still belonged to Isabel and, in 1975 — propelled by a recurrent dream in which her gaunt preacher father asked him why he wasn't with her — he looked her up in Sussex. In 1981, "Danny" divorced him so he could marry Isabel.

### A playground for outsiders

Partly because he has roots in southern Moravia, Bader endows prestigious annual prizes and a professorship in organic chemistry at Masaryk University in Brno. He also funds Bader Art History Fellowships for Czech scholars to do research, mostly abroad, and Bader Science Fellowships enabling four Czech students a year to do their doctoral work at the Imperial College in London and three U.S. Ivy League universities: Harvard, Columbia and Pennsylvania.

There is a non-elitist side to Bader's generosity, epitomized by his motto: "Save my money for somebody left out." In recent years, he and his wife have been active in humanitarian and educational aid programs for Roma (Gypsies).

One of the reasons they visited Prague in June is a case history in how philanthropy can prove profitable for everyone:

In Prague 8's flood-devastated Karlín sector, the Molákova street special school for 120 children classified as mentally or socially underdeveloped (90 percent of them Roma) was heavily damaged by last August's waters. City funds weren't readily forthcoming to repair the school. So the children were dispersed to study in special shifts elsewhere, if at all.

To encourage action, Bader pledged $20,000 (now 540,000 Kč) toward repair of the school *if* City Hall would match that sum. Neither school director Jitka Vargová nor the municipal officials to whom she brought Bader's offer had ever heard of matching grants, so the bureaucrats threw up their hands and gave her the entire 5.5 million Kč needed to restore the school.

Pleased but embarrassed, Vargová offered the Baders their money back. No way! Instead, they re-earmarked the money to dredge a sea of contaminated mud coating the school's garden. When work started, it was discovered that soil and plant contamination was much less than feared. So the money was reassigned again — this time for architect Josef Smola to create a state-of-the-art playground in the school's garden.

Complete with slides, swings, climbing wall, gazebo and wicked-witch hut, the playground was opened on Friday the 13th by the roly-poly, cherubic philanthropist and his slender, elegant wife. During the speech-making and after the ribbon-cutting, this loving and generous couple held hands, already enjoying their gift as much as the kids who couldn't and didn't wait to start using it.

*Alan Levy can be reached at alevy@praguepost.com*

## VITAL STATISTICS

**Born** April 28, 1924, in Vienna
**Career** Research chemist and group leader 1950–54 for Pittsburgh Plate Glass, Milwaukee, Wisconsin, where he and his lawyer founded Aldrich Chemical Co., supplying research chemicals, 1955, president, 1955–81; chairman, 1981–91. In 1981, Aldrich merged with biochemicals supplier Sigma of St. Louis; president, Sigma–Aldrich, 1975–80, chairman, 1980–91. Upon involuntary retirement, founded Bader Fine Arts gallery, Milwaukee.
**Author** *Adventures of a Chemist Collector*, Weidenfeld & Nicolson, London, 1995: out of print but can be ordered from amazon.com by ISBN 0-297-83461-4
**Married** Helen Ann "Danny" Daniels, 1952, divorced, 1981 two sons: David, Daniel; married Isabel Overton, 1982

PLATE 81: The article in *The Prague Post*.

## 18

# Help the Neediest and Ablest: Promoting Communication Among People

What are the roots of our efforts to be charitable? With me, these are in my early childhood. Muttili gave to many people who asked even when she herself had almost nothing, and there were so many in need in Vienna during the Depression. In my first year in school when I was six, our very good teacher, Heinrich Strehly, compared my good clothes with those of some of the other kids and asked Muttili to send money to help them. Muttili's husband, a multimillionaire, had died in 1922 without teaching her how to manage his great wealth. During the deep Depression following the inflation, the wealth disappeared, and by the time I was fourteen, there was little left.

For some time, I had been active as a stamp dealer, using my earnings to buy basic foods. When I left Vienna on the first *Kindertransport* to England on December 10, 1938, I left with one US dollar that an old friend had given to Muttili and some stamps I hoped to be able to sell in England. An elderly lady, Mrs Sarah Wolff, had paid £50 to guarantee that I would not become a burden on the community and then paid a guinea a week for my room and board. But I had absolutely no pocket money and was only too happy to sell stamps to other kids in school. I was overjoyed when one day I received a letter from old friends of my paternal grandmother, dealers in jewelry in London, who sent me a large white £5 note, which immediately found its way into the post office savings book I had opened with the money I got for my one US dollar.

The Brighton Technical College that I attended beginning in January 1940 was too far away from home in Hove for me to return for lunch, and so Mrs Ethel Scharff, where I boarded, gave me nine pence. I discovered that I could have beans on toast at the nearby Lyons Corner House for five pence halfpenny, and of course I saved the three pence halfpenny daily. I watched my expenditures very carefully: ten shillings for a pair of shoes and fifty shillings for a dark suit at Burton the Tailor.

In the internment camp in Canada, one could earn 20 cents a day, for instance making camouflage nets, but I decided to forgo this pay in order to study for the McGill Matriculation Examinations.

I was among the first to be freed from the camp in Canada. It was more than I could possibly have hoped that Martin Wolff, the son of Mrs Sarah Wolff in Hove, would secure my release. Here was a man who had just lost his wife and had five daughters, four of them unmarried, yet he took me into his small home and immediately helped me to apply to university. The day after my release, he took time off from his job to go with me to apply to McGill. On the way, he gave me CAN $5 in pocket money but did not say how long it was to last. When I was turned down at McGill, he wrote to Toronto to make an application for me there, and when I was finally admitted to Queen's on November 15, he paid for my first year's tuition; I think this was CAN $250 for the year. I could hardly believe my good fortune and was determined to do my very best.

I found a comfortable room near the campus which, with breakfast, cost CAN $3 a week. Every day except Friday I had a good lunch at the student union for 35 cents. For the evening meals, I bought bread and apples and cheese, and on Friday evening I was invited to the home of a wonderful family, the Isaac Cohens, for a delicious meal. I still have my little book (Plate 77) detailing all of my expenses: so many cents for food, so many for the occasional haircut, so many for postage stamps to write to Martin Wolff.

At the end of that academic year, I won my first scholarship, the Roberta McCullough scholarship in English, CAN $30. Mr. Wolff found me a job for the summer at RCA Victor, inspecting the soldering of radios, and although it was boring, I earned 45 cents an hour and of course saved all of it. When I returned to Queen's in September, I was invited to join the Science '44 coop. This was a great blessing. We paid CAN $8 a week for room and board and at the end of the academic year received a small refund. Also, in 1943, I received two scholarships and a bursary that took care of my tuition. That summer I found a wonderful job with the Murphy Paint Company in Montreal paying CAN $130 a month formulating paints and lacquers.

My life was changed by the kindness and generosity of the Wolff family and Queen's University. The scholarships were extremely important to me, and naturally I determined that if ever I could, I would also establish such scholarships. The first opportunity I had was in the spring of 1948 when Martin Wolff died of a heart attack while I was a student at Harvard. Though he had five daughters, he left me CAN $1,000 in his will. I used that money to establish the Martin Wolff scholarship in civil engineering at Queen's University.

From the time I went to the Murphy Paint Company for my second summer, I have been truly happy with my work as a chemist. Starting Aldrich in 1951 was a great time, because the early 1950s was the most fortuitous time to be starting a company to sell chemicals for research, a fine chemical company. There was really just the one company in the United States, Eastman Kodak, with whom I was told I could not possibly compete. They had only some four thousand products, however, and were not really interested in the business. I was, and these were the very years when the demand for new products was growing rapidly. I spoke German and was able

217

to travel to Europe and buy many new products there. In the United States more students were going to universities to study chemistry so there was an ever-increasing demand for new products for research there and in the pharmaceutical industry. I loved my work and looked forward to each day, wondering whom I could help that day. I could not pay a great deal, but wanted to provide a stable workplace, health insurance, and profit-sharing for my employees. When eventually I was able to establish the first Bader scholarship in chemistry at Queen's, it made me immensely proud to be giving back.

For the past many years, we have been in a wonderful position to help people. Isabel and I don't need much for ourselves. Our good friend Marvin Klitsner arranged for my sons' trusts each to have 6.5 percent of Aldrich—long before Aldrich was worth much—and so both are well-to-do and know that Isabel and I have wills, also written by Marvin. These wills leave almost everything to a foundation, just as Danny did. My son Daniel, who administers this charity, the Helen Bader Foundation, will administer our foundation also, but why should we not help others in our lifetime? Help for others and pleasure for us. Yet giving money away is not all pleasure, and in fact it is the most difficult of my four current jobs.

Luckily we have been helped by good and able people. Daniel has seventeen able people in the Helen Bader Foundation, and he himself is always willing to help us. He and Linda often make suggestions, particularly for local causes.

Marvin Klitsner, of course, had guided us in everything, but sadly he died in Jerusalem in August 2001. His older daughter, Frances Wolff, has taken his place on the Board of the Helen Bader Foundation, and one of Marvin's nineteen grand-children, Adina Shapiro (Plate 78), has also been most helpful to us. A remarkable young woman with a Hebrew University law degree, she was co-chair of MECA, the Middle East Children's Association, which tries to bring together Israeli and Pal-estinian teachers to discuss how best to teach children. Such meetings are very difficult to arrange with the mutual hatred engendered by the second intifada, but Adina and her able Palestinian co-chair, Dr. Abdullah Ghassan, have succeeded in arranging for several meetings, two at Herstmonceux Castle which we have funded, and other larger meetings in Turkey. MECA has also been funded by the Konrad Adenauer Foundation, and the US and EU governments.

I have long wondered whether life in Israel would be safer and better if Arab Israelis had been treated equally. Israel is a democracy, there are Arab members of the *Knesset*, and public signs are in Hebrew, English, and Arabic. But in the infrastructure of Arab towns and villages, educationally and socially, there has not been equality. Adina agrees. So now we give her several hundred thousand dollars annually through the Foundation for the Jewish Community, which she spends as she sees fit. I believe that since we are dealing with Marvin's granddaughter, we need no accounting, but she has told us that she has spent it on diverse projects, most recently on improving Israeli Arab libraries. I have asked her to explain. She wrote:

One of Israel's greatest challenges as a Jewish Democratic State has been its treatment of its Arab citizens. Although many organizations, projects, and research have addressed this issue, the past few years of intifada have also marked a significant decline in Jewish-Arab relationships within the State of Israel, indicating that strategic approaches were significantly needed. We chose to address this question by using two principles. First, private initiative with the Arab sector must replace the government agencies and should engage them in seeing their role as serving the Israeli population in its entirety. Second, the Jewish-Arab question cannot be addressed as an independent "problem" but must find its way into the mainstream issues that the State must address. In keeping with these principles we decided to

219

address the field of the public libraries in Israel, which was in dire need of incentives to reach out to their communities. Encouraging the public libraries to take a community-based approach was an optimal opportunity to look at all parts of the Israeli community with its many cultures, religions, and political beliefs.

With the help of the funds at my disposal, as well as some matching funds from our family in memory of my grandfather, we funded approximately thirty projects a year in public libraries throughout the country. The projects, which took place equally in Jewish and Arab libraries, reach out to the community in different ways such as programs for toddlers, single parents, youth in distress, and documenting the oral history of communities. All of the librarians meet once a month in a joint forum where they discuss the professional challenges of their community-based programs as well as Jewish-Arab relationships in the country. The entire program has been done in partnership with the Ministry of Education and some local municipalities, leveraging the funds with matching governmental grants for the Arab sector that did not exist previously.

The outcome of the first few years has led to the establishment of several Bedouin libraries in unrecognized villages as well as Arab libraries in Haifa and in Mukeble, where no public libraries existed prior to this. Furthermore, contents have been brought into the libraries by the directors infusing some of their experiences with the different populations to their communities. The ultimate success of the programs, however, in my eyes has been that as different peripheral populations in Israel address the needs of their communities, they see professional cooperation with their Jewish or Arab colleagues as integral and complementary parts of their pursuits. This is a sound basis for not only paying lip service to concepts of equality and diversity but actually implementing it on the ground.

Daniel is on the Board of Trustees of the American Jewish Joint Distribution Committee, the Joint, a wonderful, almost century-old organization that helps people in need—and not only Jews—around the world. We have made good friends and been helped enormously by Yechiel Bar-Chaim (Plate 79), who operates from the Joint office in Paris.

Born in Washington, DC, in 1945, Yechiel has studied at Harvard, the Sorbonne, and the Hebrew University in Jerusalem. He served in the US Army, lastly as captain in the NATO Military Headquarters in Belgium from 1969 to 1972. After his move to Israel in January 1974, he held several industrial and governmental jobs and served in the reserves as a press liaison officer of the Israel Defense Forces. Since 1986, he has been working for the Joint and in 1989 came to Vienna to help the tens of thousands of Jews then leaving the Soviet Union for the West. Later that year he was also made responsible for the JDC programs in what was then Yugoslavia and Czechoslovakia and recently in Tunisia and Algeria as well. He and his family moved from Vienna to Paris in 1991.

What a background, but most important, he is such a caring, totally reliable man.

And, of course, many like-minded people really enjoy working with him. To me, the most outstanding of these is an American writer and humanist, Paul Polansky. Originally from Mason City, Iowa, Polansky moved to Prague in 1990 where he became a Romany rights activist, documenting how the Nazis treated Roma. In 1999, he volunteered to live in Kosovo, trying to help Roma threatened by the Albanian majority. He now calls Kosovo and Nis, in southern Serbia, his homes.

The Nis gypsies live under the worst living conditions anywhere in Europe. Some of their homes were built in an historic Jewish cemetery, while another part of the cemetery became their garbage dump and open-air latrines. It was Yechiel who told us about Polansky and his work with the Roma. The scenes he described were so dreadful that we immediately

221

decided we would make a donation to fund an employment project that Yechiel and Paul hoped to set up. The idea was to employ the Roma living in one part of the cemetery to clean up the other part. These efforts with the Roma produced a remarkable cleanup of what had been a site of shame and an opportunity for the workers to earn money, often for the first time in their lives. Yechiel described this so clearly when he nominated Paul for the John Humphrey Freedom Award in 2005:

> Paul put together teams of Roma workers from the cemetery settlement (called "the Jewish village") to do the work. For better pay than they usually get, these Roma workers took out 220,000 wheelbarrows full of indescribable refuse over seven weeks' time. They spent eight hours a day in the sweltering heat, sometimes up to their chests, maneuvering heavy, seventeenth-century tombstones to get them out of the cesspools. Some of them had never had a job for so long in their entire lives.

More important than saving cemeteries is saving lives. Again to quote Yechiel when he nominated Paul:

> When the Albanian refugees came back to Kosovo, some of their extremists drove the Kosovar Roma out of their settlements and burned down their houses. Near Mitrovica the UN put the displaced Roma in camps, "temporary" ones that just happened to be located on land where the toxic wastes of nearby mines had been dumped. Paul warned the UN that the sites were dangerous, but to no avail. That was in 1999. Repeated appeals and alarming medical reports since then have never budged the authorities.
>
> The camps are still there and now there is a generation of Roma children showing lead in the blood at unprecedented levels: above 65 mg/dl (About 10 mg/dl is considered safe).

The affected children (and adults) are suffering irreparable brain damage. They stagger around disoriented, vomiting, some going in and out of coma. Paul is the one on the spot. The one taking a child in coma to a hospital in Belgrade for treatment. (Actually he had to smuggle her in, because Roma kids don't have any identification papers). The one finding a new residence for the family so Nikolina doesn't go back to the camp when she's better. The one badgering the alphabet soup of international organizations that we trust to prevent these tragedies from happening, the ones who aren't supposed to let children get lead poisoning in their camps: UNMIK, UNHCR; WHO ...

When no one stepped forward, Dr. Bader again agreed to make a grant. Now Paul has taken a new set of kids to the hospital in Mitrovica. Some of them are beyond saving, it appears. Paul will be finding ways to help the fathers become self-employed so they can move away from the camps. Now Paul has the International Committee of the Red Cross calling for their immediate evacuation and scurrying to find trailers (caravans) for the families Paul helps to escape these UN-sponsored death traps.

The world is truly blessed to have men like Yechiel Bar-Chaim and Paul Polansky working together.

Working with Yechiel and Paul was not our first involvement with the Roma. We first learned of their plight in Czechoslovakia years ago. We know that during the war, they had been treated almost as brutally by the Nazis as Jews were, but while Jews spoke up after the war and were compensated by Germany, the Roma had hardly anyone to speak up for them and even now have received little compensation. The Roma are disliked almost everywhere because they try to live in their closed society. Some are thieves, and their children, often not speaking Czech, are put into schools for disadvantaged children. It is a vicious circle that can be broken only through

223

education. We first became involved by funneling support through Charter 77 and now through to the Joint, with *Nadace Via*, an organization in Prague that supports Roma educational efforts.

Eventually I asked Yechiel what he thought of our collaboration, and his response almost overwhelmed me:

How might one characterize the philanthropic giving you channel through the Joint (and thus through me)?

There is a saying attributed to the great teacher Hillel in the Talmudic Tractate, *Pirke Avot*, (The Sayings of the Fathers II: 6), which in English goes as follows: "In a place where there are no men, strive to be a man."

Now this phrase has two markedly different interpretations, both of which you seem to fulfill.

It might be thought that virtuous behavior requires interaction with other, like-minded men. Yet here Hillel characteristically stresses the importance of individual independence. *One should be virtuous even in the absence of any partners or observers.* When it comes to supporting a soup kitchen for the poor in Novi Sad (Serbia) or vocational training for Roma refugees from Kosovo living near Skopje (Macedonia), I am well placed to assure you that when we began these projects no one anywhere in the vicinity had any idea who Alfred Bader was. And I presume that even now these places mean little to those who have known you for years.

You yourself refused any sort of plaque or naming ceremony in these locations, saying justly, "My family has never had any connection to the Balkans." The most we have been able to do for you is to name as "Bader Vests' the sweaters made by paraplegic women in Sarajevo for individuals living in institutions or homebound elderly.

The second interpretation—which I like better—has a "High Noon" ring about it. *Where no one else will step forward, you do it.* The first project we ever did together exemplifies this approach. When the Bosnian War ended, there were nearly 200 NGOs working in Sarajevo, all basically looking for ways to help the most deprived, the neediest victims of the conflict. Left out of these considerations, however, was the vital center, the capable young men and women whose potential was being ignored. You enabled us to introduce entrepreneurship training for these individuals, and based on the same rationale our local partners built an important micro-lending operation to go with it that still thrives today.

You have, I would say also introduced a so-called "Bader Corollary" to Hillel's Talmudic dictum. Phrase it this way, "Where there are men present, go elsewhere." Thus, when other funders are already helping, your tendency has been to say, "Count me out. I'll save my resources for those causes that others overlook." Thus you were distinctly reluctant to assist after the catastrophic floods in the Czech Republic in 2002, precisely because everyone else was rushing to chip in. Only when I found an overlooked, nearly orphaned school in Prague which served the youngest mentally challenged children—most of them Roma—a school with a playground dangerously polluted by two meters of floodwaters, did you come forward. If I am not mistaken a picture of a cheerfully costumed child taken during the festive re-opening of that playground should grace this book.

In your philanthropy you take special pleasure, Alfred, it seems to me in recognizing merit that has been heretofore overlooked. Just like you like discovering masterpieces of art in unsuspected paintings. How else to understand your efforts to build up the reputation of that until now less than well-known nineteenth-century Czech chemist, Josef Loschmidt, or your lonely efforts to support the Jewish School in Vienna in memory of its noble headmaster at the time of the *Anschluss*, or your re-establishment of the Ignaz

Lieben Prize for scientific achievement in the former Habs-burg Empire, a prize initially established by a prominent Jewish family in Vienna that also fell victim to Nazi depredations.

By my reading, you like to combine a certain sense of righteous indignation (drawn perhaps from your faithful teaching over the years of the Hebrew prophets) with an unswerving respect for personal character (a trait in my experience which no one who had ever studied at Harvard can ever fully escape). Thus the sterling record of the British Quakers in saving Jewish children from the Nazis (including yourself) during World War II had endeared them to you forever.

Of course you would never describe your philanthropy in the terms I have used above. As you always like to tell me, "I just like to help 'good people.'" Yet that seemingly straightforward ethical principle has proven to be one of our most challenging issues.

Thanks to one of your grants, JDC-Israel was able to train Roma—living under frightful conditions of poverty and multiple discrimination in East Jerusalem—to work as caterers or cleaning staff in hotels. But when these Roma insisted on being paid in black so as not to put their welfare benefits in jeopardy, you pulled the plug. My colleagues in Israel are still trying to figure out how to do it right.

A special trip to Vienna—and from what I could tell your entire afternoon with Isabel—was upset when I informed you that I had used some of the funds you had put at my discretion to organize through the Jewish Community of Zagreb a summer camp on the Dalmatian Coast for young juvenile delinquents. But juvenile delinquents just didn't qualify as "good people." Only when we were able to clarify much later that these youngsters were in reality only "chil-dren at risk" who had good chances of not becoming juvenile delinquents if given the right care, could the argument be settled and the project carry on.

More seriously, this debate between us has continued over your considerable philanthropic aid to projects in Serbia. Certainly before, but even after, Slobodan Milosevic was deposed as the leader of Serbia and Montenegro and put on trial in The Hague, you felt uncomfortable about such assistance. In making the case to you for putting mentally retarded adults to work producing furniture or providing a modern, sanitary kitchen for children from Kosovo still living in refugee camps years after the war ended, I have sometimes imagined the scene when Abraham had to argue with the Almighty on behalf of even the smallest number of virtuous residents in Sodom.

What a delight it is to be able to work with a man of such strong character and principles! In discussing which path to take in directing your gifts towards worthy goals we have to wrestle over questions of morality and politics. I love it.

At any given moment your thoughts and reactions seem to reach back in time. They draw on your varied past, coursing over the so markedly different phases of your own life. They touch on fierce loyalties and acute sensitivities that sometimes I can only guess at. Vienna: England; the internment camp in Quebec, Queen's University in Canada; Harvard; Milwaukee; Prague ... they all speak in many different voices through you and through your special generosity.

Alfred, I feel I am especially privileged to work with you.

The biggest challenge of course is that so much remains to be done and to be done well. Whenever I become especially overwhelmed by the opportunities you open up for me, it is another phrase from *Pirke Avot* to which I turn. This teaching is attributed to Rabbi Tarphon, and perhaps it can bring you comfort as well.

"It is not up to you to finish the work, but neither are you free to turn aside from it."

Originally I asked Yechiel to help "the neediest people you can find in the former Yugoslavia." Following these instructions, he proceeded in cooperation with his JDC colleagues and the local Jewish communities to establish a burgeoning network of micro-credit institutions called "The JFund." Operating under the slogan "Charity is Our Last Choice," the project provides non-interest-bearing investment loans to organizations that have drawn up sound business plans to create sustainable jobs for the disabled or the disadvantaged. These loans have so far helped muscular dystrophy sufferers, the deaf, paraplegics, and other disabled persons to find productive remunerative work. For more information, please visit www.thejfund.com.

We first thought about helping in the Balkans when our old friend Jane Whistler returned from Sarajevo in 1994. She had gone there with an organization called "Through Heart to Peace" of the Dandelion Trust, Women helping Women. She told us about the great help being given by the small Jewish community led by its president Jacob Finci. The old synagogue in Sarajevo was the only safe building in the city, and the community was trying to help everyone it could. Jane wondered whether Isabel and I might be able to help in Bosnia, perhaps through Queen's University.

Following her suggestion, we learned that Queen's did indeed have a strong presence in Bosnia, through an organization with the cumbersome name International Centre for the Advancement of Community-Based Rehabilitation (ICACBR). Dr. Malcolm Peat, the director of the Queen's School of Rehabilitation Therapy, spent a long time in Sarajevo where help was indeed needed so badly. During a visit to Queen's in 1995, the dean of medicine at Sarajevo University reported that "in Sarajevo alone 12,000 citizens, including

2,500 children have been killed over the past three years. Our surgery has performed over two million operations to remove shrapnel!" We were very impressed by the work of Dr. Peat and Queen's students, so in 1995, we gave Queen's $500,000 to help Dr. Peat in his work with the traumatized in Bosnia.

One of our happiest days in Prague was Friday, June 13, 2003, described so clearly by Alan Levy in the *Prague Post* of June 25, 2003 (Plate 81).

### A playground for outsiders

Partly because he has roots in southern Moravia, Bader endows prestigious annual prizes and a professorship in organic chemistry at Masaryk University in Brno. He also funds Bader Art History Fellowships for Czech scholars to do research, mostly abroad, and Bader Science Fellowships enabling four Czech students a year to do their doctoral work at the Imperial College in London and three Ivy League universities: Harvard, Columbia and Pennsylvania.

There is a non-elitist side to Bader's generosity, epitomized by his motto: "Save my money for somebody left out." In recent years, he and his wife have been active in humanitarian and educational aid programs for Roma (Gypsies).

One of the reasons they visited Prague in June is a case history in how philanthropy can prove profitable for everyone:

In Prague's flood-devastated Karlín sector, the Molakova street special school for 120 children classified as mentally or socially underdeveloped (90 percent of them Roma) was heavily damaged by last August's waters. City funds weren't readily forthcoming to repair the school. So the children were dispersed to study in special shifts, if at all.

To encourage action, Bader pledged $20,000 (now 540,000 Kc) toward repair of the school *if* City Hall would match that sum. Neither school director Jitka Vargova nor the municipal officials to whom she brought Bader's offer

229

had ever heard of matching grants, so the bureaucrats threw up their hands and gave her the entire 5.5 million Kc needed to restore the school.

Pleased but embarrassed, Vargova offered the Baders their money back. No way! Instead, they re-earmarked the money to dredge a sea of contaminated mud coating the school's garden. When work started, it was discovered that soil and plant contamination was much less than feared. So the money was reassigned again—this time for architect Josef Smola to create a state-of-the-art playground in the school's garden.

Complete with slides, swings, climbing wall, gazebo and wicked-witch hut, the playground was opened on Friday the 13th by the roly-poly, cherubic philanthropist and his slender, elegant wife. During the speechmaking and after the ribbon-cutting, this loving and generous couple held hands, already enjoying their gift as much as the kids who couldn't and didn't wait to start using it.

Through the Joint we have also helped the ablest in art history and chemistry in the Czech Republic. After some initial difficulties, both proceed relatively straightforwardly. Two awards go to young Czech chemists, one in organic chemistry and one in bioorganic/bioinorganic chemistry chosen by the Czech Chemical Society. Awards for students in baroque art are chosen with the help of an old friend, Milena Bartlova, and in June of 2003 there was a ten-year celebration in Prague, organized by Yechiel, with some thirty art historians who had received the Bader awards. We were very pleased to see that students who ten years ago were much more confined in their areas of interest have now branched out confidently after study outside the Czech Republic. Some have found positions abroad but many have returned, enriching Czech art history.

Our most ambitious and difficult effort was to establish a chair in chemistry at the Masaryk University in Brno. To be called the Josef Loschmidt Chair, after one of the ablest Bohemian-born chemists of the nineteenth century (see Chapter 15 for more about Loschmidt), it was the first chair in chemistry funded in the Czech Republic by a private donor, and a foreigner at that. The only difficulty we foresaw at the beginning was that the academics in Brno insisted that the salary offered be very low, initially $20,000, so that the Loschmidt professor would not be paid more than they were. This would mean that few who had studied outside the Czech Republic would be interested in applying because they could earn far more elsewhere. Far greater difficulties followed.

The simple contract (see Appendix, following pages) that Dean Jan Slovak, Isabel, and I signed in August 2001 established a Josef Loschmidt professorship in physical organic chemistry, this position to be in addition to the existing faculty of the department. The university did indeed have great difficulty in attracting a suitable candidate, partly because of the low salary and partly because many able Czech chemists prefer to work in Prague, where they can be in close contact with the country's most prominent chemists. Eventually, a very promising young biochemist, Dr. Jiri Damborsky, applied. He had worked at the Masaryk University for seven years after receiving his PhD there and had won the Bader Award in bioorganic chemistry in 2003. Our belief that he was an excellent choice has been borne out by the fine scientific work he does and also by his efforts to make Josef Loschmidt's chemistry known. As he came from within the university, we expected his department to find a junior to replace him. This has still not happened, probably for the same reasons that made finding the chemist for the Loschmidt Chair so problematic in the first place.

But a much larger problem arose. Professor Damborsky received ample funding for his research, particularly from the Howard Hughes Medical Institute and the Czech Ministry of Education. With seven PhD students and several assistants and

## AGREEMENT BETWEEN MASARYK UNIVERSITY, BRNO, CZECH REPUBLIC (MU) AND DRS. ISABEL AND ALFRED BADER, JOINTLY AND SEVERALLY (THE BADERS)

Before September 1, 2002 a professor of physical organic chemistry will be appointed at the Department of Organic Chemistry, Faculty of Science, MU (the department), the professor to be called the Josef Loschmidt professor and chosen as professors are chosen in the department.

The position of the Josef Loschmidt professor shall be in addition to the existing faculty of the department.

Preference in the position shall be given to Czech citizens. Knowledge of German is desirable.

The professor shall present at least one lecture annually dealing with the life and work of Josef Loschmidt.

The Baders shall personally give the department US $20,000 (twenty thousand dollars) annually, beginning in 2001. This commitment shall last for a period of thirty years and thereafter at the discretion of the Trustees of The Isabel and Alfred Bader Foundation.

Every three years the Baders (or the Foundation) and the department shall discuss whether inflation suggests an increase in the sum given.

The Baders will make the gift via The American Jewish Joint Distribution Committee (the Joint) which has agreed to this. Should circumstances make it impossible in the future to make payment via the Joint, it will be the Baders' and the Foundation's obligation to find another venue of payment.

The $20,000 given in 2001 will be used to facilitate the Loschmidt Professor's move to Brno and for equipment for his or her work.

The department will submit an accounting to the Joint by March 31 of each year. The first accounting, for the $40,000 given in 2001-2, shall be submitted by March 31, 2003.

August __2*__, 2001

Professor Dr. Jan Slovak
Dean of the Faculty of Science
MASARYK UNIVERSITY

August __10__, 2001

Dr. Isabel Bader

August __10__, 2001

Dr. Alfred Bader

postdocs, he has produced world-class biochemical research. But the Masaryk University was building a new chemistry building, to be completed in 2005, and the department was unwilling to give him sufficient laboratories in the new building! Clearly nasty politics were involved. Dean Slovak, who had signed our contract, was really sympathetic, and at first so was his successor, Dean Milan Gelnar. But at least one senior professor created such opposition that Professor Damborsky seriously considered accepting a position in Prague. It had not occurred to us to put into the contract that the Loschmidt professor should be provided with adequate space. We have been staggered by all this, since he is clearly an excellent research professor and his care for his students is admirable.

To force him to leave would, of course, end the Loschmidt Chair, as the university would have broken its contract. Perhaps we should have taken legal counsel before establishing the chair, but donors seldom question the good faith of the recipients. At first we only questioned the wisdom of the low salary, which was easily raised.

We visited the Masaryk University in June 2005 and spoke strongly with the key players. That helped, and Professor Damborsky was really happy in his new laboratories. But not for long.

In July 2003, Yechiel Bar-Chaim wrote to Dean Gelnar, "Do we understand correctly that the Loschmidt Chair will be a tenured university position (for life) since Dr. Bader has assured that the chair will continue to be funded for the foreseeable future?" and the dean replied that month:

> There is no doubt that the Loschmidt Chair will be a tenured university position for life. However, in the agreement between MU and Drs. Isabel and Alfred Bader from August 24, 2001, The Josef Loschmidt professor has to be chosen as professor in the department (Dept. Org. Chem.). According to our rules there is need to have first contract for shorter

time (maximum five years) and after it is possible to have contract for longer time, in our case for life.

We discussed all these matters with Dr. Damborsky and again with full agreement with him we decided to have first contract for five years. However, it is important to know, within six to eights months Dr. Damborsky will defend his habilitation thesis to be formally appointed as professor here. After this event, we can have another contract for him and there is no administrative barrier to have this contract for much longer time even for life.

After this correspondence and our meeting in Brno in June 2005, we assumed that Professor Damborsky would receive tenure, and were truly staggered by a letter from the vice-rector for science, Jana Musilova, sent in January 2007 advising us that Professor Damborsky's employment contract expires on August 31, 2008 and that "the dean of the Faculty of Science is bent on to open a competition for Loschmidt Chair."

Professor Damborsky is an excellent teacher who has done world-class research that has been published widely. Through his website, www.loschmidt.cz, he has made Josef Loschmidt well known. He was promised tenure, and now he would be asked to leave in August 2008. If this happens, there will be no point in the dean looking for another chair, because we will take the position that the university has broken the contract and we will not continue to support it.

What a nightmare! Isabel and I were so proud to help establish the first chair in the Czech Republic funded by an outsider. An excellent scientist and great teacher was found, and the university administrators do not understand their good fortune. This is such a mystery to us. On August 15, 2007 a very important patent was issued to Professor Damborsky and his group and later that month the university organized a press conference about this patent and the projects going on in the Loschmidt Laboratories. On October 4, 2007 Mirek

Topolánek, the prime minister of the Czech Republic, visited the Loschmidt Laboratories to congratulate personally the team working on the development of the patented technology. Yet Professor Damborsky still has not been assured that he will receive tenure! And as of this writing, we still do not know whether the Loschmidt Chair will survive beyond the August 2008 expiration of Professor Damborsky's initial contract.

One of our ongoing gifts that brings us a lot of pleasure is to Project SEED (Summer Educational Experience for the Disadvantaged) of the American Chemical Society, about which I wrote in some detail in my first *Adventures* (pp.263–266). Project SEED provides economically disadvantaged high school students with opportunities to conduct mentored research in academic, industry, or government laboratories during the summer. The original program was for one summer. Because we believed that it would be a great advantage to offer these students a second summer's research, we helped start the SEED II program, and have recently given funds that the ACS has matched for about twenty college scholarships to support former Project SEED students who are accepted at universities. We have been so happy to see how well many of these students are doing, most in chemistry and chemical engineering, but some also in other disciplines, medicine and dentistry for instance.

In Milwaukee, we have been really impressed by the many educational efforts of Chabad, the Lubavitch organization. Two of my grandsons, Carlos and Alex, have gone to their nursery school. Chabad now directs the Hillel Academy, one of the local Jewish day schools, and one of the rabbis, Mendel Shmotkin (Plate 80), has become our good personal friend. We have been able to help to get them completely out of their debt, and Rabbi Shmotkin has guided us to help elsewhere, for instance the Chabad orphanage in Dnepopetrovsk.

Establishing bursaries for able students who need some financial help seemed eminently sensible to Isabel and me, because both of us benefited from scholarships and bursaries when we were students. Isabel established the first such bursaries at Victoria University in Toronto where she graduated in 1949. Bursaries at University College in London, at Edinburgh University, and the University of Glasgow followed. Victoria and Edinburgh have been clear and punctual in their reporting to us, and it gives us such pleasure to see how well some of the students have done. At University College, the funds for the bursaries were mixed up with the funds for an annual prize I had given earlier, but that has now been straightened out. With Glasgow, we have had the surprising problem that time and again we do not receive its promised annual reports about the students receiving the awards.

We have often said that of my four jobs, three are easy; the fourth, giving money away sensibly is the most difficult.

Helping the ablest is *relatively easy*. Bursaries, scholarships, and fellowships help the ablest and most, though not all, are easily monitored. Problems can arise in the most surprising places, totally unexpectedly. For instance, I made two gifts to the Department of Chemistry of the University of Sussex. In 1990 I gave the funds for an annual prize in organic chemistry and in 1992, funds for another in organometallic chemistry. I urged the university to invest the capital in long-term government bonds then yielding well over 12 percent so that the awards would be assured. This the university did not do. Interest rates declined, as did the capital, and by 2001, the funds had declined to the point where it was no longer possible to make the awards; the university last gave them in 2001–2 and then stopped. Although I visit the Chemistry Department each year, no one mentioned this to me until I inquired about the prizes in 2006. Professor Philip Parsons wrote to me in November:

During 2003–4 Robert Smith, the then dean of chemistry, physics and environmental science, was informed by Finance

237

Administration that the capital value of the fund was being eroded given that the annual interest no longer covered the annual prizes of £1k. It was therefore felt that the prizes could not be covered from interest alone and the option of offering a prize every third or fourth year was considered. However, it was felt that this was not in line with your intention that a £1k prize should be awarded annually. It was therefore concluded that these funds would have a finite life and be treated as donations. However, the records held do not indicate precisely what was agreed finally.

Of course, I was really saddened and annoyed. I asked whether I could not increase the capital so that the interest would be sufficient to give the two awards in perpetuity. I have been told that this is possible and made this gift in December 2006. Naturally, from now on I will inquire every year who the award winners are.

*Caveat donor.*
How do we help the neediest? Again, in Milwaukee it is relatively simple, particularly with the advice of Linda and Daniel and the Helen Bader Foundation. But in the world, in Africa and Asia? In the Balkans we have the help of Yechiel and Paul Polansky, and there even fifty or a hundred thousand dollars help. But in Africa, our gifts would be drops in a bucket and we feel so helpless.

Still, Isabel and I are so happy that we have been able to help many of the neediest and the ablest.

# Index